SPORT, POLITICS, AND SOCIETY IN THE MIDDLE EAST

DANYEL REICHE
TAMIR SOREK
(eds)

Sport, Politics, and Society in the Middle East

GEORGETOWN UNIVERSITY QATAR

Center *for* International *and* Regional Studies

OXFORD
UNIVERSITY PRESS

OXFORD
UNIVERSITY PRESS

Oxford University Press is a department of the
University of Oxford. It furthers the University's objective
of excellence in research, scholarship, and education
by publishing worldwide.

Oxford   New York

Auckland   Cape Town   Dar es Salaam   Hong Kong   Karachi
Kuala Lumpur   Madrid   Melbourne   Mexico City   Nairobi
New Delhi   Shanghai   Taipei   Toronto

With offices in

Argentina   Austria   Brazil   Chile   Czech Republic   France   Greece
Guatemala   Hungary   Italy   Japan   Poland   Portugal   Singapore
South Korea   Switzerland   Thailand   Turkey   Ukraine   Vietnam

Oxford is a registered trade mark of Oxford University Press
in the UK and certain other countries.

Published in the United States of America by
Oxford University Press
198 Madison Avenue, New York, NY 10016

Library of Congress Cataloging-in-Publication Data is available
Danyel Reiche and Tamir Sorek .
Sport, Politics, and Society in the Middle East.
ISBN: 9780190065218

Printed in India on acid-free paper

CONTENTS

CONTENTS

ACKNOWLEDGMENTS

This volume is the product of two working group meetings held under the auspices of the Center for International and Regional Studies (CIRS) at Georgetown University in Qatar. We would like to thank Mehran Kamrava, Director of CIRS, and Zahra Babar, Associate Director for Research, for initiating and guiding this project. We would like to also thank Suzi Mirgani, Managing Editor at CIRS, whose support and advice in the editing process was tremendously helpful. We also benefited from the assistance of the staff at CIRS: Elizabeth Wanucha, Jackie Starbird, Islam Hassan, Misba Bhatti, and Sabika Shaban. In addition to the authors of the chapters in this volume, we would like to acknowledge the contribution of the following scholars to this project: Mahfoud Amara, Ferman Konukman, Nnamdi Madichie, Monèm Jemni, and Betsi Stephen. Finally, grateful acknowledgment also goes also to the Qatar Foundation for its support of research and other scholarly endeavors.

ABOUT THE CONTRIBUTORS

Nida Ahmad is a PhD student at the University of Waikato in New Zealand. Her research examines the digital lives of Muslim sportswomen and how they use social media to represent aspects of their identities. Ahmad has co-authored a number of publications, including 'SDP and Action Sports', in *Routledge Handbook of Sport for Development and Peace* (2018) with Holly Thorpe and Neftalie Williams; 'Youth Sport in the Middle East', in *Routledge Handbook of Youth Sport* (2015) with Holly Thorpe; 'Youth, Action Sports and Political Agency in the Middle East: Lessons from a Grassroots Parkour Group in Gaza', *International Review for the Sociology of Sport* (2013) with Holly Thorpe; and 'Transnational families in Armenia and Information Communication Technology Use', *International Journal of Communication* (2013) with Katy Pearce and Janine Slaker.

Simon Chadwick is Professor of Sports Enterprise and Director of the Centre for Sports Business at the University of Salford (UK). He is also Professor of Eurasian Sport and Director of CESI (Centre for the Eurasian Sport Industry) at emylon, based in Shanghai (China). Chadwick is currently engaged in work examining the links between sports sponsorship and soft power; the industrial development of sports in the Gulf region; China's quest to become a leading football nation; the phenomenon of transnational sports fandom; the role social media plays in sport; and the way equity in sports brands is built through experiential marketing.

Craig L. LaMay is a journalist, an Associate Professor at Northwestern University in Evanston, Illinois, and currently Associate Professor in Residence at Northwestern University in Qatar. He is author, co-author, or editor of several books, among them: *Measures of Press Freedom and Media Contributions to Development: Evaluating the Evaluators*, with Monroe Price and Susan Abbott (Peter Lang, 2011); *Institutional Failures: Duke Lacrosse, Universities, the News Media and the Legal System*, with Howard Wasserman (Ashgate, 2011); *Inside the Presidential Debates*, with Newton Minow (University of Chicago, 2008); *Exporting Press Freedom: Economic and Editorial Dilemmas in International Media Assistance* (Transaction, 2006); *Journalism and the Problem of Privacy* (Erlbaum, 2003); *Democracy on the Air*, with Ellen Mickiewicz, Donald Browne, and Charles Firestone (Duke, 2000); *To Profit or Not to Profit: The Commercial Transformation of the Nonprofit Sector*, with Burton Weisbrod (Cambridge, 1998).

Charlotte Lysa is a PhD Candidate in the Department of Culture Studies and Oriental Languages at the University of Oslo. Her academic interests include politics and society in the Middle East and North Africa. She is currently researching female football participation in the Arab Gulf monarchies. Lysa published an article about Qatar and the World Cup in *Babylon—Nordic Journal of Middle Eastern Studies* in 2016, for which she won the Babylon prize for young researchers; 'The Banality of Protest? Twitter Campaigns in Qatar', with A. Leber in *Gulf Affairs: Identity & Culture in the 21st Century Gulf* (2016); and 'Women's Sports Programs are Challenging Saudi Arabia's Gender Divide', with A. Leber in *Gulf Affairs*, special issue, 'Gender (Im) Balance in Gulf Societies' (Spring 2018).

Nadim Nassif is Assistant Professor and Academic Advisor of the physical education major at Notre Dame University–Louaize, Lebanon. His most recent publications include: 'World Ranking of Countries in Elite Sport', *Rivista Di Diritto Ed Economia Dello Sport* (2018); 'Factors behind Lebanon's Difficulties Achieving Success at the Olympics', *The International Journal of the History of Sport* (2017); and 'Elite Sport Ranking of the "International Society of Sports Sciences in the Arab World": An Accurate Evaluation of all Nations' Performances International Sports Competitions', *Athens Journal of Sport* (2017).

Danyel Reiche is an Associate Professor of Comparative Politics at the American University of Beirut (AUB). He graduated with distinction from Leibniz University Hannover and joined AUB in 2008 after working as a Visiting Assistant Professor at Georgetown University. Reiche published *Success and Failure of Countries at the Olympic Games* in 2016 with Routledge. His peer-reviewed articles have been published in area study journals, such as

ABOUT THE CONTRIBUTORS

International Journal of Sport Policy and Politics and *Journal of Energy Policy*, as well as in broader oriented journals, such as *Third World Quarterly* and *The Middle East Journal*. Professor Reiche has also been invited to write op-eds for leading international newspapers such as *Washington Post* and *Spiegel Online* and has been frequently interviewed and quoted by major media outlets such as *Le Monde* and *The Wall Street Journal*.

Tamir Sorek is Professor of Sociology at the University of Florida. His studies focus on the intersection of culture and politics, especially in the fields of nationalism, collective memory, and sport. In his work, Sorek bridges the gap between quantitative studies and qualitative humanistic scholarship. He is the author of *Arab Soccer in a Jewish State* (Cambridge University Press, 2007), *Palestinian Commemoration in Israel* (Stanford University Press, 2015), and is currently completing a biography of the Palestinian poet Tawfiq Zayyad to be published by Stanford University Press in 2020. Sorek's scholarship has been published worldwide in multiple languages, including French, Arabic, Indonesian, Turkish, and Hebrew.

Cem Tinaz has been Director of the School of Sports Sciences and Technology at Istanbul Bilgi University since 2015, and a board member of the Turkish Tennis Federation since 2009. He authored "Policies for Naturalisation of Foreign-Born Athletes: Qatar and Turkey in Comparison," with Danyel Reiche, in *International Journal of Sport Policy and Politics* (2019); "Football in Turkey," with Emir Güney and Ahmet Talimciler, in *Routledge Handbook of Football Business and Management* (2018); "Globalizing a Brand through Sport Sponsorships: The Case of Turkish Airlines and its Sport Marketing Efforts," in *Routledge Handbook of International Sport Business* (2018). Tinaz was awarded a 2016/2017 Advanced Olympic Research Grant by the IOC Olympic Studies Centre, for the project "Examining Positive Outcomes of Unsuccessful Olympic Bids."

Dag Tuastad is Senior Lecturer in Middle East Studies at the University of Oslo, where he led the New Middle East Project, and currently heads the Rebel Rule Project. Tuastad's academic interests include political culture, power, resistance, and politics as seen from below. His publications include: *Palestinske Utfordringer* (Palestinian Challenges) (Cappelen Damm, 2014), and authored "'A Threat to National Unity'—Football in Jordan: Ethnic Divisive or a Political Tool for the Regime?" *The International Journal of the History of Sport* (2014); "From Football Riot to Revolution: The Political Role of Football in the Arab World," *Soccer and Society* (2013); "'State of Exception' or 'State in

Exile?' The Fallacy of Appropriating Agamben on Palestinian Refugee Camps," *Third World Quarterly* (2017); "The Violent Rise of Palestine's Lost Generation," *Middle East Critique* (2017); and "Nationalist Patriarchy, Clan Democracy: How the Political Trajectories of Palestinians in Israel and the Occupied Territories Have Been Reversed," *Die Welt des Islams* (2017).

Murat C. Yıldız is Assistant Professor of History at Skidmore College. He specializes in the cultural and social history of the modern Middle East. Yıldız is currently working on a book manuscript that focuses on the development of a shared sports culture among Muslims, Christians, and Jews of late-nineteenth- and early-twentieth-century Istanbul. His work has appeared in the *Middle East Journal of Culture and Communication*, the *Cairo Papers in Social Science*, the *Journal of Middle East Women's Studies*, and the *Arab Studies Journal*. He is an Assistant Editor for the *Arab Studies Journal*, a peer-reviewed, multidisciplinary research publication in the field of Arab and Middle East studies.

LIST OF ILLUSTRATIONS

LIST OF ILLUSTRATIONS

INTRODUCTION

FROM SPORTS IN THE MIDDLE EAST
TO MIDDLE EASTERN SPORTS

Tamir Sorek and *Danyel Reiche*

Sports in the Middle East have become a major issue in global affairs: Qatar's successful bid for the FIFA World Cup 2022 (won in a final vote against the United States), the 2005 UEFA Champions League Final in Turkey's most populous city Istanbul, the European basketball championship EuroBasket in 2017 in Israel, and other major sporting events, such as the annually staged Formula 1 races in Bahrain and Abu Dhabi, have put an international spotlight on the region. In particular, media around the world are discussing the question of whether the most prestigious sporting events should be staged in a predominantly authoritarian, socially conservative, and politically contentious part of the world.[1] The influence of sports in the Middle East extends beyond the region: professional sports clubs around the world have signed sponsorship deals with Middle Eastern airlines, and stadium-naming rights have also been signed with those companies. Major football clubs like Paris Saint-Germain Football Club and Manchester City have been bought by investors from the Gulf–Qatar and Abu Dhabi, respectively.

The growing visibility of Middle Eastern sports has only recently attracted the attention of scholars. Although some sporadic academic studies appeared

1

as early as the 1980s, we can identify the beginning of a 'wave' of scholarship in the mid-1990s, which intensified in the early 2000s. These studies were mostly socio-historical, sociological, and anthropological, and they tended to focus on the particular dynamics of certain countries, including Egypt,[2] Turkey,[3] Iran,[4] Yemen,[5] Israel/Palestine,[6] and Jordan.[7] While more recent scholarship continues similar patterns, and extends to cover new countries,[8] since 2010 we may also identify the addition of two new trends. The first is related to the power shift in international sports towards Middle Eastern countries, with the awarding of mega-sporting events to countries such as Bahrain, Qatar, Turkey, and the United Arab Emirates. As a result, in the 2010s more scholarship appears to be focused on business, management, and policy.[9] The second trend is the contextualization of various case studies related to specific countries within a broader regional frame. Numerous volumes on sports in the Arab world, Middle East, or MENA (the Middle East and North Africa),[10] and particularly about soccer,[11] have been published since 2012. This volume is part of both emerging trends, but with its own particular characteristics.

First, following Abbas Amanat's question, 'Is there a Middle East?',[12] we ask 'is there a Middle Eastern sport?' In other words, beyond the aggregation of case studies, can we identify common regional dynamics typical for the Middle East? This volume, therefore, emphasizes the interdependence between regional patterns and local developments in particular countries. For example, chapters in this volume identify common patterns in the historical developments of Middle Eastern sports, illustrate the common experience of Muslim female athletes throughout the region, analyze the diverse effects of regional mega-sporting events on Lebanon, and outline common trends in the sport business in the six Gulf Cooperation Council (GCC) member states. Second, the contributors to this volume share a common understanding of Middle Eastern sports as a contested terrain, where struggles over resources, meanings, and identities are constantly taking place, and there is no inevitable outcome for these struggles. We demonstrate the role sports play in the battle over social memories related to the Palestinian–Bedouin divide in Jordan, or over competing definitions of 'Israeliness' among Israelis with different approaches to religion, as well as different ethnic and class backgrounds. In Lebanon, mega-sporting events have been playing an indirect role in struggles over the definition of Lebanese national identity, as well as the degree to which this identity is embedded in the broader Arab world.

These struggles are also related to the various roles sports can play in societal change in the Middle East. While a major goal of policies aimed at pro-

INTRODUCTION

moting sports in the Middle East is international recognition,[13] to what extent can sports also contribute to changes within the region? In most Middle Eastern countries sports participation is much lower compared to that in other regions of the world, which has had severe consequences on the health of the population, with obesity becoming a major problem, particularly in the Arabian Peninsula. Does the interest in hosting mega-sporting events, and using sports as a promotional tool, also lead to improved promotion of sports at the grassroots level? Since sports in the Middle East has traditionally been considered a masculine sphere,[14] are women in sports gaining acceptance? And are sports such as football, which are considered to be masculine arenas, becoming more popular and accepted among girls and their families?

The Middle East is not a homogeneous group of countries: there is political stability in some countries while others are facing civil wars. Most Middle Eastern countries are Muslim-majority countries, but some also have large Christian populations, as well as other religious minority groups. Arabic is the most widely spoken language in the Middle East, but there are also other languages spoken, such as Turkish, Persian, Kurdish, and Hebrew. What most Middle Eastern countries have in common is their colonial legacy and complicated present-day relations with the West. In addition, most of them share a low ranking on indexes tracking gender equality, as well as on those tracking democracy and press freedom.[15] Can mega-sporting events awarded to Middle Eastern countries contribute to societal reform, and can they positively affect, for example, freedom of expression? While such a scenario is possible, this volume rejects the romantic and deterministic idea that sport always contributes to societal improvement. Nonetheless, it does highlight specific case studies where this is indeed the case, for instance the empowerment of women in particular circumstances and under particular conditions.

As this book shows, the state assumes different roles in various Middle Eastern sports sectors. In wealthy Middle Eastern countries such as Qatar, and in emerging market countries such as Turkey, the state plays a central role in the sports sector. A challenge discussed in the volume is how the private sector must grow to assist governments in meeting the ambitious visions and targets for sports. For states such as Lebanon with weak—and some might even argue, failing—governments, the challenge is different: to fight corruption around mega-sporting events, especially regarding the allocation of sports budgets. They also need to develop a more strategic approach that gives some guidance to stakeholders in order to meet targets such as increased sports participation and elite sport success.

This book is the product of a research initiative conducted by the Center for International and Regional Studies (CIRS) at Georgetown University in Qatar. In 2017, CIRS invited the contributors to this book as well as other experts in the field to attend two working group meetings in Doha focused on 'Sport, Society, and the State in the Middle East.' All participants contributed to the review process and provided feedback on the drafts of this edited volume. The final group of contributors was carefully selected, and includes some of the most renowned experts in the field. The selected contributions cover a broad range of Middle Eastern countries, although some nations are more in focus than others. Two chapters (Lysa and LaMay) entirely, and another chapter partly (Chadwick), focus on Qatar, largely because of the growing international interest in the country ahead of the 2022 FIFA World Cup, but also because Doha hosts multiple international universities and is relatively easy to access for most researchers from all over the world to conduct their studies. Similarly, there are two contributions focusing on sports in Lebanon (Nassif and Reiche), a country with both strong academic and sporting traditions.

Although great effort was made to identify scholars working on all major Middle Eastern countries, and to include them in the two working group meetings that ultimately led to this edited volume, not all countries could be included. For example, there is no chapter in the volume that deals exclusively with Egypt or Iran. However, Murat Yıldız's chapter provides an overarching regional history of sport, and dedicates extensive attention to these two countries.

The volume is thoroughly interdisciplinary, and integrates different academic disciplines from the humanities and social sciences, including business, cultural studies, communication, history, journalism, sociology, sports management, and political science. The ten chapters of this book offer original, in-depth, theoretically grounded, and richly empirical chapters. The contributions rely on diverse research methodologies, ranging from ethnographic work, surveys, and in-depth interviews to reviews of government files and the growing body of academic literature and media articles on sports in the Middle East.

The first part of the book (chapters 1 to 5) considers sport a contested terrain, where various struggles over meaning, resources, and rights, are fought. The book begins with a historical overview. Some popular discussions give the impression that sport is something new to the Middle East, or that it is no more than a Western import. Competitive organized physical activities, however, have been known in the region for centuries, long before the Western colonial enterprise.[16] Still, it is true that the codified and stand-ardized versions of modern global sports as we know them today were imported to the Middle East in the late nineteenth century—soon after their codification in Western countries.

The representation of modern sport as a 'Western' institution is the origin of the first tension we discuss. In the opening chapter, Murat Yıldız traces the activities of educators, government officials, sports club administrators, students, club members, editors, and columnists who helped turn sports into a regular fixture of the urban landscape of cities across the Middle East. Furthermore, these actors frequently saw themselves as agents of Western modernity, and, in this capacity, they aspired to turn the physical activity from 'fun' into a broader project of training, disciplining, and educating the self. His chapter highlights the tension between these two interpretive poles, and how it is related to the construction of the West vs. East dichotomy. Yıldız's chapter is also a response to the rapidly growing study of the history of sports in various Middle Eastern countries, and questions whether we can talk about a shared and distinct history of sports in the Middle East. Based on press research and integration of secondary sources, the chapter traces the emergence and spread of team sports and physical exercise throughout the urban centers of the Middle East from the late nineteenth century until the 1930s, and demonstrates that there were important shared discursive and institutional features across the region. The chapter shows that the tension between sports as fun and sports as a disciplinary tool is by itself an important characteristic of Middle Eastern sporting history.

The next two chapters deal with struggles over the definition of collective identities. Dag Tuastad analyzes football's role in how societies remember. Based on several phases of ethnographic work over two decades, the chapter demonstrates how football constitutes a dominant arena for battles over national social memories related to the Palestinian–Bedouin divide in Jordan. Social memory processes in football arenas represent two related social phenomena. First, collective historical memories are produced. Second, during football matches, with their symbolic and physical confrontations, these collective memories are also enacted and embodied. Palestinian–Jordanian encounters on the football field have been especially important in this context, and have served as a stage for reprocessing and embodying the memory of the 1970 civil war. For Palestinians, as a stateless ethno-national group that lacks the formal national institutions to preserve a national past in the form of museums or archaeological preservation, football, and particularly the Wihdat team, has become an important alternative. While until the early 1990s the fans' chants emphasized identification with the armed struggle, today the dominant themes are Palestinian common descent, unity, and refugee identity. At the same time, the team's alter ego, FC Faisali, has served as a focus of East Bank Jordanian nationalism, emphasizing tribal roots and values, Islamic tradition, Hashemite loyalty, and the tribal roots of the monarchy.

Similarly, in chapter 3, Tamir Sorek analyzes sport as a sphere of struggle over Israeli collective identity. The chapter combines analysis of the rhetoric of Hapoel Tel Aviv hardcore football and basketball fans with a quantitative demographic examination of the wide circle of sympathizers of various teams. The bifocal examination reveals that the stadium rhetoric is actually an expression of fundamental struggles between competing definitions of Israeliness. The rhetoric of Hapoel fans is an uncommon combination in Israeli sports: socialism, anti-nationalism, anti-racism, but it also includes violent, sexist, classist, and Germanophobic content. In addition, hardcore Hapoel fans make provocative use of Holocaust terminology. This rhetoric is partly related to the demographic basis of both the hardcore fans and the wider circle of sympathizers who tend to be more middle class and significantly more secular than the fans other teams. The chapter argues that the transgressive rhetoric of Hapoel fans is partly related to the decline in the political power of the secular elite in Israel. The insights are based on an online survey, and studying websites and forums of Hapoel Tel Aviv fans, fan songs available on YouTube, and phone and Skype interviews with fans.

From struggles over meanings and symbols, the next two chapters take us to struggles over inclusion of women. In chapter 4, Charlotte Lysa discusses how Qatari female footballers negotiate gendered expectations in football. On the one hand, these players are being encouraged by government policies, in accordance with pressure from international organizations, to pursue sports careers. On the other hand, these women are subject to a conservative culture, upheld by specific societal and family values, in which it is largely unacceptable for a woman to play football. This tension has driven some Qatari women to create a safe space for their activities by initiating university teams, allowing them to bypass established norms regarding women and femininity. Based on interviews with young women engaged in football activities, this chapter shows that these spaces do not carry the same negative connotations of masculinity that the official clubs and the national team do, thus allowing women to challenge the perception that it is not possible for a female to play football, while at the same time preserving their femininity and adhering to societal moral codes. By relabeling women's football as a university activity, rather than something that conflicts with their academic priorities, they are able to play football without getting into conflict with their families. The women seek to gain a positive freedom to pursue their objectives and to reclaim control over shaping their own lives.

While Lysa examines the tensions between athletic aspirations and social norms on the field, in chapter 5, Nida Ahmad investigates them in the virtual sphere. Social media creates unique opportunities for sportswomen to engage in a form of self-branding by sharing aspects of their lives online, but the study of this phenomenon has so far been limited to the Western context. The chapter presents the findings from a digital ethnography of the social media accounts of sportswomen from Saudi Arabia, Kuwait, the United Arab Emirates, Egypt, and Iran, as well as semi-structured interviews with these women. In contrast to research findings that show Western sportswomen using social media for self-branding and their tendency to offer intimate details of their lifestyles, Ahmad shows that Middle Eastern sportswomen carefully consider what and how they share with their audiences, applying different strategies to safely and effectively navigate the digital terrain. Family and cultural constraints are central to their digital decision-making.

In chapter 6, Craig LaMay takes us to another sociopolitical conflict, as he elaborates on the effects of the 2022 FIFA World Cup on Qatar's restrictive media system. How does the World Cup affect rights of expression and publication in a country that criminalizes, for example, blasphemy and criticism of the emir? The analysis is based on the author's conversations with newspaper editors in the country, assessing internationally known indices of press freedom, and the growing body of academic literature on Qatari sport and media politics. Being home to broadcaster Al Jazeera, Qatar is the most progressive member of the GCC in matters of free expression, but ranks low on international indicators. Qatar's successful bid for the 2022 World Cup has brought the country both new attention and criticism, with the latter focusing especially on the *kafala* labor system. Neither China nor Russia's media regimes changed after hosting the Olympics in 2008 and 2014 respectively, but the chapter argues that Qatar has been relatively open to its critics, and the award of the World Cup has advanced conversations in the country about sensitive subjects. To be recognized as a modern and influential state, LaMay predicts that Qatar will liberalize its media environment, but on its own terms, which might deviate from Western standards.

The next three chapters deal with other aspects of Middle Eastern sports politics. In chapter 7, Cem Tınaz examines Turkish sports policy with emphasis on the period since 2002 when the tenure of the Justice and Development Party (AKP) government began. Based on in-depth interviews with former Turkish sport ministers and other sport authorities, as well as a review of academic literature, government files, and press articles, the chapter concludes that a main focus of Turkish sports policy is on gaining domestic and international prestige rather than on increasing sports participation. While Turkey was five times unsuccessful in its bids for the Olympic Games in 2000, 2004, 2008, 2012, and 2020, it has had several other accomplishments, including hosting other high-profile international sporting events such as the 2005 UEFA Champions League Final and constructing football stadiums. The country also gained elite sport success at international championships and the Olympic Games, with the naturalization of foreign-born athletes a main driver. The chapter stresses the central role of the state, and the sport sector's dependence on government subsidies, since most financial resources come from the sports betting company Iddaa. When it comes to the low sports participation in Turkey by international standards, Tınaz argues that the government has so far failed to properly integrate sports with the education system, making school sports one of the most problematic areas of sport development in Turkey.

Compared with other Middle Eastern countries, Turkey has been relatively successful in international sports. For example, the Turkish men's national soccer team finished third in the FIFA World Cup in 2002; the men's basketball national team finished second in the 2010 World Cup; and the country has won ninety-one Olympic medals in its history of participation (up until 2018). Lebanon, on the other hand, is located at the other end of the achievements scale. It has never qualified for the FIFA World Cup, and has only won four medals at the Olympic Games since it started participating in 1948. To date, the country's best achievement is coming sixteenth in the men's Basketball World Cup. This is far less than, for example, Estonia, Georgia, and Jamaica, which are countries with smaller populations and lower GDP than Lebanon. In chapter 8, Nadim Nassif asks why Lebanon is failing in international sport. The chapter argues that the promotion of elite sport has never been a priority for the Lebanese government. Nassif reviews the academic literature on elite sport success, and discusses political, economic, demographic, and cultural factors. It is argued that the meager annual budget allocated by the Lebanese government to the Ministry of Sport is a necessary but insufficient explanation for Lebanon's failure in international sport. The Ministry of Youth and Sport issued a 'Sport Strategy 2010–2020', but never implemented the proposed policies. Beyond the government, there is the problem of the corruption that is prevalent in the national sport federations. Nassif highlights how administrators occupy key positions based on their political affiliations, rather than on their skills and capacities.

Danyel Reiche provides a different perspective on sports in Lebanon. In chapter 9, he engages with the scholarship that emphasizes the benefits of mega-sporting events to host countries, from increasing their international prestige and influence on global politics, through mobilizing national pride, to serving as a tool of economic development. Reiche investigates the benefits accrued to Lebanon as a result of hosting four regional mega-sporting events after the civil war ended in 1990. He examines the similarities and differences between these four events by examining, in particular, the tangible and intangible legacies. Apart from a review of academic and press articles, primary data were collected by interviewing key stakeholders in the Lebanese sports sector who were involved in the events. The chapter concludes that while the events provided the country with some short-term promotional benefits, they introduced a heavy financial burden, especially regarding stadium and sports hall construction. Resources to maintain those facilities became a source of corruption. The chapter suggests that, in the future, Lebanon should consider co-hosting mega-sporting events with other countries in order to limit the financial risks. It should also integrate legacy management programs into the event planning to avoid unused facilities after the events.

Finally, Simon Chadwick discusses sports as a business. He presents an overview of sports business in the six Gulf Cooperation Council states. GCC member states stage sporting mega-events and invest in global sports, for example, by acquiring football clubs. The shirt sponsorship and stadium naming-rights deals of the region's national airlines aim to create favorable perceptions of those companies and their nations, as well as to diversify economies beyond oil and gas. The chapter provides a statistical profile of sport in each GCC member state and shows that Bahrain, Kuwait, and Oman are lagging far behind Saudi Arabia, United Arab Emirates, and Qatar in terms of sport industry size. Fluctuating oil prices, political tensions between GCC states, and weak attendances at games are serious threats to the future growth of the sport industry. Chadwick concludes that the private sector needs to seriously develop in order to replace the state as the industry's central focus.

In sum, this book brings together leading scholars of Middle Eastern sports to portray the complex social, political, cultural, and economic aspects of sports in the region. The common thread in this volume is that sports in the

Middle East are much more than an 'interesting angle' through which to popularize academic themes. They are themselves a major political and economic force that not only reflect but also shape both individuals' lives and large-scale social processes. Sporting competitions gain immense visibility in the media, elicit high levels of emotion by producing drama, and hold great potential to shape dominant meanings, identities, discourses, and ideologies.

1

MAPPING THE 'SPORTS *NAHDA*'

TOWARD A HISTORY OF SPORTS IN THE MODERN MIDDLE EAST

Murat C. Yıldız[1]

Introduction

In February 1933, King Vittorio Emmanuel III and Queen Elena of Italy made an official state visit to Egypt. The visit was a well-publicized event, aimed at celebrating Egypt's relationship with Italy.[2] Leading western newspapers, such as *The New York Times* and *The Illustrated London News*, pointed to the 'true Oriental hospitality' that the Egyptians demonstrated to their royal guests and the exotic spaces the Italian royal family visited.[3] *Al-Abtal* (the champions), an Arabic physical culture magazine published in Cairo, focused its coverage of the visit on an entirely different topic: a 'sports exhibition.'[4]

The event was a smashing success. A large crowd of spectators gathered around the track and in the stands to watch male students from Egyptian primary and secondary schools put on a show. Dressed in white shorts and long pants, the 'sons' and 'cubs' of Egypt marched in unison, performed gymnastics exercises, and contorted their bodies. As the photographs and text of *al-Abtal's* article make abundantly clear, this was a highly choreographed spectacle (Figure 1). According to *al-Abtal*, it was none other than King Fuad himself who ordered Egypt's 'Inspector of Physical Education' (*muraqaba al-tarbiyya al-badaniyya*) to organize the sporting performance.[5] The organization of the event raises questions about the significance of sports in Egypt, more specifically, and the Middle East, more broadly, during the period. What was so important about demonstrating the athletic acumen of Egyptian students?

Figure 1: Egyptian students performing gymnastics exercises for Italy's King Vittorio Emmanuel III and Queen Elena during their trip to Egypt, *al-Abtal*.
Source: 'Al-hafla al-riyadiya al-kubra li-wizara al-ma'arif bi munasiba tashrif hadrati sahibi al-jalala malik wa malika Italiya,' *al-Abtal*, March 4, 1933, p. 4.

Al-Abtal's description of the event offers some important clues. The magnificent display of Egyptian male bodies at the event, according to the article, was nothing less than the manifestation of the glorious 'sports awakening' (*al-nahda al-riyadiyya*) that Egypt and its children were experiencing during this 'auspicious age'.[6] *Al-Abtal's* use of the word *nahda* to refer to sports is significant. *Nahda* literally means awakening or renaissance;[7] however, the term also connoted an entire movement of reform during the late nineteenth and early twentieth centuries. *Al-Abtal's* usage established a discursive connection between sports and a broader reformist project that emerged in urban centers of the Middle East. In other words, sports was inextricably connected to a region-wide *nahda* project that brought together thinkers from a diverse array of professional and intellectual backgrounds and traditions who were committed to refashioning and modernizing the self, institutions, the state, and nation.

Historians of the Middle East have recently started to explore the plurality of intellectual exchanges and features that constituted the *nahda*.[8] Nonetheless, the corporeal and popular sporting facets of the *nahda* remain underexamined.[9] The writings of sports enthusiasts in *al-Abtal* and other publications unequivocally establish that they were witnessing and contributing to the formation of a sports *nahda*. Across the region, sports enthusiasts persuasively proclaimed that physical exercise, gymnastics, and team sports, namely football, were educational and leisure activities that young men—and, increasingly during the 1920s and 1930s, women—needed to be exposed to in order to become healthy, moral, and modern citizens. How might the inclusion of this discursive framing in consideration of the *nahda*—of the relationship between sports, the body, the self, and community—augur new lines of inquiry? Did the spread of sports clubs, publications, and venues across the broader Middle East expand the geography of the *nahda*? Does the intellectual and ethnoreligious diversity of the actors and institutions that indelibly shaped the spread of sports reveal an even more capacious cultural *nahda* than originally envisioned?

This chapter's approach to the sports *nahda* builds on an exciting body of literature on sports in the Middle East. Over the past decade, scholars from a diverse array of academic stripes, non-professional academics, journalists, and museum directors have deployed different methodological approaches to examine sports and physical culture throughout the Middle East. However, they published manuscripts, edited volumes, and articles; organized conferences, workshops, and panels; and curated exhibitions at museums that largely focus on sports either in a specific nation-state, mainly Egypt, Iran, Israel,

13

Palestine, and Turkey,[10] or in a region within the Middle East, particularly the Arab world.[11] This chapter builds on this important body of literature by exploring sports across the region.[12] It examines the discursive and material transformations that shaped the emergence, vernacularization, and spread of sports during the late nineteenth century until the interwar period in the Middle East. More specifically, it examines how people, from Istanbul to Jerusalem, Cairo to Beirut, and Baghdad to Tehran, performed gymnastics in schools, played team sports for athletic clubs, cheered for their favorite team in the stands, and read (or listened to people read aloud) descriptions of the latest matches and the importance of regular exercise in periodicals.[13] Drawing from a diverse array of primary sources, such as newspapers, magazines, memoirs, diaries, government and school reports, western travel literature, as well as photographs, and secondary literature, this chapter maps the ideas, practices, and institutions that constituted the sports *nahda* in the modern Middle East.

Educating the Body and Having Fun: Physical Exercise and Sports in Clubs and Schools

Throughout the mid- to late nineteenth century, educators, doctors, government officials, and ordinary people across the globe started to look to physical exercise and team sports as both a panacea for society's perceived ills and a fun pastime. In a speech at Harvard, in 1893, Francis Walker, president of the Massachusetts Institute of Technology (MIT), praised the ability of physical exercise and team sports to cultivate 'courage, steadiness of nerve ... resourcefulness, self-knowledge, self-reliance ... the ability to work with others ... readiness to subordinate selfish impulses, personal desires, and individual credit to a common end.'[14] The modern assumptions undergirding this discursive framing about reforming the body and the physical activities through which people disciplined and trained their bodies gradually spread throughout urban centers of the Middle East. Foreigners, in general, and Europeans and Americans, more specifically, played an integral role in the spread of the ideas, practices, personnel, and objects of the sports *nahda*.

Sports clubs and schools served as two of the main organizations in urban centers of the Middle East through and in which people encountered team sports and exercise as both an educational and leisure activity. By no means did foreigners exclusively establish and serve as the administrators of schools and sports clubs; denizens of urban centers throughout the region also established, joined, and administered clubs and schools. Nevertheless, foreigners played an instrumental role in the introduction of sports in these spaces.

The presence of foreigners in Alexandria, Beirut, Cairo, Istanbul, and Tehran, as well as other cities around the region, was inextricably connected to the integration of Khedival Egypt, the Ottoman Empire, and Qajar Iran into the global economy and the modern nation-state system.[15] In particular, three transformations during the nineteenth and twentieth centuries made this possible: capitulations, imperialism, and increased western competition throughout the region. Together, these transformations and their attendant political, social, economic, and cultural rearrangements facilitated the spread of Europeans living in urban centers of the Middle East.

These foreign passport holders played a significantly large role in the creation of football teams and sports clubs in the Middle East. Foreign merchants, educators, as well as military and bureaucratic personnel envisioned sports clubs as spaces in which they could organize and spend their leisure time. Members of these clubs played a number of physical activities, such as football, cricket, and polo. However, football developed into the most popular and widespread of the team sports.

Across the region, foreign men from different professional backgrounds joined these clubs and played sports. In the Ottoman Empire, visiting British sailors and entrepreneurs living in Istanbul created football teams during the late nineteenth century.[16] In Egypt, British military personnel and officials organized football matches in Cairo and Alexandria during the British occupation of Egypt (1882–1923).[17] In Iran, British officers, employees of the Anglo-Iranian Oil Company, educators, as well as missionaries played an integral role in the introduction of football throughout the country.[18]

Many of these clubs embraced an elite foreign identity by restricting membership to foreigners. Clubs in Alexandria and Cairo, for example, catered to the British community that increased dramatically after the military occupation of Egypt in 1882. According to western guidebooks, by 1897, Alexandria and Cairo each had four foreign sports clubs.[19] These clubs offered the British community of both cities an elite homogenous space where they could assert and perform their foreignness while socializing and playing sports, such as lawn tennis, cricket, golf, and polo.[20] The Gezira Sporting Club in particular was popular among British officers stationed in Cairo. The club was established in 1886 in order to provide a space for British officers to exercise and play sports. According to historian Lanver Mak, British civilians were also allowed to become members of the club "'by courtesy" of the military.'[21]

Despite its initial exclusion of Egyptians, the Gezira Sporting Club gradually allowed a coterie of elite Egyptians to become members. Mixed clubs gradually started to emerge in other cities in the Middle East. In 1911, for example, foreign European and local Arab residents of Jaffa created the Circle Sportive (al-Muntada al-Riyadi).[22]

Within ten to twenty years, 'locals' also established their own sports clubs in urban centers of the Middle East. In cities across the region, such as Alexandria, Ankara, Baghdad, Beirut, Cairo, Damascus, Ismailia, Istanbul, Izmir, Jaffa, Jerusalem, Port Said, and Tanta, elite and middle-class young men created and became members of sports clubs. The spread of these clubs reflects the growing popularity of sports as well as the emergence of a new type of civic organization: the voluntary association.

Across the region, residents of cities created a diverse array of voluntary associations, such as literary, political, religious, scientific, as well as sporting. Their emergence coincided with the spread of the idea that men and women from an expanding middle class needed to fill their 'free time' with beneficial activities. Reformers writing in a variety of languages argued that it was a moral imperative for people to create and join spaces that were committed to improving their minds and bodies. For example, *al-Hilal* (the crescent), one of Cairo's leading Arabic magazines, offered readers updates on the formation of clubs. In 1894, *al-Hilal*'s section on 'Egyptian events' informed readers of a 'new club' (*nadi jadid*) that 'a group of Cairo's notables' (*ayan al-Qahira*) created.[23] According to the publication, the club provided this group with a space in which they could engage in the pursuit of beneficial activities during their 'free time (*awqat al-faragh*), instead of wasting it in places of amusement (*amakin al-lahw*).'[24] Other early twentieth-century publications, such as Muhammad Umar's book *The Present State of the Egyptians, or, the Cause of their Retrogression* (*Hadir al-misriyyin aw sir ta'akhkhurihim*), argued that sports clubs and physical exercise were central needs of Egypt's expanding middle stratum.[25]

The idea that young men needed to regularly exercise and play sports was not confined to sports clubs. For example, during the early twentieth century, lectures organized at Jerusalem's Flourishing Literature Association (Jam'iyat al-adab al-zahra) also discussed sports. Khalil al-Sakakini, a leading educator in Palestine during the late Ottoman Empire and the British Mandate, wrote about the importance of physical exercise for Jerusalem's youth at the association. 'Athletic fields' (*sahat al-le'b*), according to al-Sakakini, served as the space where youth strengthened different parts of the body, developed 'courage and resolve', cultivated 'the love of struggle and competition', and sharpened their 'intellect.'[26] In short, athletic fields were the training grounds of new Arab men.

These ideas were not confined to the walls of Jerusalem's Flourishing Literature Association. During the first three decades of the twentieth century, a number of local upper- and middle-class men from a diverse array of ethnic and religious backgrounds established and joined athletic clubs throughout the region.[27] They joined these clubs for a whole host of reasons. Playing team sports and engaging in physical exercise were definitely motivating factors; however, elite and upwardly mobile young men also joined them in order to socialize and to be part of a broader fraternity of young men.

These clubs shared a number of characteristics: first, they were organized around a shared activity or activities, the most popular were gymnastics and football; second, these clubs tended to be ethnically and/or religiously homogenous. Predominantly Arab, Armenian, Greek, Greek Orthodox, Jewish, as well as Muslim clubs popped up in cities across the region. Their efflorescence reveals the growing popularity of sports and an emerging leisure market in urban centers. In other words, clubs were not only competing on the pitch, they were also competing for the bodies of young men.

Predominantly Jewish clubs mushroomed throughout the Middle East. During the first three decades of the twentieth century, Jewish denizens of various different urban centers grew increasingly interested in playing sports, exercising, and becoming members of a sports club. These athletic clubs played an instrumental role in both responding to and cultivating this interest in cities such as Aleppo, Alexandria, Baghdad, Beirut, Cairo, Damascus, Istanbul, Jerusalem, Salonica, and Tehran.[28] Maccabi clubs were the most prominent Jewish sports organizations.[29] Like other sports organizations, many of the Maccabi clubs offered their members more than a space to exercise. For example, the Maccabi Jewish Sports and Literary Union of Alexandria (Union Juive Sportive et Litteraire Macchabée) regularly organized sporting competitions as well as conferences on 'Jewish, literary, historic, and scientific subjects.'[30]

While many of these clubs embraced and projected a shared ethnic and/or religious identity, there were also instances in which young men became members of a club that was not connected to their ethnic or religious community. For example, Muhammad Hassan was a member of the Greek Club of Port Said (al-Nadi al-Yunani Por Said). As his name suggests, Muhammad was a Muslim living in Port Said. Nevertheless, as a young man who was interested in bodybuilding and physical exercise, Muhammad seems to have maintained no qualms about joining a voluntary association that maintained a conspicuous Greek appellation.[31]

Other organizations established around an exclusive ethnoreligious identity also attracted young men from different communal backgrounds. For example, the Young Men's Christian Association (YMCA) was a Protestant organization committed to recruiting Christians, Muslims, and Jews alike. Founded in urban centers throughout the region during the late nineteenth and early twentieth centuries, the YMCA provided spaces for members to read, take classes, exercise, and play sports.[32] In the aftermath of the First World War, YMCA administrators made a concerted effort to make team sports and gymnastics integral components of the organization's activities across the region.

Young men exercising, competing, and socializing in ethnically and religiously mixed spaces troubled some educators. A group of Muslim educators and reformers in Cairo were particularly critical of the YMCA's activities. The presence of Muslim members in the YMCA infuriated Muslim reformers, who viewed the organization as a Christian missionary one. It is in this context that the Young Men's Muslim Association (YMMA, in Arabic Jam'iyat al-Shuban al-Muslimin) was formed in Cairo in 1927.[33] Established in response to the YMCA, the YMMA looked to the organization as both a competitor and model, incorporating a number of athletic, cultural, social, as well as religious activities. The YMMA was not limited to Cairo; during the 1920s, the organization opened branches in other cities in Egypt as well as in Palestine.[34] Like other clubs during the twentieth century, the YMMA turned to photographs as a means to record and share its associational identity. Figure 2 is an example of the group photographs that members and administrators of the YMMA posed for. The image captures the YMMA's wrestling team posing in athletic attire. The YMMA shared the group portrait with *al-Abtal*, which subsequently published the image.

By the 1920s and 1930s, sports clubs became a regular fixture of urban centers in the Middle East. The efflorescence of these institutions also resulted in greater diversity. For example, football clubs in Turkey were divided between large and small. Large clubs were members of larger sports federations, had multiple sports branches, and had better amenities, such as fields, courts, gymnasiums, and equipment. Smaller clubs made up the vast majority of sporting organizations in Turkey during the first three decades of the twentieth century. They tended to be largely independent of larger federations and connected to a local neighborhood.

المصارعوبه الناشئوبه

بجمعية الشبان المسلمين

تمثل هذه الصورة فريق

جعية الشبان المسلمين من

المصارعين الناشئين الذي

سيشترك في بطولة القاهرة

للناشئين المحدد لاقامتها

يوم ٣ ابريل سنة ١٩٣٣

Figure 2: The wrestling team of the Young Men's Muslim Association (Jam'iyat al-Shubban al-Muslimin), *al-Abtal*.

Source: *Al-Abtal*, March 11, 1933, p. 22.

Sports clubs were not the only spaces in which ordinary people of the Middle East played sports and trained their bodies; young men—and, to a lesser extent, women—also played team sports and exercised in primary and secondary schools and colleges. Starting in the nineteenth century, educators in the Middle East started to envision sports as a means to create strong, healthy, and moral youth. As a result, they gradually integrated physical exercise into the daily lives of students in government, private minority, and foreign schools alike. Government schools in the Ottoman Empire and Egypt gradually integrated physical education into their curriculum during the late nineteenth century.[35] This development led to educators penning works in Arabic, Armenian, Greek, Ladino, Ottoman Turkish, and Persian about education that included discussions about physical exercise.[36]

The integration of physical education in government schools did not take place at the same time across the region. For example, educators in Iran started to integrate physical exercise into government school curricula after the First

World War.[37] The 1920s and 1930s, in particular, were important decades for the integration and spread of physical education courses as well as team sports in government schools. According to Issa Khan Sadiq, an Iranian who completed his PhD at Columbia University in 1931 and served as minister of education in Iran, after a school was established in order to teach physical education in 1925, 'a law was passed requiring daily physical exercise in all schools, at first in the larger cities, and gradually, within three years, in all parts of the country.'[38]

Physical exercise and sports were not limited to government schools. Jerusalem's Constitutional School (al-Madrasa al-Dusturiyya) also introduced students to the importance of exercising their bodies. Khalil al-Sakakini established a private school in 1909, envisioning the institution as a trendsetter in its approach to education.[39] The Constitutional School accepted students from different religions and confessions, banned corporeal punishment, and introduced a number of pedagogical innovations, including stressing the importance of 'sports' (al-alʿab al-riyada) and 'military exercises' (al-harakat al-ʿaskariyya).[40] Wasif Jawhariyyeh, who studied at the school during the early twentieth century, highlights the importance the school placed on the body and physical exercise. During the early twentieth century, an instructor from Lebanon taught the students sports the 'French military way' (ʿaskariyya Fransiyya).[41] In addition to stressing the salubrious benefits of exercise, al-Sakakini also encouraged students to eat well by regularly consuming meat, especially chicken. Together, the emphasis placed on exercise and diet, according to Jawhariyyeh, exposed students to the maxim: 'a sound mind [lives] in a sound body' (al-ʿaql al-sahih fil jism al-sahih).[42] This idea was not confined to the walls of the Constitutional School. Educators across the region and beyond, writing and teaching in a variety of languages, such as Arabic, Armenian, English, French, German, Hebrew, Ladino, Persian, and Turkish, institutionalized this modern reading of the interconnection between the body and the mind, and looked to sports as the most effective tool to develop a healthy body.[43]

Foreign missionary schools, in particular, served as some of the first spaces where people played team sports, exercised, and participated in athletic competitions. Administrators at American schools, such as the American University in Cairo (AUC), the Syrian Protestant College in Beirut (later the American University of Beirut), Robert College in Istanbul, the St Paul Institute in Tarsus, Anatolia College in Marsovan, Central College at Aintab, Alborz College in Tehran, and the English Church Missionary College in

Isfahan treated physical exercise and team sports as necessary components of a modern education.

American missionary schools were not the only institutions that valorized physical exercise. Jewish educational organizations spread across the Middle East also gradually integrated physical education into their curriculum. One of the most prominent and widespread was the Alliance Israélite Universelle (AIU). Operated as a French Jewish organization, the AIU created schools for boys and girls in cities throughout North Africa, the Ottoman Empire, and Iran.[44] The AIU's Central Committee considered gymnastics an effective means of modernizing Jews in 'the countries of the East or Africa' (*les pays d'Orient ou d'Afrique*),[45] or more specifically, that physical exercise helped strengthen the bodies and minds of Jewish youth.[46]

Educators in government, private, and foreign missionary schools, alike, viewed exercise as a necessary component of primary and secondary schools as well as colleges; however, American schools in particular played a leading role in institutionalizing team sports, such as football, basketball, and baseball, during the early twentieth century. Gymnastics and exercise enabled students to develop their bodies; however, team sports served as activities through which young men of different ethnic, religious, and socioeconomic backgrounds built bonds and developed a commitment to fair play, selflessness, honesty, and camaraderie.[47]

American colleges offered a number of amenities for students to exercise. Together, gymnasiums, athletic fields, and basketball and tennis courts enabled students to play team sports and exercise year-round. The American University of Beirut (AUB), for example, maintained a 'modern athletic field', which the college's administrators envisioned serving 'the purpose of an out-of-doors gymnasium.'[48] Many of the colleges also had indoor gymnasiums and outside gymnastics equipment. For example, both administrators at Robert College and Anatolia College built indoor gymnasiums. Robert College's gymnasium, Dodge gymnasium, maintained an indoor track, a complete set of gymnastic equipment, as well as a basketball court.

In many American colleges across the region, administrators often stressed the benefits of team sports. For example, Howard Bliss, president of the Syrian Protestant College, looked to 'foot-ball' as a team sport that enabled students to develop a number of noble qualities.[49] This sport, according to Bliss, 'develops the ability to receive a hard blow without showing the white feather or drawing a dagger. This means that when the men get out of the college they will stand upon their feet as men.'[50] In addition to cultivat-

21

ing these characteristics, the game also had the potential to bring together students from different socioeconomic classes. At the Syrian Protestant College, according to Bliss, the son of a prince and cook not only played together, the cook's son even served as the captain of the team.[51] In the 1930s, the English Missionary College in Isfahan also introduced football to its students.[52] In short, football was one of the most popular sports on campuses around the region.

Although educators at different American colleges highlighted the importance of football among students, college athletic departments also introduced a number of other team sports. Educators at the AUC introduced basketball to its students. By 1927, basketball, according to the school's newspaper, *The A.U.C. Review*, had become the 'favorite sport' at the AUC.[53] While the university's basketball team struggled to find another team to play against during the early 1920s, by 1925, a number of teams were formed in Cairo and Alexandria, such as the Lycée Français of Alexandria, Secondary Training College, Tawfiq Coptic, Training College, the College AUC Faculty, Assiut College, YMCA, and the Armenian National School.[54] AUC's basketball team did not only compete against teams in Cairo and Alexandria, but also played games against the American University of Beirut,[55] whose basketball team was highly competitive.[56]

Let's Talk about Sports: Exercise and Team Sports in the Press

Throughout the nineteenth and early twentieth centuries, sports enthusiasts penned articles in newspapers and magazines and authored pamphlets and books that contributed to localizing the practices and ideas espoused in schools and sports clubs. These writings shaped the discursive contours of the sports *nahda*. For example, starting in the 1890s, Cairo's Arabic press started to feature irregular articles on sports clubs, sports, and physical exercise. *Al-Hilal* featured these discussions in different sections of the publication, such as 'Question and Suggestion' (*bab al-su'al wa al-iqtira*) and 'Scientific News' (*bab al-akhbar al-'ilmiyya*). Together, they reveal a growing interest in physical exercise and sports.

There was also a concerted effort to frame these activities as indigenous to the region. For example, Doctor 'Abd al-Aziz 'Abd al-Mowjud's article 'Physical Exercise among the Ancient Egyptians' (*al-riyada al-badaniyya 'and al-masriyyin al-qudama*) offered illustrations of, and a discussion about, ancient Egyptians wrestling and playing a 'foot game' (*le'b al-kura*).[57]

Figure 3: Basketball game at the American University at Cairo's Field Day, AUC Archive.
Source: American University of Cairo Archive, Box 5, Athletics and sport—1920s –1980s—Sports day.

The article is significant because it presented a long history of physical exercise among the Egyptians. In doing so, the author conveyed the idea that at the height of their greatness, Egyptians were exercising their bodies. In short, sports were an *Egyptian* tradition. Whether or not this is historically 'accurate' is irrelevant. What is significant is the modern way in which the author marshalled historical facts about physical culture in ancient Egypt and deployed fundamentally novel assumptions about the body, nation, and historical continuity. Egyptians, according to the author, exercised and played sports before Westerners popularized team sports and gymnastics during the nineteenth century.

Illustrated magazines focused exclusively on sports and physical culture emerged throughout the Middle East during the first three decades of the twentieth century. Journals such as *al-Abtal* (the champions), *al-Medmar* (the track), and *al-Al'ab al-Riyadiyya* (sports) in Cairo, *Keihan-e varzeshi* (world of sports) in Tehran, and *Spor Alemi* (the world of sports), *Türkiye İdman Mecmuası* (Turkey's sports magazine), *Şa Şa Şa* (hooray), and *Marmnamarz*

Figure 4: The 'physical training' section of *al-Abtal*.
Source: 'al-Tarbiyya al-Badaniyya,' *al-Abtal*, February 4, 1933, p. 10.

(physical training) in Istanbul, provided readers with an abundance of information about sports.[58] The founders, editors, and authors of these publications drew insights, both in terms of content and format, from physical cultural magazines published in the United States and Europe during the period. Nevertheless, by selectively running similar sections and translations of articles, they also localized the debates and discussions that sports enthusiasts were having in the west. In short, Arabic, Armenian, Persian, and Turkish sports magazines simultaneously reflected the growing spread of discussions about sports in the west and the growing demand for information about sports in a local idiom.

These publications, as well as leading weekly magazines that ran sporting editions,[59] provided the space needed for thinkers to establish the discursive boundaries of these novel physical activities in the region's press.[60] According

to historian Wilson Jacob, nineteenth-century writers in Egypt reconfigured
the Islamic concept of *riyadat al-nafs* (caring for the soul) and redeployed it
as *al-riyada* (sports).[61] *Al-riyada* consisted of a diverse range of physical activities, such as team sports, physical education, and gymnastics. Educators writing in Ottoman-Turkish, Persian, and Armenian also refashioned terms and/
or developed neologisms to describe new practices. Ottomans writing in
Ottoman-Turkish deployed the terms '*idman*' and '*spor*' to mean sports, and
the terms '*terbiye-i bedeniye*' and '*riyazet-i bedeniye*' to mean physical education. In Persian, people deployed '*varzesh*' for sports and physical exercise, and
'*tarbiyat-e badani*' for physical education.[62] Iranian educators often used *tarbiyat-e badani* in a more specific context of the school system, while *varzesh*
was used as a comprehensive term. In short, people writing in a variety of
languages treated physical education, both institutionally and discursively, as
part of a broader category of sports.

These discussions presented novices and experts, sports enthusiasts and
skeptics, with a diverse array of content. Articles in sports magazines focused
on particular team sports—mostly, but not exclusively, football—physical
exercise, and scouting, as well as on bodily care. Magazines often ran articles
describing how to play sports. For example, *Spor Alemi*'s first edition featured
a two-page article titled 'How Do We Play Football?' (*Nasıl Futbol
Oynuyoruz?*).[63] In addition to team sports, many magazines also featured regular sections on how to perform physical exercise and calisthenics. A section in
al-Abtal titled 'Physical Exercise' (*al-tarbiyya al-badaniyya*) stressed the
importance of regular exercise: 'spending ten minutes a day doing physical
exercises is enough to keep your body in a good state (*hala jayida*) of health,
strength, and activity.'[64] These textual and visual guides offered detailed
instructions for the reader, especially the novice, to follow.

Publications also offered impassioned editorials that stressed the moral
benefits of physical exercise. According to *al-Abtal*, 'the majority of Egyptians
still believe that physical exercise is a bunch of deviance and nonsense, and
that the good sportsman does not have any special qualities besides the growth
of his body and the prominence of his muscles.'[65] The editorial argues that in
addition to molding bodies, physical exercise also shaped the defining contours of a person's morality. This gendered athlete, irrespective of whether he
was a football player, wrestler, gymnast, boxer, or swimmer, developed praise-
worthy characteristics, such as bravery, discipline, endurance, and a commitment to the 'spirit of collaboration' and 'brotherhood' that made him the ideal
man. In addition to cultivating these positive traits, 'the correct sportsman'

(*al-riyadi al-sahih*) developed the discipline to stay away from three of the most significant vices that ostensibly damaged the moral fiber of people: 'alcohol, smoking and staying out late.'[66] In short, sports facilitated the creation of a modern, moral, and healthy generation of men.[67]

Sports publications also created a strong discursive connection between sports 'abroad' and 'home.' *Spor Alemi*, for example, accomplished this by running sections entitled 'the world of sports in Turkish regions' (*Türk diyarında spor alemi*), 'the world of sports' local news' (*spor aleminin dahili havadisleri*), and 'news of the west' (*garp haberleri*).[68] These sections included both the results and short descriptions of football, hockey, and boxing matches. Sports magazines also featured photographs of local and foreign athletes on the cover, and published regular spreads dedicated to discussing the feats of these modern, healthy athletes, the sports they played, and the teams for which they competed. In doing so, magazines like *al-Abtal* created a pantheon of moral athletic 'heroes' (*abtal*) at home and abroad. Over the next few decades, books were also published on these heroes, extolling their athletic feats.

Figure 5: Anwar Ahmad on the cover of *al-Abtal*.
Source: *al-Abtal*, February 25, 1933.

Figure 6: Egypt's early-twentieth-century football star Hussein Higazi.
Source: Al-Sayid Faraj, *Kabtin Masr: Hussein Higazi* (Cairo: al-Majlis al-A'la li-Ri'ayat al-Shabab, 1961).

The press also served as the leading instrument through which educators stressed the importance of women's exercise. Such calls date back to the late nineteenth century, when women's magazines published caricatures of women performing gymnastics.[69] During the 1920s and 1930s, however, this irregular coverage significantly expanded, both in quality and quantity. The press textually and visually celebrated young women's performance of physical exercise and, to a lesser degree, team sports. Sports and cultural magazines regularly ran articles that examined the important athletic and educational achievements of young women, developments in the institutionalization of sports in girls' schools, as well as why and how girls, young women, and older women should exercise. For example, *Spor Alemi* ran a lengthy article that textually and visually highlighted the importance of sports in the Istanbul Girls' High School (İstanbul Kız Lisesi).[70] The article featured images of female students playing basketball and volleyball (Figure 7).

While both men and women were increasingly encouraged to play sports, some sports enthusiasts also contributed to a gendering of sports by highlighting the idea that certain athletic activities were more appropriate for women.[71]

Tennis, according to a doctor writing in *al-Muqtataf* (the collection), one of Cairo's leading journals, was not suitable for women. 'The violent game' was considered dangerous for women, but not men, because it created a disproportionate physique.[72] During the 1920s and 1930s, Iran's press also expressed a gendered reading of sports. According to historian Mikiya Koyagi, Tehran's press argued that swimming and dancing and, to a lesser extent, volleyball and skiing were more appropriate physical activities for women because they maintained weaker bodies than men.[73] Publications like *Ta'lim va Tarbiyat* (instruction and education) highlighted the different benefits that physical exercise offered boys and girls: exercise prepared girls for housework, while it prepared boys for the military and work outside of the house.[74]

Sports enthusiasts founded, edited, and contributed to these magazines. The magazines were anchored in the debates and discussions surrounding sports, athletics, and physical exercise of the cities in which they were produced. Nevertheless, the content of the magazines also resonated with a growing Arabic, Armenian, Persian, and Turkish reading public throughout the

Figure 7: Full two-page article in Spor *Alemi* (The World of Sports) about the institutionalization of sports in the Istanbul Girls' High School.
Source: 'İstanbul Kız Lisesi'nde Spor,' *Spor Alemi*, March 3, 1926, pp. 10–11.

Middle East. As a result, these magazines circulated beyond the city and country in which they were produced. For example, a growing Arabic readership read the Cairene *al-Abtal* in other cities in Egypt, such as Alexandria, Port Said, and Tanta, as well as outside of Egypt, in Baghdad, Beirut, and Damascus. Historian Stacey Fahrenthold demonstrates that intellectuals and educators writing in the Syrian *mahjar* (diaspora) were also active contributors to a transnational discussion in Arabic about sports.[75] Jurj Atlas' Arabic literary magazine *al-Karma* (the vineyard), which was published in São Paulo, Brazil, included discussions about the moral benefits of physical exercise and team sports.[76]

Other magazines reveal the transnational dissemination of these ideas throughout the Middle East. For example, *al-Abtal* published a section that featured photographs of young athletes sent to the journal by readers from different parts of Egypt and other cities in the region.[77] According to the section, 'on this page, we are printing some photos of novices in Egypt and other places from "sister regions" (*al-aqtar al-shaqiqa*), to encourage and promote their development and brilliance.'[78] Figure 8 depicts one of the regular sections that *al-Abtal* published of these neophyte athletes. The section features photographs of young men with contorted and well-defined bodies, posing in athletic attire, as well as captions describing who they are, what physical activities they regularly perform, and where they are from. For example, according to the section titled '*Min Damashq*' (from Damascus), 'Abbas and Baha' al-Din, who were interested in wrestling and boxing, respectively, were among Damascus's most brilliant 'young athletes.'[79]

These photographs and descriptions are significant for three reasons. First, they reveal a growing Arabic reading public throughout the Middle East read the magazine. In other words, the magazine circulated among sports enthusiasts in urban centers of the region. Second, by sharing images and short biographies with *al-Abtal*, young men like 'Abbas and Baha' al-Din from Damascus, Muhammad Bakkar from Beirut, and Rasheed Hasan and 'Abd al-Sattar 'Abd al-Latif from Iraq actively shaped the content of the magazine.[80] As a result, the magazine cultivated a transnational Arab identity. Third, these vernacular photographs firmly established the widespread dissemination of sports photography throughout urban centers of the Middle East during the early twentieth century.[81] Young men from Egypt, Iraq, Lebanon, and Syria had their photographs taken dressed in tightfitting athletic attire, while they flexed their muscles and contorted their bodies. These images served as tokens of friendship and 'gifts' that young men shared with friends, colleagues, as well as the press. Many of

Figure 8: Photos of athletes from Egypt and 'sister regions' (*al-aqtar al-shaqiqa*), *al-Abtal*.
Source: *Al-Abtal*, January 28, 1933, p. 20.

these images, like the photograph of al-Sayid 'Abd al-Wahed (Figure 9), were signed and addressed to the recipient.

Illustrated sports magazines were not the only publications that provided the region's growing reading public with information about sports; daily newspapers also offered an abundance of information about the importance of physical exercise and team sports, and provided readers with regular coverage of football matches. Daily newspapers had a significantly larger circulation than illustrated physical culture journals. As a result, these publications probably played a more significant role in spreading and popularizing discussions about sports throughout the region. During the first four decades of the twentieth century, articles in Arabic, Armenian, English, French, Greek, Hebrew, Ladino, Persian, and Turkish were published about team sports and athletics;

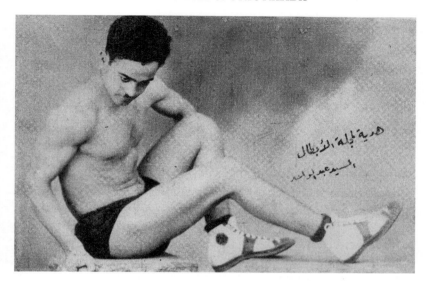

Figure 9: Signed photograph of al-Sayid 'Abd al-Wahed that he gifted to *al-Abtal*. Source: *Al-Abtal*, February 11, 1933, p. 18.

many of these publications also created regular sports columns. The development of these discussions in popular newspapers, such as *al-Nahar* (the day) in Beirut,[82] *al-Ahram* (the pyramids) in Cairo,[83] *al-Qabas* (the firebrand) in Damascus,[84] *Cumhuriyet* (the republic) and *Takhidromos* (postman) in Istanbul,[85] *Filastin* (Palestine) in Jaffa,[86] and *Etilla'at* (information) in Tehran,[87] ensured that sports was considered part of daily news. English and French newspapers, like *The Egyptian Gazette* in Alexandria and *L'Orient* (the Orient) and *Le Jour* (the day) in Beirut, provided sports coverage to many of the foreign passport holders in the Middle East during the transition from empire to nation-state and the mandate system. It is safe to assume that when people of the region sat down in a coffee shop either to read or listen to someone read the daily news,[88] they would have encountered discussions about team sports, gymnastics, and exercise.

This coverage exposed readers to the outcome of local, regional, and international matches. *The Egyptian Gazette*, for example, provided coverage of the various football tournaments organized in Cairo and Alexandria as well as a 'football calendar' for readers to follow.[89] Newspaper columns often described the performance of teams in local, regional, and international competitions as indicators of the nation's development and progress. However, international matches between national teams, namely football, were particularly loaded with symbolic meaning.[90]

In addition to coverage of sports in newspapers and magazines, advertisements from the press during the first three decades of the twentieth century also reveal the growing popularity of sports. It was during this period that department stores started carrying athletic apparel, and sporting goods shops opened across the region.[91] For example, Istanbul's 'sporting store' (sporting mağazası) regularly ran ads in the sporting press of the city, informing readers that the store offered 'football, tennis, golf, hockey, cricket, baseball, boxing, basketball, volleyball, and scouting apparel.'[92] The New London House in Cairo also carried a diverse array of goods.[93] The store's impressive selection of athletic apparel included 'football shoes, boxing gloves, tennis rackets, sport shirts, sweaters, trunks, traveling bags, boy scouts equipment, as well as hats.'[94] According to one advertisement, the store's inexpensive selection attracted students and sports aficionados alike.[95] Together, these and other advertisements reveal the expansion of a sports market that offered consumers sports

Figure 10: Advertisement for Istanbul's 'sporting mağazası' (sporting store), *Spor Alemi*.

Source: *Spor Alemi*, April 19, 1922, p. 10.

apparel that could be used for both educational and leisure activities in cities across the Middle East.

Matches and Sporting Events

During the first three decades of the twentieth century, sporting events served as popular forms of entertainment and educational displays. Football matches, athletic competitions, and gymnastics exhibitions played an integral role in the spread and popularization of the sports *nahda*. These events were organized in a variety of spaces. Formal and informal matches were played in open fields, on the grounds of sports clubs, as well as in stadiums. Stadiums and open fields provided football fans, sports enthusiasts, and the casual observer with outdoor venues where they could socialize and watch clubs compete and young athletes display their athletic acumen. These spaces differed, however. For example, some of the earliest football matches in Jerusalem were organized in a makeshift field in the Palestinian quarter of Herod's Gate (Bab al-Sbat).[96] The growing popularity of sporting events in Istanbul encouraged denizens of the city to build multiple venues across the city.[97] In other cities, football matches were often played on club grounds. For example, in Cairo and Damascus, matches were played in the Ahli Sporting Club's stadium and the Mu'awiyya Club's stadium, respectively.[98]

Matches, leagues, tournaments, and cups played an important role in popularizing football. For example, the creation of the Sultan's Cup in Egypt marked a watershed moment in the institutionalization and vernacularization of football in colonial Egypt.[99] The Sultan's Cup served as the first nationwide football championship in Egypt. Both the timing and founders of the championship are significant. The Mixed Sporting Association in Alexandria formed the championship during the First World War in 1916. Because the Mixed Sporting Association exclusively consisted of foreign personnel, a number of Egyptian football clubs refused to participate in the competition. The boycott seemed to have an effect on the association, because the Mixed Sporting Association decided to allow three Egyptians to serve on its committee. In response, the Egyptian teams leading the boycott participated in the championship in 1917. Together, the inclusion of Egyptian personnel in the Mixed Sporting Association and the participation of Egyptian teams in the national championship resulted in people showing up for matches. Coverage of the Sultan's Cup in *The Egyptian Gazette*, for example, regularly praised the sizeable number of football fans at the matches.

The spread and localization of football through the construction of clubs, the organization of matches and tournaments, and the regular coverage of such matches in the daily press made football an immensely popular pastime for people of the region. According to *The Egyptian Gazette*, by 1918, 'football serve[d] to be the principle attraction for all lovers of sport.'[100] Cairo was not the only city that experienced football fever. Residents in Baghdad, Damascus, Jerusalem, and Istanbul also regularly attended football matches. By the 1920s, newspapers and magazines increasingly commented on the development of a fan culture at football matches, more specifically, and sporting events, more generally.

The growing popularity of sporting events as social spaces also served as a source of concern. Commentators criticized both the ability of athletes and spectators, or lack thereof, to maintain proper etiquette when playing or watching a match. For example, a US report on the state of sports in the Republic of Turkey during the 1930s describes football matches as events where 'feeling runs high', 'riots ... develop', and 'players and spectators alike' engage in 'free-for-all fights.'[101] The author of the report, Eugene M. Hinkle, Third Secretary of the United States Embassy in Ankara, was particularly concerned with the spectators at the match, which he referred to as 'the Turkish crowd.' According to Hinkle, 'in any match one has the feeling that the crowd while listless has latent enormous unrestrained emotions which may be unleashed at some unforeseen provocation.'[102]

Such descriptions were not unique to football in Turkey. *The Egyptian Gazette*, for example, criticized what it regarded as the Egyptian Football Association's inability to foster a culture of sportsmanship and respect. The association, according to an article published in 1925, did not have 'the slightest idea of control of players, clubs or spectators.'[103] Events at a match at the Prince Farouk Cup Final, which consisted of 'fighting, arguing, and foul play', revealed that the Egyptian Football Association, 'either individually or collectively', did not have 'the slightest intention of willingness of "playing the game".'[104]

Not Modern Enough? The Problem with Sports among the 'Locals'

Westerners living in the Middle East often displayed a patronizing view of football, specifically, and sports, more generally. These views were embedded in a broader late-nineteenth-century colonial discourse that often claimed that people of the region were both inherently different and in a transitional state in which they had neither properly modernized nor fully embraced the blessings of western civilization.[105] Newspaper articles written by foreigners living in the region reveal both an appreciation for the development of football as well as the inability of 'locals' to play, watch, and/or referee the sport like Westerners. *The Egyptian Gazette*, for example, explicitly challenged Egyptians' ability to serve as referees. In February 1924, the newspaper ran a series of articles and letters about the dismal performance of an Egyptian referee at the Prince Farouk Cup. According to one of the letters, '[a]s far as can be gathered from reports regarding the referee in a recent match at Cairo, there does not appear to be the least doubt that the referee was not only weak, but biased.'[106] The anonymous writer suggested that in the future 'an absolutely neutral referee' should be appointed for such matches where 'feeling ... runs high.'[107] More concerning to the author was the potential of Egyptians to tarnish the name of football in Egypt: 'one can see at no far distant date that football in Egypt (the locals) will spoil the very name if the European element is not allowed to have more power on the various committees.'[108] In other words, the author was worried about the ways in which 'the locals' would dilute the European characteristics of honesty, sportsmanship, neutrality, and discipline that ostensibly undergirded football.

According to this nineteenth-century colonial discourse, punctuality was also a defining feature of the west, which the Egyptians failed to properly respect and comprehend. *The Egyptian Gazette* ran articles admonishing Egyptians' disregard for punctuality on the pitch, noting that Egyptians' 'prevailing custom these days' of showing up late to matches ensured that the sporting events were less exciting.[109] On 1 March 1924, the newspaper ran such an article about a delayed friendly match between Egyptian State Railways Institute (ESRI) and Royal Air Force (RAF) at the Railways Ground.

> The match having been arranged to begin at 3–15, a good number of spectators were present, but they had to wait along with the visiting team who punted the ball about the field until 3–30 when Hegazi lead [sic] out most of his men, the others following like Mary's little lamb.[110]

The fact that Hussein Higazi was leading the late team is significant. His feats on the pitch in Egypt and England—serving as captain of the Egyptian National Football team in the 1920 and 1928 Olympic Games and competing on different football teams across Egypt—led many to deem Higazi one of the most important Egyptian football players of his generation.[111] The article implied that even Egypt's most respected player was unable to be punctual.[112] Moreover, the article suggested that this indifference to punctuality on the pitch stemmed from a more fundamental disregard for the importance of time throughout Egypt, which it described as 'the "maalesh" spirit'.[113] Such indifference to punctuality might be acceptable among Egyptians, but it would definitely not be tolerated in the west. This was particularly troubling to the author of the article, given that the Egyptian National Football team was to compete in the 1924 Olympic Games in Paris:[114] 'A little less of the "maalesh" spirit will have to be shown by the Egyptians when they take part in the Olympic Games, as punctuality is enforced rigidly.'[115]

The Turkish sports press was cognizant of such views. *Spor Alemi* even ran satirical cartoons of stereotypical European views of Turks. A cartoon published in February 1922 exemplifies this approach (Figure 11). The image features a Turkish man dressed in a turban, sitting cross-legged on the ground, and smoking a water pipe. While postcards and descriptions of traveling throughout the empire and broader Middle East often featured images of Turks smoking in cafes, this character is particularly novel: The 'idle' tobacco-consuming Turk is dressed in athletic attire, shorts, jersey, and football cleats. Together, the image and satirical caption, '*Avrupalılar Türkleri Nasıl Biliyorlar?*' (how do Europeans know Turks?), present a well-established Orientalist trope and reveal its reconfiguration.[116]

Despite the implicit critique of this image, many sports enthusiasts, whose writings and activities shaped the sports *nahda*, internalized the idea that Westerners were ontologically more developed than they were. Writing in Egypt during the early twentieth century, Muhammad 'Umar, for example, argued that Europeans were modern, developed, and successful in large part because of their embrace of sports and physical exercise.[117] Sporting columns in Mandatory Palestine's Arabic press stressed that Arabs were athletes in the past; however, they had come to abandon physical exercise for a long period, which had resulted in their perceived decline.[118] In short, these and other discussions reveal the ways in which contributors to the *nahda* simultaneously accepted and challenged the idea that they were inherently less modern.

Conclusion

Can we talk about a shared history of sports in the Middle East? Tracing the emergence and spread of team sports and physical exercise throughout urban centers of the Middle East starting in the late nineteenth century until the 1930s, this chapter demonstrates that there were important shared discursive and institutional features across the region. There were striking similarities in

Figure 11: 'How do Europeans know Turks?', *Spor Alemi*.
Source: 'Avrupalılar Türkleri Nasıl Biliyorlar?' *Spor Alemi*, February 8, 1922, p. 2.

terms of the institutions and actors that popularized sports. Schools, sports clubs, the press, public squares, and stadiums served as the main venues in which, and through which, people institutionalized and popularized sports. The activities of educators, government officials, sports club administrators, students, club members, editors, and columnists in these spaces helped turn sports into a regular fixture of the urban landscape of cities across the region.

People across the region displayed a similar reading of sports. Articles in the press, school reports, and the experience of fans in the stands across the region reveal that people envisioned and treated sports as a form of education and a form of pleasure. Sports enthusiasts teaching in schools, working in sports clubs, and penning articles in the press, certainly foregrounded the importance of sports as an educational activity that enabled young men and, increasingly, young women to develop into ideal, modern citizens. However, their focus on the educational benefits, as well as their implicit and explicit critique of sports as a form of leisure, also speaks volumes about the different ways in which ordinary people took pleasure in watching a football match or athletic competition, reading about it in the press, as well as arguing and fighting about a goal with strangers and friends. Together, the institutional and discursive arenas of sports reveal that people living in urban centers across the region envisioned and experienced sports as a form of pleasure and discipline.

Despite these similarities, there were important differences that emerged out of the intersection of space, people, time, and circumstance. The history of sports, like other embodied forms of knowledge and practice, were interwoven with the social, cultural, and political history of cities, empires, and new polities that emerged after the First World War. For example, sports clubs, schools, and the press introduced physical exercise and team sports at different moments throughout the region. Newspaper and magazine articles, government and school reports, as well as diaries and memoirs reveal that residents of Cairo, Istanbul, and Jerusalem encountered football, gymnastics, as well as other team sports as early as the late nineteenth century. On the other hand, with the exception of students at missionary schools, Iranians living in cities across Iran had to wait until the 1920s and 1930s.

This chapter establishes that the sports *nahda* was a regional phenomenon. However, additional research could offer important insights into the degree to which particular cities emerged as regional sports hubs in the Middle East during the first three decades of the twentieth century. In other words, did sports aficionados across the region look to specific places for information about sports and physical culture? Did exchanges of people, ideas, objects, and practices take place in some cities more frequently than others? This chapter suggests that by the 1920s and 1930s, Cairo, Istanbul, and Tehran served as, what historian Ilham Khuri-Makdisi calls, nodal cities.[119] This does not mean that there was a dearth of sports clubs, football matches, and discussions about physical exercise in cities like Baghdad, Beirut, Damascus, and Jerusalem; nevertheless, a growing Arabic, Turkish, and Persian speaking and reading public increasingly turned to these places for the latest trends in, and discussions about, the world of sports.

The regional sports *nahda* also reveals the profound intellectual and ethnoreligious diversity of the individuals and institutions that shaped the defining contours of sports throughout the Middle East. As a result, these historical actors offer a unique window into the inclusivity of the cultural *nahda* that engulfed the Middle East during the early twentieth century.

MAPPING THE 'SPORTS *NAHDA*'

Much of the traditional literature focuses its analysis of the *nahda* as an Arab awakening; however, the sports *nahda* demonstrates that it was inclusive of Muslim wrestlers in the Young Men's Muslim Association in Cairo, American Protestant educators in Istanbul, Zionist sports clubs in Jerusalem, and footballers in Tehran.

2

FOOTBALL'S ROLE IN HOW
SOCIETIES REMEMBER

THE SYMBOLIC WARS OF
JORDANIAN–PALESTINIAN FOOTBALL

Dag Tuastad

Introduction

My aim in this chapter is to demonstrate, using a case study from Jordan, how
the football arena constitutes a dominant stage for battles over national social
memories. Social memory, as Maurice Halbwachs argued, has two dimensions.[1] The first has to do with memorization as a cognitive process with a
social dimension. In a continuous stream of impressions, what becomes
selected as memories in the mind is determined by group dynamics—by the
social interaction with others who share the same experience(s) or have the
same understanding of events. Remembering, Halbwachs noted, takes place
in individual minds, but through group membership.[2]

The second dimension of social memory is related to how group identity is
produced through the active remaking of the past. As members of a social

group commemorate and attach meaning to the past, their self-awareness and self-consciousness is created. Memory is, as understood by Olick and Robbins, 'a central, if not the central, medium through which identities are constituted.'[3] Social memory is also a battlefield. Just as there are struggles over dominant narratives and discourses in society, there are struggles over memories. Where one finds mnemonic hegemonic strategies of states and other powerful actors, one also finds counter-memories challenging these.[4]

The role of football and the sports arena in how societies remember, I will argue, is an understudied field in the social science of sport.[5] In the case at hand, I will analyze how football matches contribute to preserve social memories of ethnic communities. The chapter is organized into three phases of symbolic battles between Palestinian Jordanians and East Bank Jordanians observed during football matches. First, from 1970 to the Oslo process in the 1990s with the Palestinians' social memories of the civil war to reassert their national identity. Second, after the Oslo process until the Arab uprisings in 2011, the East Bank Jordanians' assertions of the historic roots of the alliance between East Bank tribes and the Jordanian monarchy. And finally, Palestinian refugees' social memories of their common ethnic origin, confirming their refugee identities while being Jordanian citizens.

Methodology

This study is methodologically based on multi-sited ethnographic fieldwork in Jordan over a period of twenty years. This includes participant observation in the Wihdat camp, deciphering of fan chants during matches, as well as interviews and conversations with various informants, including Wihdat fans and club leaders, and antagonists with Jordanian army and East Bank backgrounds. My first fieldwork was in the Wihdat camp in the summer of 1994, focusing on Palestinian refugees' coping strategies.[6] Having learnt about the camp football club and the political dimensions of football in Jordan, I returned to Jordan the subsequent year to do ethnographic fieldwork in Amman focusing on the political role of football in the country.[7] Since then, I have followed developments in Wihdat and its football club during several rounds of fieldwork. The two latest field trips to Wihdat took place in 2012 and 2014. In 2012, I carried out fieldwork for a study of the role of football in the Arab revolutions.[8] While I base this chapter on material gathered going all the way back to my first visits, the main fieldwork was conducted in 2014. Following Wihdat matches during the end of that football season, I observed how ethnic roots and symbols, like the iconic status of *mulukhiya*,[9] appeared to have gained a more dominant place in the chants of supporters than what I had registered earlier. This was what made me contemplate the crucial role of football in social memory, preserving the two sub-nations of Jordan: the Palestinian Jordanians and the East Bank Jordanians.

The First Phase: Social Memories of the Civil War during Football Matches

In 1948, with the establishment of Israel and the Arab defeat in the Israeli–Arab war, no country received more Palestinian refugees than Jordan. After the war, King Abdullah of Jordan annexed the West Bank, which had until then been part of the British mandate of Palestine. With the annexation of the West Bank, and the massive influx of refugees from within what became Israel's border in 1948, Jordan was demographically Palestinianized. The 340,000 indigenous Jordanians saw 450,000 West Bank Palestinians and 450,000 Palestinian refugees become not only new inhabitants of Jordan, but also new citizens, as Abdullah thought of himself as the king of the Palestinians and East Bank Jordanians alike and granted the Palestinians citizenship.[10]

When Israel occupied the West Bank in 1967, this partly represented a moment of liberation for the refugees.[11] The Arab monarchies, like Jordan, were weakened, while the Palestinian Liberation Organization, the PLO, was taken over by Palestinian guerrilla groups, mainly based in Jordan. The PLO guerrilla groups could barely absorb all the refugees streaming to their offices to take part in the armed struggle. Fatah, the main PLO group, had an explicit strategy of engaging Israel in armed struggle launched from Israel's neighboring states. When Israel responded, this would force these states to participate on the Palestinian side against Israel. The strategy was largely successful until 1970. Other PLO groups wanted to first use armed force to bring down what they saw as reactionary regimes of the Arab world, like Jordan, and to subsequently unite the Arab world against Israel.[12]

By September 1970, King Hussein had had enough and cracked down on the PLO. The PLO headquarters in the Wihdat camp on the outskirts of Amman was dealt the heaviest blow as the Palestinian resistance movement in Jordan was crushed, eventually fleeing to Lebanon. The Palestinian refugee camps, and first among them, the Wihdat camp, were in ruins.

After the 1970 civil war, an 'East Bank first' policy was employed in Jordan. It meant that the Palestinians from then on confronted innumerable problems within the Jordanian bureaucracy in order to obtain a driving license or passport, register a business, etc. The Palestinians were discriminated against because of their national identity. Nevertheless, their exclusion from any middle ground, and the increased segregation and discrimination, inadvertently strengthened internal Palestinian social interaction and solidarity, and thus also Palestinian national identity. Suppressing Palestinian nationalism ended up reinforcing it. The only arena where Palestinian national identity could be openly expressed became, from then on, the football arena. From the ashes of the Wihdat camp, the headquarters of the PLO during the civil war, and the most heavily damaged of the camps, was born the most successful sporting phenomenon in Palestinian history.

Wihdat Football Club evolved as a result of the activities of the youth centers established in the camps by the United Nations Relief and Works Agency for Palestine Refugees in the Near East (UNRWA), the UN agency administering the camps. Initially, the various refugee camps organized their own separate league system, outside the national Jordanian system. From 1975, however, teams from the Palestinian refugee camps were admitted into the Jordanian league. Wihdat evolved into a tremendous success story. Through its matches, the refugees would get to know the rare taste of victory.[13] Thus, while most matches in the Jordanian league attracted an audience of a couple of hundred, the Amman stadium was packed with 20,000 supporters when Wihdat played—and not only in Amman; wherever Wihdat played in Jordan, the Palestinian refugee population rushed to the stadiums. Wihdat became a symbol of Palestinianness, with the club insignia visible all over Jordan wherever there were Palestinians. Wihdat's jerseys, shorts, and socks were black, green, red, and white, the colors of the Palestinian flag. There was a heavily enforced law against exposing or supporting Palestinian nationalism, but there was no law against supporting a football team in the Jordanian league. A special car horn sound came to be associated with Wihdat, and the green Wihdat shirt was everywhere to be seen. Wihdat became an unequivocal expression of Palestinianness, an identity elsewhere forbidden.

Each year, Wihdat climbed within the league system. In 1980, they sensationally won the league. The supporters celebrated this and subsequent victories as if they were indeed national victories. 'Wihdat is something holy, it is Palestine. ... When Wihdat lose, Palestine loses' said an inhabitant of the Wihdat refugee camp.[14] The role of the football team in raising the morale and self-respect of the refugees was explicit in supporter chants: 'Arrange the chairs, arrange the chairs, the green Wihdat raises our heads' (*suffu al-karasi, suffu al-karasi, al-Wihdat al-akhdar byirfaʿ al-raʾsi*). In the football arena, the refugees reformulated their identity. They replaced the stigma of abandoning their lands and losing their honor by becoming *fida'iyun*, or armed guerrilla fighters, chanting, 'we don't want wheat or sardines, we want bombs' (*ma bidna thin wala sardin, bidna anabil*). In the Jordanian context, a reference to armed struggle would inadvertently be interpreted as a reference to the 1970 civil war as much as to the Palestinian liberation struggle. Supporters of opposing teams from East Bank origin ridiculed Wihdat for being cheap—it being the location for the largest and cheapest tomato market in the Amman area—often chanting: 'The whole of Wihdat sells tomatoes.' Wihdat supporters responded with 'we are all Palestinians,' and 'we are all *fida'iyun*' (guerrilla soldiers).[15]

This symbolic war between the supporters at matches—Palestinians against ethnic Jordanians as during the civil war—would increasingly be accompanied by physical clashes between the supporters. Crowd violence peaked at a match in 1986. As police forces fired warning shots during the disturbances, several people were injured and one supporter of the Faisali team—the team most associated with East Bank nationalism—was killed. The incident represented a breaking point regarding the Jordanian regime's tolerance for the mini civil war fought anew every time the Faisali and Wihdat teams met. The board of Wihdat was dissolved and the club was put under direct control of the Jordanian government. Moreover, a name change was imposed. The new name, al-Difftain—or, the two Banks, referring to the East Bank and West Bank of the Jordan river—was designed to express the government's desire that the club no longer be the property of Palestinian refugees. But it would take much more than a name change to remove the most distinctive feature of the club—the only arena in Jordan where Palestinian national identity could be expressed in public. Wihdat supporters continued to chant heavily politicized chants during matches. 'Take off, take off, from the Amman stadium to the West Bank' (*shalit, shalit, min stad al-'Amman li-Daffa al-Gharbiya*) they chanted, turning the Two Banks name into one of return and re-conquest.

In 1988, the Palestinian uprising in the West Bank and Gaza stirred up the deadlocked Middle East conflict. One consequence was King Hussein withdrawing Jordan's claims over the West Bank. Jordan thus abandoned its ambition to represent Palestinians in the West Bank and Jordan alike. A year later, Jordan abolished emergency rule and opened the way for democratic elections. The new parliament elected in 1989 promptly decided to abolish the al-Difftain impositions. Control over the club was returned to the

Wihdat camp, and its board could again gather at the club's headquarters inside the camp.

With the 1993 Declaration of Principles between the PLO and Israel, and Jordan's peace agreement with Israel in 1994, a new political reality dawned for the Palestinians in Jordan. Visualizing Palestinianness and acquiring international recognition of the PLO were no longer collective Palestinian issues, with the PLO being internationally recognized as the sole representative of the Palestinian people. The focus of the Palestinian national movement was now state building in the self-ruled areas of Palestine.

The Second Phase: FC Faisali, Asserting the Common Roots between the Monarchy and the East Bank Tribes

It takes two to tango. If the civil war was fought all over again symbolically during football matches, the club foremost representing East Bank nationalism was FC Faisali. From 1957 until 1977, they were unrivalled in Jordan, winning the league every single year. When Wihdat rose to fame it was chiefly at the expense of Faisali. The symbolism could not be missed. Wihdat replaced the Jordanian team that had been the symbol of East Bank success and of the alliance between Jordanians of tribal origin and the Jordanian throne. It was the story of Palestinians in Jordan; if Wihdat could replace Faisali, the Palestinians could eventually take over the whole country. Wihdat matches against Faisali would consequently bring to the surface East Bank Jordanians' deeply felt resentments.

The civil war had severely crushed the illusion of Jordan as a united country, and room for a middle ground had disappeared. An East Bank neo-nationalism had emerged alongside Palestinian nationalism. East Bank neo-nationalism represented those who regarded the Palestinians as ungrateful for the hospitality of Jordan, a country that granted them refuge as well as citizenship. Some saw the Palestinians as traitors.[16] The core of East Bank neo-nationalism was thus anti-Palestinianism, emphasizing values opposed to that of the Palestinians. The PLO's nationalism had been largely secular, pan-Arabic, and leftist. Neo-Jordanian nationalism emphasized tribal roots and values, Islamic tradition, and Hashemite loyalty. Importantly, East Bank neo-nationalism emphasized the tribal roots of the monarchy itself.

Historically, Jordan was never a political community. It was made a country because of British interests in controlling the unruly tribal people of some 300,000 living in the area between Syria, Palestine, and Iraq. Unlike the Arabs of the Arabian Peninsula who sided with Britain during the First World War to bring the Ottoman Empire down, the Bedouins of Transjordan sided with their Ottoman rulers. The reason was that the Bedouins wanted to preserve the status quo rather than have borders limit their freedom of movement. However, while the British faced rebellions in Iraq, Egypt, and Syria, their colonial rule in Transjordan turned out to be a great success. The key to this success was the benevolent form of indirect rule practiced, through the shaykhs of the tribes, not instead of them.[17] To understand the alliance between the Faisali football club and the Jordanian throne, these historical ties are of essential importance.

'Abdullah bin Husayn, the son of the *Sharif* of Mecca, was brought in as the ruler of the tribal confederacies, operating under British supremacy and receiving a monthly salary and a budget to administer the area. When the nomadic tribes gradually settled, they were handed plots of land and they adjusted to a mixed system of pasturage and cultivation. Moreover, the sons of shaykhs were recruited to military desert control, administered by the British. This turned the former nomadic raiders into the core of the armed forces of Transjordan—a well-trained professional army with modern weaponry. By the time the Kingdom of Jordan was established as an independent state in 1946, replacing the British mandate of Transjordan, tribal opposition had been transformed into a founding element of the new state. The co-option of dominant tribes implied that Jordan was a state-building project as opposed to a nation-building project. Rather than nationalizing tribal identities, the tribes 'tribalized' the nation.[18] Some subgroups—the co-opted tribes—were privileged at the expense of others. To this day, various sub-national identities have been sustained within the Jordan regime. It might be argued that the Palestinians, in spite of being granted citizenship in Jordan, were never really integrated, as the tribal core of the state asserted itself again and again. When Faisali became a main proponent of East Bank neo-nationalism, it related to this history and how the club came to symbolize the alliance between the East Bank tribes of Jordan and the crown.

Faisali is the oldest football club in Jordan, founded in 1932 during the British Mandate. It was the club of the Adwan tribe—one of the most powerful tribes in Jordan—in the Balqa region where Amman is located. During the British Mandate, King Abdullah, the ruler under British supervision, recruited members from the Adwan tribe into the elite troops of the Transjordanian army.[19] This meant that close ties were forged between the throne and Faisali—the tribe and the club—long before the influx of Palestinians to

Jordan. With the demographic Palestinization of Jordan, however, the club gained a new meaning: as a symbol of the royal–tribal alliance in which Palestinians played no part. Its success in football reflected the hegemonic power of this alliance in Jordan. Thus, during football matches, unlike in any other domain, Wihdat's challenge to Faisali's dominance and references to the civil war bring out exclusivist anti-Palestinian East Bank nationalism. This was partly triggered by political developments in the 1990s. In 1991, martial law in Jordan was abolished and in the subsequent year political parties were legalized. The prospect of genuine democratization constituted a threat to East Bank tribes and elites who had benefited from nepotism and close relations to the throne. There was a prospect that Palestinians might take over Jordan through the ballot box. Moreover, with the Israeli–Palestinian peace process of 1993, the establishment of a Palestinian state in the West Bank and Gaza was no longer quite so unimaginable. For Palestinians in Jordan the scenario represented a dilemma regarding the prospect of having to move to a part of Palestine that was not their original home. Many therefore preferred their Jordanian citizenship. For the East Bank nationalists, however, a Palestinian state would solve the problem of democratization; the Palestinians could 'go home.'

While the deep respect of the East Bankers for the late King Hussein would contain more radical East Bank neo-nationalism, this ended with the ascendance of King Hussein's successor, King Abdullah II. With the death of King Hussein in 1999, the perception that the state was under full East Bank control was shaken. The long-time heir to the throne, Crown Prince Hassan, had largely been considered a leader of the hardline camp against normalization with the Palestinians, and was strongly opposed to the PLO.[20] As King Hussein fell out with his brother Hassan during the last days of his reign, he chose his inexperienced, eldest son, Abdullah II, in what was widely perceived as a shocking decision. With the new king being married to a Palestinian, Rania, East Bank nationalists started pondering what the future could bring. Two years after Abdullah's ascent to the throne, it was at the Amman football stadium where an unprecedented East Bank message challenging the monarchy was first heard: '*wahid, ithnan, talaqha, Abu Husain*' ('one, two, divorce her Abu Hussein [Abdullah]'), and '*talaqha wa tazawwaj ithnan minna*' ('divorce her and marry two from us'). The message was clear: Abdullah should divorce Rania, and marry someone from the tribes for Jordan to separate from the Palestinians. This led Wihdat supporters to counterattack rather than bow their heads. Playing on the threat of Palestinians taking over the country, Wihdat supporters started chanting '*Um Husain jibi awlad, khalina nuhkam al-bilad*' ('Umm Hussein [Queen Rania], give us children, so we can rule the country').[21]

The anti-Rania chants of Faisali supporters were allegedly also a cause for clashes during the Wihdat–Faisali derby in 2009 in Zarqa, which received international attention following the leaks of an American embassy report.[22] The match was interrupted and cancelled as Wihdat players were bombarded with bottles and other items by Faisali supporters. In spite of the seriousness of the incident, which was notably underreported in the Jordanian media, the disturbances during the Wihdat–Faisali derby the following year, in Amman in December 2010, were even worse.[23] After Wihdat won the match, as part of the normal procedure, their supporters were kept inside the stadium. They were pelted with stones thrown by the Faisali supporters from outside. The situation got out of hand, creating panic, unrest, and clashes, with cars set on fire and property damaged. Two hundred and fifty people were injured, with many hospitalized.

The neo-nationalist spirit was inflamed at the football stadium, and eventually also found its way to the Jordanian public. In 2011, at the start of the Arab uprisings, what had hitherto only been heard during football matches suddenly appeared in Jordanian media in a public letter signed by thirty-six tribal leaders. Echoing chants from Faisali fans against Queen Rania, the letter called upon the King to 'return lands and farms given to the Yassin family (Rania's family). The land belongs to the Jordanian people.'[24] Moreover, Queen Rania was accused of 'corruption, stealing money from the Treasury and manipulating in order to promote her public image—against the Jordanian people's will.' The letter also included an unprecedented warning for the king: 'King Abdullah has to stop his wife and her family from taking advantage of their power, otherwise the crown might be in danger.'[25] Offending the royal family is forbidden by law in Jordan and could lead to prison terms of up to three years. But the signatories of the letter were powerful, and the campaign was initiated by a committee of tribal army officers, the National Committee for Retired Officers. One of the signatories, the army veteran Ali Habashneh, noted that the government would not send generals to jail. He also said that he was explicitly against a democratic, constitutional monarchy in Jordan: 'We are against democratization.'[26] Democratization would mean a change in the election system, where votes from the Palestinian areas would count as equal to the votes from Jordanian areas, and 'could lead to civil war.'

The letter deeply shocked the Jordanian monarchy. Steps toward democratization, including changing the heavily gerrymandered election system disfavoring the Palestinians, were reversed.[27] Jordanian–Palestinian relations have since been at a freezing point. When Fatah convened its seventh congress in Ramallah in November 2016, its twenty-six delegates from Jordan remained notably absent. They had allegedly been threatened with revocation of their Jordanian citizenship if they attended.[28]

In societies less divided than Jordan, football supporters who blame the police for unrest would often be dismissed as biased. The category of fanatical football supporters known as 'ultras' have, after all, made confronting the police a part of their ethos. However, in the Jordanian context, there appears to be some truth to Wihdat's claims of bias against their supporters during these unrests. According to Wihdat's dirtector, Tareq Khoury, the same flavor of East Bank neo-nationalism that animates Faisali ultras also exists in the special police branch of the Jordanian security apparatus, the *darak*, or gendarmerie, deployed during Faisali–Wihdat matches.[29] When describing the disturbances that took place during a match in 2010, Khoury argued that the *darak* had all but orchestrated the unrest: 'We won the game and were celebrating. All of a sudden the *darak* started to push and hit our fans. I felt that a disaster happened, and that there would be many killed ... 99 percent of the *darak* are Faisali sympathizers, thinking that those of Palestinian origin are taking everything in the country, in stead [sic] of themselves taking control.' The unrest subsequently spread to other places in Amman, and the Wihdat camp was bathed in tear gas. According to Khoury, the *darak* forces wanted all of the Palestinians to suffer. Cracking down on the Palestinians was an attempt to rebalance the imbalance of Wihdat deposing Faisali, and equally reconfirmed where the true power of the state was and should be located: in the historic national ties between the East Bank tribes and the monarchy.

The Third Phase: Reasserting Ethnic Roots

What then is the current status of football as an arena for social memory production for the two competing sub-nations constituting Jordan? In May 2014, I visited Jordan to follow the end of the season, with Wihdat seeking to win their thirteenth league championship. In Irbid, Wihdat played Al-Hussein, whose supporters appeared to be a lighter version of Faisali supporters, basically sharing their anti-Palestinian East Bank nationalism. In a battle of Arab Palestinian Jerusalem against Hashemite Jerusalem, Wihdat supporters chant: '*Allāh, Wihdat, al-Quds al-'Arabiya*' ('God, Wihdat, Arab Jerusalem'), and Al-Hussein supporters respond: '*Allah, Husain, al-Quds al-*

Hashimiya' ('God, Hussein, Hashemite Jerusalem'). Al-Hussein supporters use the Hashemite tie to Jerusalem—the Jordanian royal family has actually taken care of the Muslim holy sites in Jerusalem since 1924—to challenge Al-Quds as a national Palestinian symbol.[30] However, for Faisali ultras, the core Bedouin East Bank neo-nationalists, Al-Quds was never really a historical symbol, anti-Palestinianness being more important than the Hashemite descent of the monarchy. During the 2016 derby, when Wihdat supporters chanted, 'with soul and blood we will redeem you, Al-Aqsa', Faisalis reportedly responded, 'With our soul and blood we will redeem you, *Israel*',[31] in a move to support the enemy of the enemy. After another derby in 2014, during skirmishes between the supporter groups outside the stadium, a Wihdat leaflet alleged that Faisali supporters burnt a picture of the Dome of the Rock, the iconic mosque of the Al-Aqsa compound in Jerusalem.[32] Thus, although regional unrest after the Arab uprisings and the civil war in Syria led to calls for national unity in Jordan from King Abdullah II,[33] this apparently has not reduced East Bank Jordanian–Palestinian tensions at the football stadiums.

While East Bank neo-nationalist Faisali ultras have grown even more antagonistic, however, a new trend has apparently gained momentum among Palestinians, emphasizing common descent, unity, and refugee identity rather than armed struggle. I argue this is the case, in spite of an old rebel song that is still being sung. As I entered the home ground of Wihdat in Amman in May 2014, the supporters sang the *fida'i* song, *Habbat al-nar*:

> The fire swelled and the rifles sang:
> Calling to the youth, O nation, give hope.
> The fire swelled from 'Akka to al-Tira;
> A handful of children raised on straw mats
> Became youth and never forgot the homeland,
> For who could forget the paradise of Palestine?
> The fire swelled, dignity, dignity!
> They became martyrs and woe unto
> Those who blind themselves.
> The dawn of freedom will come through
> Drawing the henna in blood.

Habbat al-nar was originally composed after the Israeli invasion of Lebanon in 1982, and was used as a call for young camp refugees—'children raised on mats'—to join the armed struggle and to become martyrs.[34] Today, however, the song's appeal for Wihdat supporters may be understood in relation to how the song evokes memories of a common struggle in the Wihdat refugee camps. One of the lyrics explicitly refers to al-Tira, a village in Palestine that was destroyed by Israel after 1948, and from where Wihdat's refugees originated.

The ethnomusicologist David McDonald observed the catalytic effect of the song. During a commemoration of the Nakba in the outskirts of Amman, a skirmish developed between supporters and non-supporters of the armed Islamist Palestinian resistance group, Hamas. When the performing ensemble observed this, they hurried to sing *Habbat al-nar*. The fighting instantly stopped. Later, the singer said he knew that most of those present were from Wihdat, and that singing about memories from al-Tira would have secular and Islamist Wihdatis alike forget their differences. Referring to al-Tira would remind them 'of their shared history.'[35] In the current political circumstances, the shared history of the Palestinians in Jordan, their ethnic origin, more than the state-building project of the Palestinian national movement, is what matters. Apparently, this increasingly dominates Palestinian social memorialization during Wihdat matches.

In fact, during Wihdat's matches at the end of the 2014 season, there was a peculiar increase in references to ethnic origins. When Wihdat played Al-Hussein in Irbid, the latter's supporters chanted, 'grass-eaters, grass-eaters', to which Wihdat supporters answered, 'shepherds, shepherds.' Yanal, a young Palestinian who accompanied me at the match said, 'they say we used to eat grass', referring to the years of famine. When Palestinians arrived in Jordan in 1948 in shattered conditions, they found refuge in camps made of flattened petrol cans, before the UN provided them with tents.[36] The Al-Hussein home supporters continued chanting, "*a'tinkum buyut, 'a'tinkum masari, 'antum ta'ishum bisababna*' ('We gave you homes, we gave you money, you live because of us'). The Wihdatis responded with, '*Allah 'a 'tana al-haqq*' ('God gave us our rights').

The Wihdat supporters went on to chant, 'shepherds, shepherds', referring to Al-Hussein supporters' East Bank origin as shepherds—that is to say, primitive Bedouins, still walking their goats on the outskirts of town. The 'grass-eaters' and 'shepherds' chants may thus be interpreted as going beyond the Nakba to the heart of the distinctive historical features of the two ethnic subgroups of Jordan: the historical *badu–hadar* cleavages of the region, between the nomadic pastoral Bedouin and the *fallah*, sedentary peasant, which is used to distinguish local Palestinians in the region from the Bedouins. The Bedouins regard the peasants' attachment to land as a source of humiliation, and consider peasants to be enslaved by others who control the land, not autonomous and free like Bedouins; while in the peasants' worldview, controlling the land and cultivation is a source of dignity, contrasting with the nomadic *badu* bands of thieves and robbers.[37]

The cultural relevance of this historical difference can also be found in food practices—one that has also entered the football pitch. Food is, as Efrat Ben Zevi has outlined, something that connects refugees to their land. This is especially so for dishes made of plants found in Palestine. Each village had its own distinctive olives and oil, like *'aqubd* (tumble thistle), *maryamiya* (sage), *za'tar* (hyssop), *sabr* (prickly pear), *zaitun* (olives), and *'alat* (winter greens). Plants, and food made from them, thus act as mnemonic devices. When non-Palestinian Jordanians refer to Palestinians as 'grass-eaters', this is also related to how grass-plants are integrated in traditional Palestinian dishes. In Jordan, one dish in particular—*mulukhiya*—has come to symbolize this tie between Palestinian ethnic identity and grass-plants. This green, thick liquid dish is considered a classic rural *fallahin* food, and is common across the Arab world, not only in Palestine. Nevertheless, in Jordan, it has become the symbol of what is *not* Bedouin food, and consequently, is a symbol of Palestinianness.

During the match in Irbid, a reference to *mulukhiya* suddenly broke out during the game: '*Ma'iah, ma'iah, Rafat Ali, sub al mulukhiya*' ('Go, go, Rafat Ali, drink the *mulukhiya*'), the Wihdat supporters chanted. This was a reference to how Rafat Ali, a legendary Wihdat captain who was originally a refugee, came to appropriate the *mulukhiya* as a symbol for Wihdat and the Palestinians. It goes back to Wihdat returning some years ago from a cup match abroad, having been crushed 7–1. In the subsequent match in Jordan, non-Palestinian supporters brought a banner to the match reading, 'Wihdat will not win the cup before MacDonald's [sic] starts selling *mulukhiya*.' Wihdat supporters picked up on this, printing and bringing their own posters of McDonald's menus, which included the *mulukhiya* dish. When Wihdat became the Jordanian champions later the same season, the Wihdat captain Ali brought a branch of *mulukhiya* as he received the trophy and pretended to drink it, thus connecting it to the Wihdat victory. During derbies, Faisali supporters chant '*al-mulukhiya wa al-jisr*' ('*mulukhiya* and the bridge'), implying that the Palestinians should take their plant and leave Jordan through the Allenby bridge crossing over to the West Bank and Israel. While *mulukhiya* as a Palestinian symbol has thus become contested, the chant '*ma'iah, ma'iah, Rafat Ali, sub al mulukhiya*' ('Go, go, Rafat Ali, drink the *mulukhiya*') has become one of the most characteristic Wihdat chants in recent years.

Back at the Amman stadium in May 2014, Wihdat played the East Bank Jordanian team That Ras. Wihdat only needed one point to win the league.

The match ended with a 2–0 victory and Wihdat became the champions. Amidst a huge police presence, one Wihdat supporter managed to enter the pitch to celebrate, and was chased by police. To the tremendous joy of the Wihdat crowd, as he ran towards the main stand of the Wihdat supporters, he waved his victory banner: a *mulukhiya* plant.

Conclusion

The Palestinians have historically lacked the formal national institutions to preserve their national past. Without state authority, they were prevented from establishing museums, conducting archaeological digs, or making historical sites accessible within a national framework.[38] While this was especially the case prior to the establishment of the Palestinian Authority, the situation has remained dire for the Palestinians in Jordan. They lack the formal apparatus for the preservation of their national past, one that constitutes them as a national group. This has made informal forms of collective memory exceptionally important in forming Palestinian identity in Jordan.

As for the East Bank Jordanians, Abu-Odeh has noted that they never really fought for their independence—the tribes were merely co-opted by an imported monarch—and so they have no national heroes, martyrs, or monuments to celebrate. This left East Bank nationalists with 'the Palestinian moment', the 1970 civil war, as their prime nationalist narrative. Anti-Palestinianism thus became the core and essence of East Bank neo-nationalism.[39] As neither of these nationalist narratives of the Palestinians and the East Bankers are in harmony with the Jordanian monarchy and its Hashemite descent, they need alternative arenas for their expression. This explains the unique role of football matches for ethnonational social memorialization in Jordan.

Social memory processes found at the football stadiums represent two equally important and intrinsically related social phenomena. First, collective, historical memories are produced. Second, during football matches, with their symbolic and physical confrontations, these collective memories are also enacted and embodied. Through football performativity, individual experience and collective identity formation are brought together. This is a process generating tremendous synergies. Football, as one of the world's greatest popular culture phenomena, tends to be analyzed as *reflecting* deeper social, cultural, and political streams.[40] However, as this chapter has shown in the Jordanian context, football does not merely reflect sociopolitical and cultural processes.[41] It is in itself a process through which people and nations are socially constructed.

3

HAPOEL TEL AVIV AND ISRAELI LIBERAL SECULARISM

Tamir Sorek

Introduction

The cheering repertoire of Hapoel Tel Aviv's fans in football and basketball includes a puzzling paradox. On the one hand, the banners on the bleachers, such as 'Workers of the World Unite', reflect a well-articulated universalist ideology stemming from the meaning of *Hapoel*, 'worker' in Hebrew. 'Anti-racism' is part of the collective self-image of the fans, and they frequently express an explicit inclusive orientation toward the Arab citizens of Israel. In contemporary Israel, which since the turn of the century has witnessed a drastic deterioration in Arab–Jewish relations,[1] this attitude is not self-evident. On the other hand, the fans' repertoire is far from being 'politically correct' in any other dimension. The cheering songs include violent, sexist, classist, and Germanophobic content, and the fans do not refrain from frequent mocking of the personal tragedies of the rival team's players and managers. Even by the rough standards of Israeli culture, Hapoel's fans are notorious for their lack of self-censorship.

To complicate the matter even more, a non-negligible number of fans do not hesitate to challenge some well-established sacred Israeli taboos, including explicit anti-patriotic slogans and frequent use of Holocaust terminology for expressing their hatred of their ultimate urban rival, Maccabi Tel Aviv. While accusations of being Nazi-like are far from being new to the Israeli public sphere, Hapoel's fans are the only group who frequently use this analogy in the sporting sphere.

Norbert Elias and Eric Dunning see the evolution of modern sports as a major element in the 'civilizing process' of British society, a process that is characterized by decreasing tolerance for sights of violence in the public sphere. As a result, the need emerged for a social sphere where regulated forms of violence were permitted.[2] One of the spheres in which this feature of modern sport is the most evident in contemporary sport is the fans' discourse, where they practice forms of verbal aggression that they would not dare to display in other contexts. In the same vein, the Israeli sociologist Amir Ben Porat called the football bleachers a 'permission zone.'[3] The permission zone, which can be found in other sports as well, is not a zone where everything is permitted. Rather, it is a zone where the boundaries of the legitimate and the illegitimate are constantly negotiated. The 'fanatic' sports fans are those who consistently flirt with the boundaries of legitimacy in their societies, challenging the most sacred taboos and bringing to the surface unarticulated emotions and opinions, which are usually covered by layers of a common aspiration for social equilibrium or political correctness.

This is what makes the rhetoric of these fans so valuable for sociological inquiry. It turns out that the fans of different teams use the permission zone for displaying different sets of ideas and for challenging different sacred taboos. These differences tell us much about internal tensions and contradictions in a given society. In this chapter, I analyze the rhetoric of Hapoel Tel Aviv's hardcore fans and the demography of the wider circle of sympathizers. This bifocal examination reveals that the stadium rhetoric is actually an expression of fundamental struggles between competing definitions of Israeliness. The transgressive rhetoric of Hapoel fans, I argue, is partly related to the decline in the political power of the secular elite in Israel. The insights are based on: 1) A 2012 online survey of 500 respondents who constitute a representative sample of the adult Hebrew-speaking population in Israel;[4] 2) a survey conducted by the Israel Democracy Institute (IDI) in 2009, including 2,803 respondents who constitute a representative sample of the adult Jewish population in Israel;[5] 3) analysis of Hapoel Tel Aviv fans' website; 4) collecting and examining fans' songs available on YouTube; and 5) semi-structured interviews with six hardcore fans of Hapoel Tel Aviv conducted between November 2012 and January 2013.

Hapoel Tel Aviv, Betar Jerusalem, and the Boundaries of Citizenship

Social scientists Gershon Shafir and Yoav Peled identified a continuous tension between three partly contradictory political goals and commitments characterizing Israeli political culture: the colonial project of settling the country with a specific group of people; the ethnonational project of building a Jewish nation-state; and the liberal project of establishing a democracy.[6] In the case of Socialist Zionists, another goal complicates the picture—the cosmopolitan vision of 'brotherhood of people', which only partially overlaps with the liberal discourse of citizenship. Therefore, from its very first steps in the early twentieth century, socialist Zionism in Palestine contained a tension between the aspiration for universal justice and the nationalist-colonialist particularistic agenda that aspired to settle the country with Jews and to build up autonomous Jewish political and economic power. Ze'ev Sternhall argues that the internal division among Zionist socialists between 'nationalists' and 'Marxists' was quickly decided in favor of the faction that represented the former, and consequently the universalist elements were subordinated to the national agenda.[7]

Since the late 1970s, however, the republican discourse has been weakened, while both the liberal and the ethnic discourses have gained power. The competitions between these discourses highly overlap with self-definitions of religiosity, where secular Jewish Israelis tend more to support the liberal discourse, and religious Israeli Jews tend to promote the ethnic discourse.[8] The realm of sport fandom, as a 'permission zone', allows extreme articulations of this competition to be displayed. It seems that the most dramatic expression can be found in the cheering rhetoric of Hapoel Tel Aviv and its political rival, Betar Jerusalem. In 2014, the journalist Motti De Picciotto conducted an online survey with 1,646 Israeli football fans, and found that when asked to describe their team, Hapoel Tel Aviv fans tend, much more than fans of any other team, to use emotional vocabulary, relying on terms such as 'us', 'love', 'soul', 'heart', and 'exciting'. Second to them in using emotional vocabulary were the fans of Betar Jerusalem.[9] Interestingly, these two teams have the most distinct political orientation among Jewish Israeli football teams. I argue that this association between sports, emotion, and politics is not incidental and reflects deep sociopolitical currents in Israeli society.

At their establishment in the first half of the twentieth century, Zionist sports federations were organized along political lines. Historically, Hapoel was associated with the trade union congress (Histadrut) and the socialist wing of Zionism that dominated it until 1977. Maccabi was affiliated with the General Zionists, a bourgeois party;[10] and Betar was the outgrowth of the militant revisionist Zionist youth movement founded in 1923, later linked to the Herut (and afterwards, the Likud) party. Each federation established local branches throughout the country.

Hapoel Tel Aviv

The Hapoel Tel Aviv football team was established in the 1920s, and the club's basketball team was founded in 1935. Until the mid-1990s, both Hapoel Tel Aviv teams were considered the flagship teams of the veteran socialist, mostly Ashkenazi (Jews of European origin) establishment. Then, following the drastic decline in the status and power of the Histadrut in Israeli society—which was a major reflection and materialization of the decline in the relative power of the republican discourse of citizenship—both Hapoel Tel Aviv teams were sold to private owners. This was part of a general process of privatization and commodification of Israeli sport.[11] The process has loosened the political identities of most professional clubs, while Hapoel Tel Aviv and Betar Jerusalem remained prominent exceptions. Even though most of the traditional demographic base of support of Hapoel has experienced upward mobility, the rhetoric and symbols remained connected to a globalized cosmopolitan working-class language. Red is the team's color, the hammer and sickle icon is still part of the logo, and even the face of Che Guevara can be spotted periodically on banners.

These symbols have become more visible since the end of the 1990s as part of a broader 'professionalization' of fan culture in Israel. Fans have become more organized and coordinated, and official fan organizations have been established, some of which are verging on illegality, or even crossing it, in terms of their aggressiveness. In 1999, the Hapoel Tel Aviv Ultras was established. The organization was inspired by Italian fan organizations,[12] and this inspiration is reflected in its name, its antiestablishment orientation, its macabre logos, its transgressive tendencies, and its flirting with violence. The hardcore of this organization—whose boundaries are blurred since there is no formal membership—includes no more than several dozens of activists, but their agenda and cheering style dominate the bleachers.

Demographically, most of the Hapoel Ultras are men in their 20s and 30s. In terms of class and origin they are diverse, but almost all of them are secular in their lifestyle. Some leaders of the group were raised in families with a clear socialist consciousness, while some adopted the ideology later in their lives, but the ideological orientation of the group is socialist with a clear inclination toward an inclusive discourse of citizenship. As Bar (pseudonym), an Ultra activist, told me: 'Most of us are left wing but this is not a requirement. The requirement is not to be racist.'[13] It is noteworthy that secular liberal Israelis are mostly upper and middle class (see Table 1), and therefore in Israel, the terms 'left' and 'right' do not always refer to the usual political or economic realm but to one's position regarding the Israeli–Palestinian conflict, the place of religion in politics, and the boundaries of Israeli citizenship.

The Ultras are members of Antifa, a global network of militant anti-fascists to whom many left-leaning football supporters pledge allegiance, including dozens of clubs across Europe.[14] This small group of activists is also responsible for the banner that accompanied the team when it played in Europe in the twenty-first century: 'We represent Hapoel, not Israel', an anti-nationalist statement that is far from being consensual among Hapoel fans.[15] The Ultras are politically active, and participate in the annual May Day parade in Tel Aviv. In 2008, they officially endorsed a candidate in the election for the city mayor, Dov Hanin, a parliament member of the Communist Party and a fan of Hapoel Tel Aviv.[16]

Unlike most professional teams in Israel, the process of privatization in Hapoel Tel Aviv has been reversed recently. The basketball club is owned and managed democratically by an association of more than 1,800 fans, and, in late 2012, the fans purchased 20 percent ownership of the football club. Evidently, this anti-privatization process is compatible with the political agenda of the Ultras.

Betar Jerusalem

Betar Jerusalem football club was founded in 1936. In the 1940s, most of the team's players were members of either the Irgun or the Lehi underground militias, which resulted in the British authorities expelling some of them from Palestine.[17] After the State of Israel was established, Betar's image as a bastion of oppositional voices was intensified. Whereas the various Hapoel teams were related to the establishment, Betar attracted the outsiders, the oppressed, and the victimized. Jerusalem absorbed many of the Jews who emigrated en masse from Arab and Muslim countries during the 1950s and 1960s, who are referred to in contemporary Israel as Mizrahim (Easterners, or Orientals). The immigrants from the Middle East, and especially those from the Maghreb, were met with a patronizing, Orientalist attitude by government agencies responsible for integrating them, and within a short time found themselves relegated to the bottom of the socioeconomic hierarchy and to the margins of the political system. Furthermore, those who did not belong to the ruling Mapai party—one of the incarnations of the Labor Movement—suffered from additional discrimination in employment and housing. In those years, Betar's circle of fans developed into a kind of political and cultural opposition. Politically, the team continued to be identified with the right-wing Herut party that was populist, anti-socialist, and committed to territorial expansionism. Culturally, the Betar Jerusalem bleachers resounded with songs and slogans borrowed and adapted from old Sephardi Jewish religious tunes, which were usually excluded from the government-monopolized media until the early 1980s.

Betar's transformation from a locally based club to a team with a national following is related to the close link between the team and Likud leaders, as well as Betar's first major achievements—winning the state cup tournaments in 1976 and 1979—coinciding with the political upheaval that brought Likud into power in 1977. In fact, the demographic coalition enabling Likud's victory was reflected in the growing circle of Betar fans. Throughout the 1980s, the triangular relationship of Likud–Mizrahim–Betar was crystallized. Betar's successes over the course of the 1980s and 1990s—three championships and three state cups—made the team popular among wider circles of fans, including many Ashkenazim and even Arab citizens. However, it remained especially popular in what was once termed 'the second Israel', namely, among Mizrahim. In recent years, Betar's right-wing image has made it popular among settlers in the West Bank. Like Hapoel Tel Aviv, Betar was privatized, but this did not affect its popular image as a bastion of the Israeli political right.

As shown in Table 1, the current demographic characteristics of the sympathizers of Hapoel Tel Aviv and Betar Jerusalem distinguish them from other football fans in the Israeli Premier League. I refer to them as 'sympathizers' rather than 'fans' since the requirement for inclusion in this category is minimal. It includes anyone who considers himself/herself a fan, even slightly. This means that it does not necessarily reflect the character of the fans in the bleachers, but rather the demographic profile of those who have a sympathetic view of the team. According to this survey, Hapoel supporters are more educated, and tend to define themselves as Ashkenazi and much less as Mizrahi. The most salient feature, however, is their secularism. Israeli Jews defining themselves as secular are either non-observant of religious law or, alternatively, observant of some Jewish traditions without ascribing religious meanings to them, and a clear majority of Hapoel Tel Aviv fans feel comfortable with this labelling. The sympathizers of Betar, on the other hand, tend to be more Mizrahi and much more religious than the rest of Israeli football fans. Betar also has the largest ratio of supporters who live in the occupied West Bank, while none of the Hapoel Tel Aviv supporters in the sample lives there.

Table 1: Demographic attributes of sympathizers of Hapoel Tel Aviv and Betar Jerusalem[18]

	Hapoel Tel Aviv (N=37)	Betar Jerusalem (N=67)	Fans of all clubs (N=154)
Religious	14%	38%	16%
Secular	62%	21%	41%
Ashkenazi	54%	36%	42%
Mizrahi	24%	46%	40%
College education	49%	30%	39%
Living in the West Bank	0%	10%	3%

While the right-wing leaning of Betar is not new, a new vocal anti-Arab tone has developed among its fans since the 1990s. Betar is also the only professional team in Israel that has never hired an Arab player. Up until the 1990s, only a few professional Jewish teams hired Arab players, but the influx of Arab players since then has passed Betar by. Today, some hardcore fans even consider anti-Arabism as inherent to the identity of the club.[19] Initiatives by the management to bring in Arab players were thwarted by fan pressure, and, in recent years, the opposition has been extended to Muslim players, even if they are not Arab. In a study of Israeli football fans, 113 Jewish fans of four large Israeli clubs (thirty of them fans of Betar) were asked if they support or oppose the inclusion of Arab players in their teams. Only fourteen fans opposed the idea—twelve of them were Betar fans.[20] This means that even among Betar fans there was a majority who support the inclusion of Arab players, but that the significant minority is strong enough to prevent any change in the policy.

The repertoire of Betar fans includes some rather unrefined anti-Arab and anti-Muslim messages. Here is an example of a popular Betar chant, dedicated to the Arab star of Hapoel Tel Aviv, Salim Tuama, with music based on a song from *Sllah Shabati*, a 1964 Israeli comedy film about the difficulties Jewish Mizrahi immigrants faced in the early years of the state:

> What does Salim do here?/ I don't know!/What is it here? I am asking/ From every side I am hearing:/ Tuama, here is the Land of Israel/ Here is the Land of Israel, Tuama/ Here it is the state of the Jews/ I hate you, Salim Tuama/ I hate all the Arabs!

Other offensive content includes scorning the prophet Muhammad and violent slogans like 'May your village burn', 'I swear to God that Arabs won't be here', and the best-known rhythmic slogan, 'death to the Arabs.'

Since 2000, the anti-Arab stand of Betar's fans has become more militant. The fan organization La Familia, established in 2005, has close ties to far-right politicians and it openly identifies with the outlawed Kach movement that supports a theocracy and the expulsion of all Arabs. This movement,[21] which is officially defined by Israel, the US, and the EU as a terrorist organization, has a flag that is sporadically seen in Betar's stadium, and political leaders of the far right—some of whom are former Kach activists who are active now in parties with different names—are commonly seen on the bleachers. It is noteworthy that in the 1970s, when Kach was established, the veterans of the Irgun tried to distance themselves from Kach and even appealed against the movement's use of the Irgun's logo. But many things have changed since then. This does not mean that the majority of Betar fans support Kach's ideology, but the extent of support is not negligible and is seen and heard in the stadium.

Scholars of Israeli society have tried to explain anti-Arab sentiments among Mizrahim either through their competition with Arabs over the same low-paying jobs,[22] or their need to deny the Arab component of their identity in a political atmosphere where Arab identity is stigmatized in a state that discriminates against Arabs.[23] Adopting and emphasizing nationalistic, hawkish, and, at times, Arab-hating views seemingly enable Mizrahim to blur what they have in common with Palestinian Arabs. However, these dynamics provide a very partial explanation for Betar's racism because there are many other teams with a dominant Mizrahi fan base that did hire Arab players, and their Mizrahi fans did not organize to prevent their inclusion. In addition, nowhere is the anti-Arab rhetoric as extreme as in the case of Betar. Betar's unique stand might be related to the interaction between the ethnic background of the team's fans, the political extremism that has developed specifically in Jerusalem since 1967, and the calculated and instrumental investment of movements like Kach and its offshoots among Betar's fans.

Anti-Racism among Hapoel Fans

Whatever the reason for the anti-Arab sentiments among Betar fans, these racist expressions enable the fans of Hapoel Tel Aviv to see Betar as the ultimate political 'others.' The anthropologist Daniel Regev conducted in-depth interviews with Hapoel fans and asked them 'what is, in your opinion, Hapoel's spirit?' and 'what values does Hapoel represent for you?' The most frequent answers were 'being different', 'co-existence', 'tolerance', 'community', 'anticonformism', and 'anti-racism.'[24] In other words, the anti-racist message has a wider appeal among the fans, beyond the Ultras. While blatant anti-Arab slogans and chants have become very common on the bleachers of the Israeli Premier League, they are rarely heard among the crowd of teams where the inclusion of Arab players has become part of the tradition of the club, as in the Maccabi Haifa or Hapoel Tel Aviv football clubs. This anti-racist attitude is also common among the fans of the Hapoel Tel Aviv basketball club, although Arab representation in Israeli basketball is negligible and attitudes toward Arabs is a non-issue in this sport.[25]

The anti-racist discourse is also embedded in a concrete social reality, and, in certain periods, relied on active support of the management. This reality includes, for example, a long tradition of including Arab players and fans. On the fan website *Adom Oleh*, one can find that supporters are proud to be affiliated with a club whose football team was the first ever Jewish Israeli team to have an Arab player as captain: Walid Bdeir was appointed captain in 2007. Hapoel Tel Aviv is also a partner in the Education and Social Project, founded by the former owner of the club. This is an organization that uses football to bring children from Israel, the West Bank, and Jordan together for coexistence programs.[26]

This explicit liberalism extends as well to the attitude toward guest workers and undocumented residents. Since the mid-1990s, but especially since 2007, tens of thousands of Africans from Sudan and Eritrea have entered Israel through its borders with Egypt. Their presence in Israel has become a controversial political issue, and, in June 2012, the Israeli Immigration and Population Authority announced that 4,000 migrants who cannot attain the status of refugee, based on their country of origin, would be deported. Five youth who were supposed to be deported were basketball players at Hapoel Tel Aviv, and the club took an active part in mobilizing support for their case. In the summer of 2012, the Hapoel Tel Aviv basketball club also organised summer camps for the children of guest workers and undocumented residents. In many of the senior team's basketball games, the announcer declared the club's objection to the deportation. This enthusiasm to adopt anti-racism as part of the club's identity is, among other things, a way to distinguish Hapoel from other teams, especially from Betar. Being anti-racist became a self-flattering label of many Hapoel fans, extending far beyond the narrow circle of the Ultras.

In the Israeli context, anti-racist attitudes cannot be discussed without reference to religiosity. Studies consistently show that, in Israel, the less religious one is, the stronger one's commitment to democratic values. To be sure, an exclusionary understanding of citizenship that emphasizes Jewishness as a criterion for acceptance has been common among secular Jewish Israelis as well, who, after all, were the founders of Israel as an ethnic nation-state. However, when Jewish Israelis were asked in a 2015 survey about the relative importance of the democratic and Jewish components of state identity,[27] the majority of seculars (53 percent) prioritize the democratic over the Jewish. Among ultra-Orthodox,[28] zero percent prioritized the democratic elements; among those who declare themselves as religious,[29] 6 percent; and among traditional Jews,[30] 17 percent. Furthermore, 80 percent of secular Jews disagreed with the statement 'Jewish citizens of Israel should have greater rights than non-Jewish citizens' compared with 25 percent of the ultra-Orthodox, 53 percent of those who declare themselves as religious, and 73 percent of traditional Jews.[31] In Israel, being secular is the strongest predictor for commitment to democratic values. Therefore, as secular Jews, Hapoel fans have a relatively high tendency to reject the purist Jewish ethnic discourse of citizenship.

Localism and Nationalism

The Betar–Hapoel conflict has another dimension related to the contrast between Tel Aviv and Jerusalem as two opposing poles of Israeli identity. In this context, the Israeli sociologist Uri Ram writes that:

> the retreat of nationalism; the rise of individualism; the spread of pluralism; and the overarching hegemony of capitalism—all centered actually and symbolically in Tel Aviv rather than in Jerusalem. All the while, the neo-Zionist nationalist, ethno-centric, and fundamentalist backlash—an orientation centered in and on Jerusalem—is also on the rise. Critics are right to argue that Jerusalem and Tel Aviv belong to the same system, and despite their blatant antagonism, they belong to the same Zionist colonialist project. Yet despite this commonality between the cities, each of them indicates a distinct potential.[32]

A chant recorded in 2000 by Gal Sokolovsky, a devoted Hapoel fan, is a vivid expression of these post-nationalist tendencies Ram ascribes to Tel Aviv: 'Put Jerusalem in Jordan/Divide it into two/Put Jerusalem in Jordan/ Give it to the Palestinians/ Put Jerusalem in Jordan/in the '67 borders/Because there is no need for Teddy [Betar's stadium], nor for Betar/ Nor the Wailing Wall, nor the Knesset/ because everything in this city is unnecessary.'[33]

The melody of this chant was taken from a song glorifying Jerusalem, written after the 1967 war and the occupation of East Jerusalem. The 'liberation' of Jerusalem is celebrated by an official national holiday, known as Jerusalem Day, and the above-mentioned song became a common element in the musical repertoire of the holiday. Over the years, despite its official status, the holiday has not been widely adopted nor observed by most secular Jewish Israelis, and one can spend Jerusalem Day in Tel Aviv without noticing that this is a holiday. Note that this is not a 'peace song' calling for reconciliation between Israelis and Palestinians or Jordanians. The author simply could not care less about Jerusalem and its symbolic weight. The lyrics reverberate a typical Tel Aviv, secular hedonistic perspective in which national-religious symbols such as the Western Wall are unnecessary: during encounters with Betar fans, it is common to hear the wish, 'may the Western Wall fall on you.' In this context, even a major symbol of Israeli sovereignty such as the Knesset (the parliament) is ridiculed.

Studies of the relationship between nationalism and localism have provided evidence that these orientations might maintain either relations of opposition, congruence, or even frequent alternation between these two orientations.[34] The fans of Betar and Hapoel display two opposing models for this relationship. While for Betar fans their loyalty to Jerusalem and their Zionist patriotism seems to coexist in harmony, the self-image of many Hapoel fans is based on a tension between their local and national identity. Regev argued that the anti-nationalist stand of Hapoel Tel Aviv fans is a demand to prioritize local identity over national identity, and he shows how fans use the same vocabulary to describe their team and the city of Tel Aviv ('tolerance', 'sanity', 'pluralism'). Fans of Hapoel are divided in their interpretation of the sign 'we do not represent Israel'—some oppose it; some interpret it as a protest against the wave of militant patriotism that swept the country, especially when the sign was first introduced during the second Intifada; and some see it as an aspiration to exclude nationalism from the stadium and to allow a limited autonomy for local loyalties and loyalty to the club in the stadium.[35] The balance of power between each of these orientations is in constant flux, and the anti-nationalist attitude is not always dominant. There seems to be, however, a general agreement among fans that their version of Israeliness—embodied and localized in the character of their city—has been marginalized in contemporary Israel.

The Holocaust: A Sacred Taboo or a Source of Moral Capital?

Another element that clearly sets the fans of Hapoel apart, especially the basketball team, is the frequent use of Holocaust terminology. This has been a source of tension and confrontation among the fans, as well as between fans and the management. Even though both the football and basketball clubs were penalized by their respective sport associations, the intensive attempts of the more established fans to eliminate this phenomenon have achieved so far only partial success.

Explaining the incorporation of Holocaust terminology into the fans' repertoire requires examining the central place of the Holocaust in Israeli public culture.[36] First, it is part of the family biography of a significant portion of the Israeli Jewish population, especially among the economic and cultural elites, in which Jews of European origin are overrepresented. Second, the Holocaust and its Zionist moral interpretation—the necessity of an independent Jewish power—was incorporated intensively into public education. Today, the Holocaust is popularly considered a major *raison d'être* of the State of Israel, and therefore the event has been loaded with sacral qualities and has become a major element in Israeli civil religion.[37] Fourth, the Holocaust is popularly considered a salient source of moral capital that legitimizes various aspects of Israeli policy,[38] especially in the context of the Israeli–Palestinian conflict.

There is, however, a clear tension between the third and fourth elements. The more the Holocaust is used rhetorically for legitimizing policy, the more its sacred quality as a taboo is being eroded. Holocaust metaphors are readily available 'tools' in the cultural 'tool kit' of Jewish Israelis.[39] In the internal Israeli discourse, political opponents have been compared to Nazis since the 1950s, and this comparison was frequently considered an extreme form of protest. In the first decade of the twenty-first century, the use of the Holocaust discourse intensified, both externally and internally. Internationally, and especially in Europe, Israeli governments have found it increasingly difficult to explain their policy in the occupied territories and therefore have attempted to use the moral credit of the Holocaust. Internally, the decision to withdraw from the Gaza Strip in 2005 was seen by certain religious-Zionist groups as an existential threat. Consequently, decision makers, as well as those who were assigned to carry out the evacuation, were quickly compared to Nazis.[40]

This inconsistency of the Israeli establishment—constant demand to maintain the sacred status of the Holocaust, on the one hand, and the steady instrumentalization of its memory for achieving political gains, on the other—paved the way for the provocative reference to the Holocaust by Hapoel fans. Referring to Betar fans, the philosopher Anat Rimon-Or has identified the slogan 'death to the Arabs' as a form of counter-hegemonic protest, since it interferes with the humanistic liberal rhetoric so often deployed as a cover for Zionist indifference to Arab life. Explicit demands to kill Arabs both back the Zionist ethos and disrupt it by exposing its inconsistency.[41] In a similar way, the intensive and uncensored use of Holocaust metaphors by Hapoel Tel Aviv fans exposes the contradiction between the Holocaust as a sacred taboo and the Holocaust as a political instrument. As the issue touches a very sensitive nerve, it is not surprising that Holocaust chants provoke reactions from politicians, and are formally discussed at the Knesset.[42]

Due to lack of documentation it is difficult to determine who 'started' it, but there is no doubt that the most elaborate and intensive use of Holocaust terminology has been directed by fans of Hapoel Tel Aviv toward their urban rival, Maccabi Tel Aviv—the most 'hated team' on the Ultras' list—and appeared in the early 1990s at basketball matches, later spreading to the football stadium. In the local context of Tel Aviv, Hapoel has been the underdog team. Their urban rival, Maccabi Tel Aviv, has won many more titles, both in football and in basketball. Maccabi has attracted many more fans, and the gap has been especially noticeable in basketball. Maccabi Tel Aviv's basketball team is the most successful sports team in Israel and one of the most successful teams in European basketball. Up until 2014, Maccabi had won 51 national championships, 39 state cups, and 5 European championships. From 1970 to 1990, Maccabi Tel Aviv won 23 consecutive championships. In those years, the team's success in Europe allowed it to develop an almost irreversible financial advantage over the rest of the basketball teams in Israel, an achievement that enabled it to buy any Israeli player who was seen as a potential threat to its domination. These years were especially frustrating for the fans of Hapoel Tel Aviv. The image of an unbeatable, ruthless, and efficient enemy filtered by the interpretative tools available in the Jewish Israeli collective memory led to the association 'Maccabi=Nazis', which is also partly motivated by the drive of the non-ideological Hapoel fans to retaliate against Maccabi fans who called them 'Communists.' In 1993, after Maccabi lost its first championship in twenty-three years, Hapoel fans celebrated the event by painting swastika graffiti on the car of the club's manager, Shimon Mizrahi.

In certain contexts of the Israeli public sphere, the distinction between 'Nazi' and 'German' is blurred, and the terms are used interchangeably. Therefore, Maccabi Tel Aviv was commonly referred to as a German team by Hapoel fans. Later on, this association spilled over from the basketball arena to the football stadium. In the first decade of the twenty-first century, the 'Songs of the German'—based on the melody of 'You are my Sunshine'—became popular among Hapoel Tel Aviv's fans in their games against Maccabi:

> Number one is German/Number two is German/Number three is German [etc. until number 10, skipping number 8], Gate 11 [the location in the stadium of the most vocal Maccabi fans] is German/The coach is German/ The management is German/ The masseur is German/The quartermaster is German/ Number 8 is Nimni—big time German![43]

The last line refers to Avi Nimni, a prominent player in Maccabi during the 1990s and 2000s who became the fans' favorite and a symbol of the team. An edited photo of Nimni with a Hitler-style moustache has been disseminated on the web by Hapoel fans. They also uploaded a parodic 'Hitler is Angry' clip in which Hitler is furious about the decision of Maccabi Tel Aviv's owner to fire Nimni from his position as coach in 2011.[44]

When fans label their sporting rivals 'Nazis', public reactions are hostile but relatively moderate. However, the tone drastically changed when the rhetoric switched the roles of victim and victimizer. In the early 2000s, shortly after the establishment of the Ultras, Hapoel fans started to wish 'revenge' against the 'Nazis,' and a new slogan was born: 'Let Maccabi have a Holocaust.' From then on, it became common to hear Hapoel fans cursing Maccabi players, management, and fans, and wishing upon them ghettos, gas chambers, and crematoriums. For example, the second part of the above-mentioned chant 'Put Jerusalem in Jordan' begins with 'Put Maccabi in the chambers/fill them with gas.' In another popular chant, the fans sing 'Maccabi are Nazis/Fucking whores/We wish you would die, burning alive,' with the word 'Nazi' sometimes accompanied by an arm raised in a Nazi salute. The sight of hundreds of young Jewish Israelis performing a Hitler greeting—a criminal offense in some European countries—in a major Jewish city certainly provoke the shocked reactions the fans desire. The fluidity of the victim–victimizer roles became a salient feature of the Ultras' Holocaust metaphors. The home arena of Maccabi Tel Aviv's basketball club, Yad Eliahu, is interchangeably referred to as the Reichstag or Yad Vashem, the national site for the commemoration of the Holocaust in Israel.

A fan of Hapoel who uses this terminology explained her behavior in an interview on an Israeli news website:

> The fans of Hapoel tend to declare that they are out of the mainstream. I choose this extreme behavior and the football stadium is for me a [place for] catharsis where everything is permitted. I enjoy uttering these expressions exactly because I take them in the right proportion. Those who don't—it's their right. Our high level of education enables us to use extremism without being labeled *arsim* like the other teams.[45]

The justification is multilayered. First, since 'we' are highly educated—and therefore rational—we do not ascribe magical power to words, as other less rational people do; and if they do, 'it's their right', namely, their problem. Second, we will not be perceived as '*arsim*,' the Hebrew plural for the Arabic word '*ars*', which literally means 'pimp.' In colloquial Hebrew, this is a derogatory term for the stereotype of a low-class young man, usually of Mizrahi origin—a set of attributes typical to the stereotype of a Betar fan.

Another possible reason, not articulated by this fan, is that in being part of a Tel Aviv-centered, secular post-nationalist culture, Hapoel fans feel less committed to unifying Jewish symbols and myths, and have fewer restraints that deter them from undermining these symbols—as in the case of mocking Jerusalem. Indeed, a 2003 survey revealed that secular Jewish Israelis have a lower level of Israeli national pride than people in other categories of religiosity.[46] This relative reservation about unifying Jewish symbols even affects attitudes toward the Holocaust. In the 2009 IDI survey, interviewees were asked about the importance of remembering the Holocaust as a principle guiding their life. Because Jews of European origin are overrepresented among secular Jews, one would expect that they ascribe more importance to the Holocaust than Jews of other origins. The results, however, contradicted this expectation. Although Jews of every category of religiosity see much importance in remembering the Holocaust, their level of religiosity was positively associated with this tendency. Among the aggregated category of religious, ultra-Orthodox, and traditional Jewish Israelis, 84 percent ascribed the highest level of importance ('very important'). Among those who defined themselves as nonreligious or secular, only 78 percent answered 'very important', and among those who defined themselves as 'anti-religious', the ratio was only 65 percent.[47]

Although the Holocaust, as an element in Jewish collective memory, is seemingly a secular source of collective identification and justification for

Zionism, certain social processes have alienated some secular Israelis, more than other Jewish Israelis, from its use in the Israeli public sphere—an alienation that is an extension of the general dissatisfaction with contemporary public articulations of Jewish-Israeli national identity. In the following concluding section, I suggest an analysis of these processes.

Fan Rhetoric and Crisis of Legitimacy

At both the Hapoel and Betar clubs, fans in the stadium violate social taboos. In both cases, what allows this violation is not only the context—the stadium as a permission zone—but also sentiments of marginalization and alienation. These similar sentiments, however, have very different origins. Betar's La Familia members, and by extension the large circle of Betar sympathizers, come from a relatively low-income and low-education background, and most of them are Mizrahim. Many of them might feel marginalized economically and deprived of the cultural capital that allows effective participation in shaping the discourse in mainstream media. They feel, justly or unjustly, that the public sphere is dominated by a worldview antagonistic to theirs.

Seemingly, secular Ashkenazi Israelis have no reason to feel alienated. The seculars have enjoyed numerical advantage and political prominence. To date, all Israeli Prime Ministers and the vast majority of cabinet ministers, judges, and generals have been secular Jews. When Jewish Israelis are offered four categories of religiosity (secular, traditional, religious, and ultra-Orthodox), most surveys show that the 'seculars' are the largest group, approximately 42–44 percent, a number that has been stable over the past three decades.

Furthermore, secular Jews in Israel are much better off economically than other groups. In 2015, in 54 percent of the secular Jewish households, the average monthly income per capita was above 4,000 NIS ($1,050), as compared with only 30 percent of non-secular Jewish Israeli households.[48] Similarly, 38 percent of adult secular Jews held an academic degree, compared to only 23 percent among other Jews of Israel.[49]

Nevertheless, this socioeconomic superiority, and even the apparent advantage in the political sphere, mask a prolonged crisis of Israeli secularism, especially regarding its relation to Israeli national identification and pride. As the Northern Irish sociologist Claire Mitchell argues, especially in context of ethnic conflicts, 'religion often constitutes the fabric of ethnic identity. Even if identities do not appear to be primarily religious per se, they may have latent religious dimensions that can become reactivated.'[50] Therefore, the self-definition 'secular' does not imply severance from the religious Jewish legacy. Nevertheless, Israeli secular identity is constructed through its relative distance from religion.[51] While Israeli patriotism and secularism seemed almost inseparable in the early days of the state, they increasingly develop tense relations in contemporary Israel.

The Israeli social scientists Charles Liebman and Eliezer Don-Yehiye,[52] as well as the sociologist Baruch Kimmerling,[53] see a direct link between the crisis of legitimacy experienced by Zionists and the need for Jewish religious symbols to cope with this crisis. Solid legitimacy for the Israeli national project is essential for two reasons. First, there exists a native population that has paid the price for the Zionist project. The Israeli–Palestinian conflict, therefore, is frequently managed in the moral field, whereby each side aspires to accumulate moral capital. Second, legitimacy is needed because Israelis are constantly facing demands for significant sacrifices, both individual and collective, to maintain the national project. Kimmerling believes that this crisis has dictated the choice of symbols from the very first steps of the Zionist movement. Since the Zionist project faced violent resistance by Palestinians, it repeatedly had to explain to Jews and the international community why it chose Palestine as its target territory for settlement. Since materialist reasoning could not be used to justify this choice, Zionism has been 'unable to disconnect itself from its original identity as a quasi-messianic movement. The essence of this society and state's right and reasons to exist is embedded in symbols, ideas, and religious scriptures—even if there has been an attempt to give them a secular reinterpretation and context.'[54]

Liebman and Don-Yehiye identified the 1967 war as the turning point in this scheme. After occupying the West Bank and the Gaza Strip, among other territories, Israel became the direct ruler of a large Palestinian population, whom Israel left in limbo with no defined status or civil rights. Liebman and Don-Yehiye argue that the old Israeli 'civil religion' based on statism, secularized Jewish symbolism, and invented tradition was not enough to provide legitimacy to the new circumstances. Consequently, 'Israelis were increasingly thrown back onto utilizing religious, or at least seemingly, religious arguments,'[55] the end result being the emergence of a 'new civil religion', one which 'seeks to integrate and mobilize Israeli Jewish society and legitimate the primary values of the political system by grounding them in a transcendent order.'[56] This quest for legitimacy has never subsided, and has even tended to intensify with the escalation of the Israeli–Palestinian conflict. The 'old Israeli civil religion' was closely connected to the republican secular discourse of citizenship. Under the circumstances of a growing crisis of legitimacy, this discourse was not satisfactory in terms of providing moral support. Therefore, Israelis either withdrew from collective goals by adopting a liberal discourse—and, implicitly, avoiding collective responsibility—or an ethnonational discourse, which is immersed in religious symbolism. The latter is popular among traditional and religious people, who are over-proportionally represented among Betar fans and sympathizers, while the former option is typical of certain secular Israelis, including fans and sympathizers of Hapoel Tel Aviv.

With the increasing reliance of Israeli leaders on biblical texts for justifying policy, and with the growing disregard for human rights expressed in this policy, some secular Jews who adopted the liberal discourse find themselves gradually alienated from hegemonic articulations of Israeli patriotism. The frustration of the secular liberal fans of Hapoel Tel Aviv leads to a political alienation. This is the story of a former elite who might still hold relative economic power, but whose influence over the political sphere has been in steady decline over the past four decades. The anti-nationalist rhetoric of Hapoel Tel Aviv Ultras—including the statement 'we do not represent the state', and the mockery of national symbols such as the Wailing Wall—might not be explicitly condoned by the wider circle of fans. Nevertheless, it reflects, or at least is enabled by, the alienation that many secular liberal Israelis feel in contemporary Israel.

4

QATARI FEMALE FOOTBALLERS

NEGOTIATING GENDERED EXPECTATIONS

Charlotte Lysa

Introduction

Female Qatari footballers are stuck between a rock and a hard place. On the one hand, they are subject to a conservative culture, upheld by society and families, in which it is largely unacceptable for a woman to play football. On the other, they are being encouraged by government policies, in accordance with pressure from international organizations, to pursue sports careers and to showcase these internationally in a way that is culturally acceptable for very few Qatari women. Asef Bayat uses the term 'subversive accommodation' to describe the ways young people in the broader Middle East region, including women, are redefining cultural norms, and negotiating with the dominant system to work in their interest rather than departing from it.[1] Such a pattern of engagement can be found among female footballers in Doha: in order to play football, they negotiate cultural barriers, and many have created a 'safe space' where their activity can be seen as less problematic. This chapter focuses on how the women themselves are navigating these obstacles, creating an arena to pursue their passion in a culturally appropriate way.

As Gary Whannel notes, sports can be used as a prism to understand socio-political issues on multiple levels.[2] In this chapter, football is used as a tool to examine how the women themselves maneuver the system, thus both accepting and transgressing established norms in the society to which they belong. Examining how women engage with football in particular is interesting for a number of reasons: it is generally considered a masculine sport in most societies, and certainly in the Middle East;[3] it is an arena where national, political, and ethnic identities are expressed;[4] and, especially in relation to Qatar, it is subject to an enormous effort that is developing and promoting the game both nationally and internationally.

On 2 December 2010, Qatar was unexpectedly selected as the host of the 2022 FIFA World Cup—the world's second largest sporting event after the Summer Olympics. The announcement meant that intense international attention immediately turned to Qatar. Despite Qatar's lack of international success in the sport, and Western commentators' claims that Qatar lacks a football culture,[5] football is the most popular sport in the country.[6] This is also the case among women, who often grow up watching and playing football along with male family members. Outside the home, however, it becomes challenging for females to take part in football culture as they grow older and gendered expectations prevail. As will be discussed in the following pages, this is especially true for organized, competitive football.

Over the past decade, Qatar has invested enormously in national and international sports development, partly explained by the bid for the 2022 World Cup, which demands a certain commitment to the sport.[7] These investments include efforts to develop women's sports, although these investments are limited compared to men's athletic activities. The Qatar Women's Sports Committee (QWSC) was set up in 2001 by royal decree, and has since worked on creating awareness and improving conditions for women in sports.[8] The QWSC helps to facilitate female athletes and develop women's sports along with the relevant national sports federations. Qatar's first women's national football team was set up in 2010. Despite these efforts however, women's football is still a neglected part of the Qatari sports evolution. In 2012, Kelly Knez et al. interviewed five players from Qatar's first female football team, arguing that the World Cup has already been a catalyst for change in the field of women's sports, but that cultural factors make it harder for women to participate, thus demanding serious negotiation between the players, their families, and society.[9] Four years later, however, the national team struggled to recruit Qatari players, and the activity (and funding) was notably lower.[10] Although the efforts following the awarding of the 2022 World Cup have provided formal opportunities for elite sport, such changes cannot overnight transform the societal and cultural factors that prevent women from playing football. This chapter will thus focus on the female football players for whom the national team, for different reasons, is not an option.

Many Qatari women are indeed interested in playing football, but official structures do not meet the necessary conditions for women to engage in the sport in a way that does not come into conflict with established cultural norms. By using the example of university teams, I demonstrate how some women, instead of simply refraining from playing competitive organized football, navigate existing norms and structures in order to pursue their interest in compliance with local culture. In doing so, these women create a space where their activities remain unopposed by society in general, one that allows them simultaneously to contest established customs.

This chapter builds on empirical data collected through interviews with Qatari women actively playing football. In addition, several interviews were carried out with other people involved in the sport sector, either as officials or athletes, both men and women, Qatari and expatriate. The interviews were conducted during two visits to Qatar in 2016, over a total of three months spent in the country. I conducted thirty interviews, mostly in English, where approximately half were with young (aged 18–25) women engaged in football-related activities.[11] I used a semi-structural approach, where certain themes were set, while at the same time allowing the interviewee to provide new angles, or introduce new subjects to the conversation.[12] The topics for the interviews mostly related to the women's motivations and aspirations for playing football, their interest in the sport, perceived obstacles to playing, reactions from members of society, and how they accommodated and negotiated their day-to-day lives in order to play football.

It is important to note that the women football players who serve as the main example in this chapter are, demographically speaking, a rather homogenous group. Most of the women interviewed were Qatari citizens of Qatari descent in their early twenties whose families had an interest in sports. Most of the women attend universities located in Doha's 'Education City',[13] an educational enclave comprises of mostly western satellite universities, indicating that they are likely to be from less conservative families than average. While the state-run Qatar University, for example, conducts most classes in Arabic and has a gender-segregated campus, this is not the case for the universities in Education City. In the 2014–2015 academic year, there were a total of 2,318 students in the universities of Education City, of whom 58 percent were women, and 40 percent of the total number of students are Qatari.[14] These students are generally more exposed to Western culture than Qataris from more conservative parts of society, and they are likely to have spent some time abroad. This implies that the female footballers of Education City are not necessarily representative of all Qatari women. Nevertheless, this group functions as an interesting example of how women who wish to pursue objectives that might conflict with the dominant norm negotiate conditions in society in order to create opportunities that would otherwise not be available.

The Education City women's football teams are largely initiated by the female students themselves. Up until 2016, the teams, leagues, and games were governed by dedicated individuals and through existing networks. Games, practices, equipment, and facilities were organized by the women themselves, allowing them to adapt activities to their cultural and academic responsibilities. In 2016, however, the women found support in an employee at Student Affairs, Amna, who argued that young men and women should have equal opportunities in sports.[15] In the spring semester of 2016, three teams began participating in a women's league. As many of the players on the different teams already knew each other, the games were organized through their personal networks. However, after Amna engaged the remaining universities, and contacted the students by email, in the fall semester of 2016, six teams (one later withdrew) signed up for a two-day league.[16] Both Amna and the players were surprised by the large turnout of both players and supporters.[17]

Negotiating Social Norms through Subversive Accommodation

Since the 1980s, scholars have moved beyond static analysis of male dominance, allowing for a more dynamic understanding of gender relations, which is especially useful when focusing on Muslim female agency.[18] As Abu Lughod famously points out, there has been a tendency in the human sciences to romanticize resistance, and for scholars to be preoccupied with identifying resisters.[19] In order to achieve a comprehensive understanding of how women are active participants in their own lives and in their communities, we need to move past the dichotomy of resistance and domination. Instead of starting off by searching for resistance, we should start by examining the everyday lives of women. Agency then, should be understood as an individual's capacity to make active choices, which are either in breach of, or in accordance with, existing norms.

Saba Mahmood argues that postcolonial feminist scholarship has been informed by the implicit assumption of a universal liberatory understanding of freedom. Agency, she argues, has been conceptualized within the binary of subordination and subversion. In her view, desire for freedom and subversion of norms are deeply connected to cultural and historical conditions. Writing on a female, "non-liberal" mosque movement in Cairo, Mahmood argues that agency and subjectivities are present not only in actions that challenge social norms, but also in actions that uphold them.[20] In this, she makes an important contribution by acknowledging that agency does not presuppose resistance, thus allowing a broader analysis of female agency. This is highly relevant in the case of the Qatari female footballers; these women are not necessarily subverting patriarchal structures, rather they are seeking to exercise their aspirations, albeit by simultaneously accepting certain cultural norms—as will be explained in the coming pages.

According to Sertaç Sehlikoglu, a fourth wave of feminist Middle Eastern scholarship has emerged, focusing increasingly on subjectivities not directly associated with piety.[21] Focusing on the ordinary, Asef Bayat points out, the subject's acknowledgement of gender and power relations does not necessarily mean that they are actively resisting it.[22] He argues that Iranian women, recognizing the constraints on organized campaigns, have pursued a strategy involving 'mundane practices of everyday life, such as pursuing education, sports, arts, music, or work outside the home.'[23] With examples from Iran and Egypt, he shows how youth, including women, have made claims through 'subversive accommodating', utilizing existing norms and institutions, while at the same time redefining and subverting 'the constraints of those codes and norms.'[24]

Such practices are present also among Qatari female football players; the women, instead of simply adhering to moral codes, may find or create ways to bypass these social norms in a way that does not expose them to possible sanctions by society. This does not presuppose a liberatory claim that these women are, consciously or not, subverting the moral code that imposes limitations on their ability to play. By focusing on their actions and their own retelling of them, rather than looking for resisters, this study opens up a discussion regarding how these women themselves perceive the barriers to their activity and, more importantly, how they are exercising their agency in working within and around them. Focusing on ordinary and everyday activities allows us to move beyond binaries like resistance–quietism and pious–liberatory, and to come to a more nuanced understanding of how women negotiate social norms in their everyday lives by acting in a way that is both subversive and accommodating.

Many Palestinian female football players in Israel, according to Kenda Stewart, conceptualize their participation in the sport as a hobby, thus creating a space for reshaping their Palestinian identity, while maintaining limits on how far the activity can go. In this case, women's football is treated as a hobby rather than a profession, which Stewart argues may in fact make football more accessible. She continues by arguing that sport can create a liminal space in which people are freed from the external constraints and rules governing everyday life, one in which they are able to contest, ignore, and overturn these social roles and constraints in the spirit of play.[25] Stewart's argument is thus transmissible to Qatar: by framing football activities within the context of the university, rather than a professional setting, the players bypass several of the barriers imposed upon them.

Cultural and Social Barriers to Female Football Participation

In Qatari society, the family is considered the basic unit of social organization.[26] Societal organization in Qatar is grounded in this view, and women's role in society is defined from this perspective. In Qatar's National Development Strategy, it is stated that 'the family is the basis of Qatari society, the foundation for all aspects of Qatar's social structure', and an appreciation of traditional values is listed as one of the characteristics of healthy, cohesive families.[27] This understanding places a woman first and foremost within the context of her duties to the family, and so also places certain barriers on her ability to participate in certain activities, including sports.

Despite rapid economic development and modernization, Qatari society remains culturally conservative. As formulated by one female interviewee, 'a man carries his own honor and shame, a woman carries the family's.'[28] A Qatari woman is expected to dress modestly and in line with local custom; a black abaya and a shawl to cover the hair.[29] Protecting women from exposure, or the male gaze, is central in Qatari culture. Although prominent women like Sheikha Moza bint Nasser, the mother of the emir, have an active and highly visible role, and Qatari women outnumber men in higher education by 2:1,[30] they are still less visible in politics, and society in general, than men. Only 36.9 percent of Qatari women are active in the workforce, compared to 68.5 percent of Qatari men.[31] Further, women and men have very different rights according to Qatari law, which is still dominated by an orthodox interpretation of *shariʿa* in issues relating to family law.[32] However, like their male counterparts, women in Qatar lack political representation since the state of Qatar is an absolute monarchy, with no elected bodies besides a rather insignificant municipal council.[33] When the emir appointed new members to the Shura Council in November 2017, it was the first time women were among those appointed.[34]

Writing on Qatari women and the role of segregated *majālis*,[35] Jocelyn S. Mitchell et al. argue that Qatari women find themselves under pressure to contribute to the human development of the country and to simultaneously maintain their roles at home. The researchers argue that women's increased ability to work, pursue higher education, and enter the public sphere grind against social norms. These issues necessitate complex personal and professional choices for Qatari women today.[36]

Similar conflicts are also present in the field of sports, where formal opportunities are increasing, while strict social norms remain. There are no formal laws preventing women from participating in sports, as in neighboring Saudi Arabia, but the opportunities for women are considerably fewer than those available for men. This is especially the case in organized and professional sports. Sports, including women's athletic activities, are highlighted as an important part of Qatar's development, and increasing female participation in sports, particularly for health reasons, is stated as a goal in several government documents, including the National Development Strategy, which is part of the Qatar National Vision 2030.[37] The Sports Sector Strategy, for example, highlights that women 'play a critical role in promoting healthy lifestyles through their influence on their children's health and well-being.'[38] According to Susan Dun, one of the main strategies to reach this goal is to link women's physical activity to elite sports participation by promoting female sportswomen in local media. However, as Dun points out, many Qatari families do not allow female members to show their face in public or to be featured in the media.[39]

Qatar's global investments in sport, as with the hosting of the FIFA 2022 World Cup, has put pressure on the country to increase women's participation in sports, and has, according to Dun, contributed to large investments in women's sports.[40] This pressure led Qatar to send female athletes to the Olympics for the first time in 2012 in London. Instead of sending two female athletes as requested by the International Olympic Committee (IOC), Qatar sent four—all with 'wild card' status.[41] One was even the country's flag bearer, indicating that Qatar was serious about showing the world it complied with the demands of the IOC.[42] At the 2016 Summer Olympics, however, Qatar only managed to send two female athletes.

After being introduced to Qatar in the 1940s through British workers, football rapidly gained popularity.[43] The first official season of the Qatar Stars League (previously known as Q-League) was played in 1972, shortly after Qatar gained independence from British protectionism, and two years after Qatar joined FIFA.[44] The first unofficial season, however, was played nine years earlier, according to the Qatari Football Association.[45] Thus, the generation now entering adulthood is, to a large degree, the sons and daughters of the first generation of Qataris who grew up with football, a sport that is now important to many families. As one interviewee, Haya, testified, 'I remember when I was little we used to sit with the family and watch the Qatari league. If there was a final, if the national team was playing ... it was an event that brought us together more than anything.'[46] Another woman, Aljohara, has similar memories from her upbringing: 'ever since we were kids we always played football with our cousins ... If you ask anyone, it's in every grandma's house.'[47]

Although many of the women interviewed for this chapter grew up playing and watching football with their families, and actively supported both local and international teams, after reaching a certain age, they become largely excluded from public football activities both as players and spectators. 'I believe that women are actively excluded from football. Even in my family, who is a sports family', Maryam explained.[48] Even though there is a 'family section' for women in football stadiums, Qatari female supporters are rare. Mohammed, a male professional football player, said the following when asked what he thought of Qatari female spectators in the stadium:

> It's allowed, but I wouldn't accept them going to the stadium. It's complicated. It's not usual to see ladies in the stadium. Even though they go shopping, they go out. They are around men, but I don't know ... It's like a tradition; I cannot let my sisters, or my mother go to the stadium. Even to watch me.'[49]

This kind of attitude might help explain why even though football has been played since the 1940s, and the QWSC was set up in 2001, it was not until 2010, the year Qatar placed its bid for the World Cup, that a women's national team first emerged. In 2016, however, the national team had not played any official games in over two years.[50] In a similar manner, the official female football league was not active at the time this study was conducted.[51] According to one interviewee, the national team struggles with recruitment and, due to government budget cuts, has no funding for travel or to pay the players, which in turn makes fewer of the players show up for practices.[52] For the girls who do show up for practice, many of them of foreign descent, it is for fun or as a hobby. If Qatari women are interested in playing football, as this study shows, then why are they so hard to recruit?

Firstly, the number of Qatari citizens is relatively small, which leaves a small pool for recruitment of players—both men and women. In addition, as Qataris are usually wealthy,[53] there is little room for social mobility as an incentive for a sporting career, which again plays a role in recruitment.[54] Players of foreign descent are able to obtain a Qatari passport in order to represent Qatar in sports,[55] and would, according to players, obtain a higher salary than a Qatari woman. These benefits create an incentive for female players of foreign descent to a greater degree than for Qatari women.

Geoff Harkness identified the following barriers to female sports participation in Qatar: family, hijab, gender segregation, and reputation.[56] These are, to a large degree, overlapping but not identical to the football-specific barriers. Harkness interviewed female players and coaches of basketball teams at the universities of Education City. The main difference between the basketball and football teams, and thus the sources of our respective studies, is that the basketball teams are largely made up of non-Qatari women, whereas the football teams are mainly made up of Qatari female citizens of Qatari descent.[57] As Haya, being one of the few Qatari women active on both the basketball and the football teams of her university, explained:

> For basketball it's very diverse. I think for basketball, some girls don't want to play because its open to the public and for football it's private. Only girls can come and watch. Girls coach, girls referee ... and no men are allowed. I think that's why so many of the Qatari girls are motivated to play football.[58]

Hessa, another football player, stated that the basketball team was never an option for her, as she was not comfortable with men being present, despite being better at basketball than football.[59] Thus, a major difference in how the two sports are practiced in Education City is that all-female football events are gender-segregated. With regards to cultural norms, being in Qatar and being from Qatar are two different things. Although Qatari culture is conservative, the same expectations on clothing and behavior do not apply to expatriate residents.

It is important here to note that the challenges faced by sportswomen differ not only depending on the sport, but also on the level of professionalism. Practicing physical activities for leisure or health purposes is typically more accepted than participation in semi-private and organized competitive sports. Thus, professional competitive sports are the least accepted level of sporting activities for women. Hence, there are some specific barriers regarding recruitment to *professional* football. This is reflected in a study on the lives of five female football players in Qatar conducted by Kelly Knez et al in 2012. The women take different precautions when playing in a public forum compared to playing in a male-free zone. The women also engage in careful negotiation with the media as, for example, images of the female body in movement are considered particularly taboo.[60]

Resistance from the Family

When it comes to constraints on football participation, the family has a large impact on the life decisions of both young women and men. According to Harkness, the family is the most frequent barrier to participation in basketball.[61] This is arguably valid for female footballers as well; players and coaches claim that they would have problems convincing families that playing football is an appropriate activity for girls or young women. Aljohara argued that, because Qatar is a very communal society, her actions reflect on her parents and her family. Therefore, even if her parents allowed her to play football, her extended family would have the authority to refuse.[62] She recalled her own experiences:

> I had this dream ... if I was going to die, I would die on the field as I scored a goal. So that's how I was going to be remembered. That was the dream. And then after school, I realize that's not the case, that's not even an option. My dad sat with me and explained to me, I need to tone it down. If you want to play you can play ... [but] you can never play professionally and not be associated negatively with a stereotype, and being too masculine and you know ... because we are such a small community, you can't really afford that because it's not only on you.[63]

As the above quote exemplifies, getting support from the family, especially for attending more professional or official football initiatives, is difficult for many women. The motives behind the resistance of family members may be rooted in different reasons. The prominent cause, however, is the idea of what should constitute a woman's role in society and in the family.

Receiving a good education is deemed of high importance among Qataris of both genders.[64] Qatar is a very academically oriented society, where a career as a football player is considered unstable and unfavorable compared to other vocations like engineering. This explanation was repeated by many of the interviewees, both sport officials and players of both genders. Aljohara recalled that her father did not accept her brother's wish for a career in professional football:

> Even with my brothers, when they wanted to pursue it [football] as a career, my dad would not allow it. It is not as legit as it is in Europe, because in Europe for a guy to become a football player is kind of a big deal. Here, it's not really. We still hold on to hard professional occupations, like an engineer, a doctor, whatever, and these are the acceptable ones. So, when my brother wanted to pursue a career in football, my dad was like, 'you know what, it's time for us to take you out of these trainings because they are brainwashing you.'[65]

Thus, spending a lot of time playing football, both as a hobby or as a profession, is seen as an impediment to education. Some of the women interviewed—those who considered playing for or had played for an official club or the national team—noted that one of the reasons why they did not practice properly was because training and traveling took time away from university, and often clashed with classes. They said that they would rather pursue education than athletics.

Exposure

By participating in professional or official football activities, one exposes oneself. The concept of 'exposure' refers to being exposed to men, or being without an abaya, but also in a more general way of willingly seeking a situation that will cause one to receive attention. As Mahmood notes, the ideal of modesty, or shyness (*al-ḥayā*), is central in many Muslim communities.[66] Qatari culture encourages female modesty, and moral codes are expected to be followed. For female footballers, it seems that public exposure is a reason for resistance from family members. Whereas playing for the national team would be off-limits for most Qatari girls, playing at school or university is more acceptable. One of the women interviewed, Sheikha, who had played for the national team when it first started, explained how Qatari ideas about exposure had made it particularly difficult for her to continue playing:

> Being on the national team for me was really difficult. Usually when I travel outside [of Qatar], I take my hijab off. But if you play for the national team you had to wear a bandana, because you are representing Qatar. That wasn't an issue. But the issue was [that] the first game I played was against Afghanistan—they came here—which was the first game that was going to be registered by FIFA. So, it is an important game. Some of the girls had an issue ... that the game was going to be televised. It's a new team, this is a conservative society. I mean, it should develop slowly, not just immediately. So, they told us it wasn't going to

be televised. They told us it was going to be closed off for men. Because when I went to my father, he was supportive and everything, but he told me that he would mind if it was going to be televised because the whole country would be seeing his daughter wandering around, and it's just not within our culture to do that. So, they told us it was going to be closed off for men, except for fathers. So, when my father came, there was like 5–600 Afghani men, no joke! 500 men just came and sat in the stands. Everyone was looking at each other, because they told us no men were going to come. We played and everything, and they took footage, and it was put in Qatar news.[67]

The Qatari women's national basketball team protested the International Basketball Federations' ban on the hijab, and withdrew from the Asian Games in 2014.[68] Female team members usually have to wear a kit consisting of a shirt and shorts, which is far more revealing than traditional Qatari attire or even most Muslim female dress codes. This kind of sporting gear would be considered inappropriate not only because it reveals more skin, but because it reveals the outline of the body in contradiction with customary attire.

Wishing to cater to a demand for more modest sportswear, the *Oolaa* company was established in Qatar by three women who wanted to make it easier for women to engage in physical activities. The type of clothing is less important for the university female football teams, where there is no access for men at tournaments or practices. In addition, the majority of the informants claimed that when playing football, exposure itself was the problem rather than how one dressed. Maryam claimed that, in Qatar, 'It is actually more negative [to be] perceived to be Qatari and work out with loose fitting clothes, than to be Western and wear shorts or show your belly.'[69] Another woman, Noura, stated that by pursuing sport and willingly exposing oneself, one would be considered a 'strong' woman—in a negative sense.[70] The issue of exposure thus creates challenges for professional female footballers; it is hard to find venues for practices and games that suit the demands for segregation. Many Qatari women are not comfortable being portrayed in the media, which in turn creates problems of attracting sponsors.

Transgressing the Notion of the 'Feminine'

For the majority of the women interviewees, there are negative connotations attached to playing football, especially playing in the established leagues. A Qatari woman is expected to represent not only herself but also her family, which is ultimately related to her chances of marriage.[71] A big part of a young Qatari woman's life is preparing for marriage. As Aljohara stated:

I'm not sure if you are familiar with this but, in the Qatari culture, once a girl goes to university her next target is getting married, and that's like ... shoved down your throat by your parents; mostly by your mum or female relatives. By junior year or senior year, you're supposed to be engaged already, you know. You're supposed to invest your energy in not even, like, studying; they don't care what your GPA is or whatever, but, they just care about the next step in life: 'You got into university, OK, good for you. Now the next step: you're supposed to get married.' You're not supposed to take care of your body, no, no, no, because there's plastic surgery to fix that. But you're supposed to look for a husband, and get married.[72]

As women's sports are still new to Qatari society, there are prejudices about how physical activity affects the body, potentially making it appear less 'feminine.' Football is understood, in Qatar, and elsewhere, as a masculine sport. As gender roles are specific, and the understanding of what is acceptable behavior for a female is restrictive, these pose additional barriers for women interested in playing football. According to some of the female players, it was mainly the cultural expectations of society that made it challenging for them to participate in organized competitive football. One woman who had experience in the national team, club teams, and university teams, explained that a lot of *būyāt*—women who dress and act in a way regarded as masculine—would play football in the clubs; by joining, one would be called a *būya* simply by association.[73]

Why is it a problem to be called a *būya*? That means you are gay, and you will receive scrutiny for that. You will be called a *būya* for that [playing football in the official clubs], *būya*, *būya*, *būya*, and then it travels around Qatar, which happens in like two minutes. And everyone says, oh, that girl, she's a *būya*, she plays football. So that is why not a lot of girls want to join the clubs. If you get called a *būya*, a lesbian, how would you get married?[74]

Aljohara recounts her initial experiences with professional football in Qatar:

I can understand why people have the negative connotations, externally. I understand why they have that, because when I was playing in the official league, there were girls who looked like men, acted like men, who basically did it to prove a stance to, like, kind of maintain their sexuality in a way. So, every person who played in that league would be associated with that. Because there's a majority of them who do it ... The first time I went, I saw a woman and I thought she was a man and I was like: Why isn't everyone covered up?? Fully shaved head, no breast, no butt, I thought she was a guy! Her voice was so deep, she sounded like a man. And then all of a sudden, I see a whole cult of them! And there are a lot of them! It's not people that I'm used to mixing with.[75]

Amelie Le Renard encountered the concept of *būyāt* in her work on young women in Riyadh, Saudi Arabia. She sees the *būyāt* as subverting a hegemonic model of femininity. Although she writes that the practice is denounced in different discourses relating to class, ethnicity, and religion, and that the perceived masculinity of these women makes their fellow students question their sexuality or associate them with lesbians—they do in fact in some cases engage in relationships with other women—she argues that 'owing to the absence of men, women-only spaces and gatherings probably allow digressions from dominant norms of femininity to be less violently repressed, and *buyat* are visible and numerous.'[76] Some of the *būyāt* Le Renard encountered were indeed critical about the status of women in Saudi Arabia, and what they experienced as limitations caused by a strict understanding of gender. Others among the *būyāt*, however, saw their physical appearance as simply a trend.[77]

In the case of Qatar, the women who do not consider themselves to be *būyāt* experience the label as a burden. In addition to the serious effect such a perception could have on their chances of getting married, the women expressed discomfort at being identified as a *būya*. Although the Qatari context arguably makes such a label more troubling since breaking with gender norms is indeed a taboo, similar findings appear in studies on women's football in other cultures.[78]

Even though some barriers for participation are present for both genders, it becomes clear that most of the challenges facing Qatari female footballers are not only gendered, but are also based on the customary Qatari understanding of gender. There are strict cultural norms dictating how a woman is supposed to behave, what she should wear, and what activities it is appropriate for her to engage in. Thus, the example of being labeled a *būya* for participating in organized, competitive football is telling: if you play football, you are by definition no longer fully feminine.

University Teams as a Safe Space

Despite the negative connotations attached to being associated with a club or the national team, and other barriers preventing women from joining, Qatari women still play football. There is indeed a difference in how different types of sporting activities are perceived. Activities related to health or wellness, like running or weight lifting inside an all-women's gym, would typically be the least controversial. Competing on the national team, in a 'masculine' team sport, would be close to impossible for a Qatari woman. Likewise, playing

international games on the women's national football team would be, culturally speaking, difficult, while playing football at home with other female
friends for fun is more likely to be accepted. In order to pursue organized,
competitive football, it is necessary for Qatari female footballers to negotiate
the expectations and norms of society in order to create a safe space.

The universities in Qatar's Education City function as such spaces.
Education City is a campus on the outskirts of Doha composed of a number
of universities, including six American satellite universities and the Qatari
Hamad bin Khalifa University. The main language of instruction is English,
and the campus is not gender segregated, in contrast to the more traditional
Qatar University campus. This indicates that many Qatari students at
Education City likely come from less conservative families, and many of the
students come from private primary school backgrounds with international
curriculums. Most of the universities have a women's football team, mainly
organized by the students themselves, driven by passionate individuals who
are seeking to find a way to participate in competitive football. The teams'
players are students, and are usually recruited by friends or classmates. These
activities have only been in operation for a few years and, since they still rely
on individual effort, the structures are fragile. However, they seem to be growing and, after a successfully executed tournament in the fall of 2016, there are
plans to continue developing the structures of female football in Education
City through cooperation with the Supreme Committee for Delivery and
Legacy, the local organizing committee of the 2022 FIFA World Cup.[79]

The teams were started by women who wanted an opportunity to play
organized, competitive football. These women had previously played football
in school or with friends and family, but did not see participation in official
teams as an option due to negative connotations associated with them, or due
to lack of time. They were not simply given an opportunity to play, but, rather,
worked for the opportunity to play; Alanood recounts how she used to struggle with the university administration to find someone to support her team in
order to rent fields and apply for funding.[80] Underlining the players' role in
organizing practices and games, Haya noted that since all the players are
enrolled in the universities, this proximity allows them to plan for games and
practices in a way that does not get in the way of their educational obligations.[81]
In a similar manner, Hessa explained that for her to be part of the team, the
venues of play had to be gender segregated—a rule she said the players had
decided on together.[82] When Amna in Student Affairs—not the department
that would normally organize sports events—got engaged in the female foot-

ball league, one of her motivations was to organize it in a way that would feel safe and comfortable for the players. This was in line with the ideas of the already-active players, and was based on conversations with female students.[83]

The university teams can be understood as hybrid: they are not professional, nor are they simply for leisure. By taking charge of the organization, the women can build teams that meet regularly in order to build a coherent team identity. These teams further enable women to pursue the competitive aspect of the sport, which is highlighted by many of the players as lacking when engaging in leisure-oriented initiatives, such as playing with family and friends. Since the teams are under the supervision of the universities, it becomes easier for the sport to be accepted by their families; it becomes viewed as a hobby, thus making it more accessible. For some women, it allows them to not disclose the activity to their parents at all.[84] As Stewart notes in the case of female Palestinian players, they create a space where social norms can be contested.[85]

In addition, organizing the events within Education City premises enables transgression of the borders between private and public. The environment where practices and matches are held is neither private nor public. Rather, the universities offer a semi-private, semi-public space. By creating university teams within these imagined borders of the university, the women create a safe space where societal barriers can, to a large extent, be overcome. As one of the players explains:

> In some cases, it's easier for the parents to be OK, it's a university, you just play against other universities and they are mostly your friends. And it's closed off; you are not exposed in the same way. The whole environment is different; it is two different worlds.[86]

Framing the activities in the realm of the university also gives the women the opportunity to organize practices and games in ways that accommodate their class schedules. As the games are played on university premises, they do not have to spend time traveling—something several interviewees emphasized was a problem when taking part in official teams. Playing on university campuses thus allows the women to organize games and practices in a way that does not affect academic life. By associating the activity to their education—as opposed to being an obstacle to it—they can convince their families that it is a legitimate way to spend time, since not all of the girls have families who support their football interest. In these cases, engaging with the sport at university allows them to play without having to confront their parents. Universities are trusted spaces and, therefore, it is less controversial for women to engage in these kinds of activities—this is the case for the girls themselves, for their families, or for society in general.

In addition to less resistance from their families, organizing the activities on university premises allows the female players to be less prone to exposure. Instead of playing outside on a full-scale field, the women play *futsal*, indoor football with five players on each team. This allows them to play in a more protected and enclosed space, which makes it safer with regards to exposure to males or the general public. This enclosure also allows them to play in more practical attire, as they do not have to worry about exposing body parts they would otherwise keep covered.

The example of Qatar's Education City is interesting in this regard; the two team sports mainly available to women are football and basketball. Basketball is well established and run by the administration, making it generally better organized and better attended. However, the female basketball teams consist of mostly non-Qataris, as mentioned above, while the football players are mostly Qatari. However, since the Qatari female football players organize their own practices and tournaments, they have the opportunity to engage in the game in a way that suits their needs. A player who grew up playing sports, albeit not football, explained how this affected her choice:

> By the time I moved to university, they offered football in an all ladies space. All the practices and all the games would be female only, which was more motivating for me ... Basketball is more popular, they have a proper league. But sometimes they would have a man ref and the matches are open to everyone, so I wasn't comfortable with that.[87]

Discussing the privacy and gendered spaces of Qatari homes, Rana Sobh and Russell W Belk argue that because women are made to embody morality and virtue in the local culture, gendered spaces in Qatari homes give women the convenience of being uncovered. Respect for their privacy, they argue, is important to the honor of the family. Privacy should thus be interpreted as respect rather than seclusion, giving privacy a public function.[88] In other words, gendered spaces can serve to empower Qatari women, and to 'reconcile the conflicting demands of modernity and tradition.'[89] Mitchell et al. similarly argue that Qatari women use female-only gatherings to tackle issues related to conflicts between traditional norms and increased possibilities for women in society.[90]

Playing on official teams is not an option for most of the women interviewed. By adhering to the local tradition of segregation, and keeping their activities within the safe space of universities, in both a metaphorical and a physical sense, the women are creating an alternative arena, parallel to the official societal arena, in which to exercise their aspirations. Thus, Qatari female footballers are negotiating the gendered expectations placed on them by their families and society as a whole, while simultaneously engaging in what Bayat terms 'subversive accommodation.'[91]

It is important not to underestimate the workings of power in this case. As Abu Lughod reminds us, by concentrating on finding resistance, understandings of power can be lost.[92] Power structures do not simply disappear, but are transferred into new relationships. Although the immediate effect of the women's efforts in their quest to play football is limited, it is, however, far from insignificant. Writing on women's continuous persistence through ordinary activities in post-revolutionary Iran, Bayat argues that this 'non-movement' made 'considerable inroads, empowering women through education, employment, and family law, and raised self-esteem.'[93] Qatari female footballers are indeed adhering to a number of established social norms that limit their options for playing football but, instead of accepting that there are no ways to play, they reclaim some control by *creating* ways to play. As one woman argued:

> I don't think it [culture] is a barrier [to playing football in general], because we still play. We can still amend the rules, we can say, OK, girls only, we can still have a league; we can have refs, we can have all that. It doesn't have to be open to the public, to men. So, it can function. The love for the sport outweighs everything. If you want it, you will do it.[94]

Secondly, by creating a space where their activities are not sanctioned, they are also creating a space in which they can help redefine women's football; they do not adhere to the idea that one cannot be feminine and play football at the same time. Although all of the women interviewed believe that Qatari society is undergoing transformation, and that their initiatives were contributing to change, they all thought it would take time before playing openly would be accepted. The women are what Mahmood terms 'docile agents,' exerting their agency in the quest for a contextual freedom, rather than an explicitly liberal one.[95] Thus, *playing*, rather than playing professionally or openly in public, is the objective for these women. One woman interviewed said she believed there was a glass ceiling that needed to be broken by one generation building upon the previous one, starting with the girls saying: 'Hey! I'm a girl, I can play football.' She elaborated:

> It is part of a change. It is an awakening. It is like the roots of the future. It's like planting a seed for a garden you will never see. It's not going to be easy, and it's not going to be our generation that will see it.[96]

Conclusion

By navigating limitations, some Qatari women have created a safe space for their activities that allows them to bypass established norms regarding women and femininity. These self-created spaces do not carry the same negative connotations of masculinity that the official clubs and the national team do, thus allowing women to challenge the perception that it is not possible for a female to play football, while at the same time preserving their femininity and adhering to societal moral codes.

The university football teams, largely organized by the women themselves, function as a hybrid. They are semi-private, semi-public spaces, and allow for the girls to play organized competitive football, while at the same time avoiding severe scrutiny. This is clear in the fact that while recruitment of Qatari women is still challenging for teams operating in a public or non-segregated space, the university football teams attract great interest from female students. By relabeling women's football a university activity, rather than something that conflicts with their academic priorities, they enable themselves to play football without getting into conflict with their family. The women are seeking to gain a positive freedom to pursue their objectives, and reclaiming control in shaping their own lives.

5

SPORTSWOMEN'S USE OF SOCIAL MEDIA IN THE MIDDLE EAST AND NORTH AFRICA (MENA)

Nida Ahmad

Introduction

Social media has played a significant role in the Middle East and North Africa (MENA), especially during the Arab uprisings, and its impact is far from slowing down. The ongoing and developing events in the region—tensions in the Gulf, humanitarian crises, and civil wars—are widely deliberated, and discussions surrounding the instability of the region dominate news headlines. These stories are being disseminated even more widely through social media.

The topic of social media has gained interest from a range of scholars across disciplines keen to examine its use, significance, and impact on communities. For many members of society, key aspects of our lives are mediated online, and we are increasingly living a 'digital life.'[1] We share and consume information via social media platforms like Facebook, Twitter, Flickr, and Instagram, and through various technologies like cell phones, laptops, and tablets that are capable of monitoring important aspects of our lives, such as our health and well-being.[2] Research and discussion regarding social media use in the region has tended to focus on civic, economic, political, and religious aspirations,[3] with less consideration of the everyday uses of such platforms.[4]

The discussion on how women from the MENA region use social media tends to be centered on political activism,[5] fashion, and business uses, and how they negotiate gender and faith according to their community.[6] Digital platforms allow some women from the region to negotiate social, cultural, and/ or religious norms, and to share their experiences through images and text.[7] Discussion around how women from the region are negotiating social media platforms for everyday purposes, particularly in relation to their sport and physical activities, is lacking. Due to increased use of social media by women in the region, this chapter addresses the following questions: what role does social media play in constructing and representing female athletes' sporting lives? And what are the sociocultural implications of these representations?

Theoretical Framework: Identity Formation in Digital Spaces

According to Stuart Hall,[8] understandings of identity must recognize it as highly complex, encompassing gender, ethnicity, religious and social beliefs, and class, and something that is constantly shifting. Furthermore, when it comes to how identities are constructed, they are 'within, not outside discourse.'[9] Many sports media scholars have drawn upon Hall's work to examine the power relations involved in the production and consumption of sporting representations and identities in particular historical contexts. However, fewer have used his work to inform our understandings of the multiple forms of power operating on and through individual and group identities in sporting social media contexts.

It is important to examine how sport and social media construct, reinforce, perpetuate, and challenge dominant perceptions and lived experiences of identities. According to Hall, 'identities are never unified, and, in late modern times, increasingly fragmented and fractured; never singular but multiply constructed across different, often intersecting and antagonistic, discourses, practices and positions.'[10] Yet, within Western media discourses, Muslim women are often homogenized and categorized into either 'positive' or 'negative' representations.[11] Furthermore, Western media often monolithically represent women in the MENA region through stereotypical images or content, despite the cultural, religious, economic, and ethnic diversity present in the region and between individuals. Women from the region are often represented as victims of their oppressive cultures and their male compatriots.

Whereas such representations typically focus on the growth of discrimination and the spread of racist, misogynistic, and sexist rhetoric, it is important to note that the lives of women vary across and within countries, where political, cultural, and social circumstances impact their experiences in varied ways and, in this case, their sporting and social media activities.

Methods

Over the past few years, researchers around the world have been paying close attention to the ways athletes use social media, with a growing number of scholars focusing on these issues. Most of this literature has focused on Twitter, with more recent scholarship examining the use of Instagram.[12] As a contribution to expanding the focus of the literature, this project examines Twitter, Instagram, Facebook, and SnapChat to understand how these platforms are used by sportswomen from the region. With this aim, between January and August 2017, I conducted a digital ethnography of the social media accounts of twelve MENA sportswomen based in Saudi Arabia, Kuwait, the United Arab Emirates, Egypt, and Iran, and across the four platforms mentioned above. Digital ethnography is the observation of digital space comprised of images, videos, and text showcasing the interactions of individuals, communities, countries, and geographies.[13]

In addition to this digital ethnography, between April and August 2017, I conducted semi-structured interviews in English with sportswomen aged 22 to 39.[14] The diverse range of their backgrounds, experiences, identities, social media practices, and lived experiences contributed to the richness of the data. The sporting disciplines included combat sports, action sports (surfing, climbing, and mountaineering), 'traditional' sports (basketball), fencing, CrossFit, and those engaged in physical activity (runners). The sportswomens' participation in sports varied; some were non-competitive but sports or physical activity were part of their routine, while others trained to compete at local, national, and international levels. Furthermore, I monitored developing political and cultural situations in the region through Google alerts and Twitter's 'trending' section, which allowed me to contextualize the participants' background and to inform my interview and data.

As with any method, there are strengths and limitations to digital ethnography. Although digital ethnography is rapidly gaining popularity across the social sciences and humanities, issues have arisen relating to ethics. A particularly controversial issue relates to covert online 'lurking' for research purposes.

This is a highly contested topic since images, text, and other information remain in public digital spaces and can be easily accessed by anyone without consent, rather like a newspaper or magazine article. Some researchers have embraced the covert possibilities of online research by 'lurking' in digital spaces without consent.[15] This raises ethical concerns regarding the rights of those being observed and their need to know that their participation is being recorded for research purposes.[16] In acknowledgement of such ethical considerations, I was overt about my role as a researcher. Prior to any digital observations, I gained consent from all participants who chose which platforms I could follow for the purposes of this research. To protect the identity of participants, pseudonyms are used throughout the chapter. Furthermore, I created new accounts specifically for this research, and, while I was observing the participants' social media accounts, I limited my activity in terms of 'liking' and 'commenting' on images and tweets for the safety of all the participants, and to ensure clarity of my role as a researcher. This allowed me to be mindful of ethical issues and critical of the processes when examining the digital lives of the sportswomen in question.

Social Media in the Middle East and North Africa

Due to the extent of its cultural impact, social media's wide reach has attracted the attention of researchers and practitioners from a range of disciplines. There are different definitions of social media, such as new media and Web 2.0, but, for this research, I apply Ellison and Boyd's definition:

> A social network site is a networked communication platform in which participants 1) have uniquely identifiable profiles that consist of user-supplied content, content provided by other users, and/or system-level data; 2) can publicly articulate connections that can be viewed and traversed by others; and 3) can consume, produce, and/or interact with streams of user-generated content provided by their connections on the site.[17]

This definition encompasses both online and offline connection and engagement, and users' ability to harness online platforms through 'tags,' 'likes,' and 'comments' to construct, perform, and accentuate their identities.[18] The ever-changing and fluctuating technology is part of the daily routine in the everyday lives of so many, and the purposes of social media go beyond sharing and consuming information; social media may contribute in important ways to an individual's sense of identity and belonging, to corporate and organizational strategies, and to sports media production and consumption.

Social media use is increasing in the Middle East and North Africa, though popularity and accessibility vary across countries. In 2016, there were approximately 21.4 million active users in the region, with the highest numbers found in the Gulf countries. For example, 75 percent of the population of Qatar uses social media, 69 percent in the United Arab of Emirates, and 55 percent in Saudi Arabia.[19] Digital technology is permeating different aspects of individuals' lives; digital spaces are creating opportunities for political, cultural, and social conversations to occur, and they also facilitate offline movements.[20] The impact and importance of social media are being recognized in the region, with some countries creating initiatives such as the Arab Youth Media Initiative launched by the UAE's Ministry of State for Youth Affairs to prepare a young generation of media professionals to disseminate Arab media content worldwide.[21]

MENA Women's Use of Social Media

Conversations about social media in the MENA region are often associated with the Arab uprisings, with some scholars arguing that the revolutions in Tunisia and Egypt were led by Twitter and Facebook.[22] There are ongoing debates about how social media facilitated the revolutions as an instrument enabling activists to harness digital technologies to share their stories, generate public support, and raise awareness through images, texts, and tweets.[23] It is important to note that participation in digital spaces in the Middle East is not exclusive to men, and that women are also at the forefront of digital spaces, leading to online and offline activism. For example, Lina Ben Mhenni, an internet activist from Tunisia, used her blog *A Tunisian Girl*, along with other social media platforms, to document the protests occurring in her country via the words and images she shared globally.[24] Many discussions about Egyptian women and social media during the Arab uprisings tended to portray them as passive about protesting, which overlooked the different reasons for how and why women were protesting.[25]

In many parts of the Middle East, social media had already been adopted by women prior to the Arab uprisings. In Iran, women had embraced technology and were using digital spaces to discuss issues relating to feminism, religion, gender-based discriminatory laws, and politics.[26] Prior to Iran's Green Movement in 2009, women were using blogs and social media platforms to collect signatures to address and change discriminatory laws.[27] Their activism did not stop there, and Iranian women employed the #WhiteWednesday hashtag on Twitter and Instagram to promote gender equality during the 2017 presidential election. Another example involved Saudi women using social media—Twitter, in particular—to start the #IAmMyOwnGuardian hashtag in 2016 to oppose the strict law that requires Saudi women to seek permission from a male guardian to take part in essential tasks like travel, marriage, education, and work. Caving to intense social pressure, a royal decree was passed in May 2017 giving Saudi women basic freedom, such as allowing them to travel and study without gaining consent from male guardians. Women from the region have started other online activist movements through the use of social media, and, in particular, created specific hashtags to raise awareness and make issues go viral.

Online spaces, such as blogs, allow women to practice solidarity and agency,[28] and to debunk assumptions held by outsiders. For example, to disrupt Western media narratives that often assign Muslim women the status of the 'oppressed other,' 'hijab bloggers' are harnessing digital spaces and sharing aspects of their lives through fashion.[29] Engagement in social media spaces does, however, come with consequences and risks. Issues of online harassment, racism, sexism, and even rape and death threats are common, and many female bloggers encountered such threats especially during the Arab uprisings. More recently, a Saudi woman raised controversy and became the subject of a call for punishment because she was seen on SnapChat walking around an ancient fort in Saudi Arabia in a short skirt and without hijab. The various aspects of social media are essential conversations on the impact of individuals and communities in the region. While none of the participants in this study explicitly mentioned the Arab uprisings, it is important to note that, in this context, sportswomen use social media in different ways, and often in close connection to their community and culture.

Social Media and Sport in the Region

The scholarship surrounding sports and social media is increasing,[30] and is moving beyond discussions of sports management and branding to address issues of how athletes are engaging with social media and their online *self*-representation.[31] To date, the discussion of social media and sports in the MENA region is limited and, as of yet, there has been no examination of the importance of social media in the lives of sportswomen from the region.

Technology use is a daily routine for many and goes beyond just sharing and consuming information.[32] Individuals can share personal narratives through text or images instantly, giving them a sense of identity and belonging in digital spaces. Some researchers suggest that social media platforms allow sportswomen to control visibility about themselves, to increase coverage of their sport, and to share other aspects of their identity.[33] This is significant since it can disrupt gender narratives, especially as sportswomen have often been trivialized or sexualized in the mainstream sports media for decades.[34] Furthermore, digital platforms have proven to be valuable sources of solidarity, especially for those from marginalized communities.[35] Access to information is creating a space where women from all over the world can connect and share their experiences.[36]

Digital spaces and, in particular, social media platforms, have created unique opportunities for a diversity of voices to be shared.[37] However, how sportswomen in the region are using social media is widely unexplored and requires further research. The present study addresses these issues.

The Ways MENA Sportswomen use Social Media

My digital observations and interviews with sportswomen generated a range of themes, but, for this chapter, I focus on 1) self-branding their sporting lives in digital spaces, and 2) preservation of modesty in digital spaces. In so doing, I draw upon international literature to consider how sportswomen from the MENA region are engaging with social media in similar or different ways from their international peers.

Self-Branding and Sporting Identities in Digital Spaces

As various scholars have shown, sportswomen tend to be marginalized, trivialized, and sexualized in the mass media.[38] Some have argued that social media offers sportswomen valuable opportunities to self-represent and to offer alternative visions of their sporting lives. In doing so, social media creates unique opportunities for sportswomen to self-brand by sharing particular aspects of their lives online. Professional athletes in the United States and Europe have been adept at using social media to share their journeys and training regimens, through sometimes perfectly tailored and candid images that aid in attracting sponsors.[39] In my digital observations and interviews with sportswomen, those who have public accounts explained how they used their social media platforms to draw attention to themselves and their sport, to raise awareness about particular issues, to gain followers for self-branding, or to inspire others. For example, Maya is a 30-year-old competitive CrossFit athlete and coach from Kuwait. Even though she is a mother and was expecting her second child at the time of this research, she continued to train throughout her pregnancy. She not only shares her sporting journey on social media, but uses it to attract clients. Speaking about why social media is important to her career as a trainer, Maya stated that, 'my Instagram account is not just a document of my journey, it is kind of like I am advertising myself as trainer. A lot of my clients and members, they come to the gym because they want to be coached by me.'[40]

Maya also discussed being sponsored by different local companies, such as those that provide supplements to active individuals or athletes. As part of her sponsorship agreement with one company, she was required to post 'twice a week' about the brand on her social media account. She no longer works with that brand, stating there was no specific reason for the departure; however, she is currently sponsored by a health food company, about which she actively posts on her Instagram stories because 'I am showing them support because I am very happy with their service, and its free food', she said, laughing. When asked how her relationships with sponsors emerged, she explained that she attracted a range of opportunities because her Instagram account was 'open' to the public, and because she was 'consistently active,' documenting her sporting journey through images, text, use of hashtags,[41] and engaging with followers. In 2016, she was featured as one of the 'influencers' of her sport in a prominent magazine in the region,[42] and she is regularly included in ongoing major sporting campaigns and events, such as those for Reebok and Nike in the MENA region. Social media plays an important role in enabling athletes to develop relationships with brands,[43] and those who are able to successfully brand themselves gain higher salaries and progress in their athletic careers. This can be seen with Maya and her use of Instagram, and there are plenty of other examples of sportswomen from the region utilizing social media to that effect.[44]

Maintaining a business and attracting clients and/or potential sponsors is not an easy task. Maya stated that she has to remain 'consistent' with the information she posts, and often prepares ahead of time: 'I will prepare something in advance in case I get a day where I am too stressed or I am not in the mood.' She further stated that it is not only important to remain 'consistent' but 'it is important to keep your followers engaged', which is especially challenging since Instagram has over 400 million daily users sharing over 40 billion images.[45] Maya further stated: 'you will either be forgotten or people will lose interest.' To stay abreast of the developing changes in social media, such as new features and trends, Maya participates in social media marketing courses to

further develop her brand, sport, and gym. While Maya was the only participant to have taken online marketing courses, others mentioned seeking advice
from social media experts.

Another important aspect of social media usage is time spent posting or
engaging with followers. Athletes who successfully use social media for the
purposes of self-branding tend to spend a significant amount of time on social
media.[46] The twelve participants in my study confirmed these findings. 'I will
spend at least one hour or two hours on social media just either posting or
replying or checking', stated Hiba, a 29-year-old Olympian.[47] The same goes for
Dina, a 30-year-old mountaineer who is from the United Arab Emirates and
works in marketing, and for Shirin, a 33-year-old action sportswoman from
Iran who competes in national and international events and who works as a
brand and marketing influencer in her country.[48] They both stated that they
spend 'a lot of time' posting content. Shirin has the upgraded business version
of Instagram, which allows her to analyze her Instagram posts. She notes, 'I
look at which picture gets the most engagement, insights into the impression
of the post, and the time of day, week and stuff like that.' This allows her to
strategically post her images and videos to reach a larger audience.

Maya, Hiba, Dina, and Shirin were not the only sportswomen spending a
significant amount of time on social media. Another participant, Sarah, a
33-year-old CrossFit trainer and competitor from Saudi Arabia stated that 'it
takes me a good hour just to post one post.' Sarah not only focuses on developing her brand via social media, she also uses it to 'inspire' men and women to
live an active lifestyle. Many of her videos show how she trains, what she eats
(healthy or not), what she wears (mostly sports clothes), and other sport-
related activities (such as speaking at public events). She uses hashtags like
#Nike, #Reebok, #Puma, along with #ArabWomen, #lifestyle, #sport, etc. to
reach a larger audience. For Sarah, social media is an important tool. Due to
limited opportunities in her country, she turned to social media to 'market'
herself and build her brand. Her Instagram account and engagement with her
followers has given her opportunities such as working with the Ministry of
Youth and Sports to lead local fitness and/or sporting events, and she has been
featured in a well-known regional magazine along with several news articles
and video promos. Sarah is also aware of her audience and the uses and abuses
of social media. Sarah stated:

> I understand how social media works. If someone wants to show their abs, or
> show their whatever, just for more likes, then okay, but you can't fool your true
> followers for long. If you really want to inspire people, they will not get inspired
> by your bum in the camera.[49]

For her, the focus is not on the number of followers or 'likes', but more about using social media to inspire other women through sports. Like many of the sportswomen interviewed for this research, Sarah is aware of what others post on social media but avoids mimicking movements or images based on their sports, and refrains from posting 'sexy selfies.' These sportswomen share images that are focused on their sport, their lifestyle, and their identity; they shy away from the objectification/sexualization of their body, preferring to share images in order to engage with their audience and build their brand.

As these examples suggest, sportswomen in the MENA region are actively posting, sharing, and producing carefully considered content to share aspects of their sporting identities for self-branding. This is interesting, since the literature about how sportswomen are using social media for self-branding has mainly focused on Western women, many of whom embrace traditional notions of heterosexual femininity—for example, with sexualized images of their 'bum in the camera' or wearing revealing clothes to attract more audience members.[50] Some women are encouraged to celebrate their bodies as a 'source of power,'[51] which, for some, is a form of empowerment to freely make a choice and share aspects of their lives online.[52] When sportswomen focus on their heterosexual femininity they are likely to attract viewers, but their comments sections are peppered with salacious and sexist remarks (for example, 'nice ass', 'I'd bang that'), which do not suggest that they are being respected for their athletic prowess or achievements. Despite sharing images that do not sexualize their bodies, the women in this research were not exempt from receiving such online comments. Some stated that they received private DMs (direct messaging), asking for their hand in marriage and/or commenting on their looks (for instance, 'you are so beautiful').

As previously stated, social media provides athletes with opportunities to self-brand and self-represent. With the ability to personally craft images and text, they can share aspects of their sporting identities with their audience.[53] This allows them to develop relationships with stakeholders, fans, and potential sponsors,[54] which is accomplished by the sportswomen in this research. Even though some researchers have indicated that women are likely to be more sexually expressive in their social media posts,[55] this was not the case for the sportswomen in this particular study; they stated that they kept their culture and society in mind when they shared their sporting identities online. The participants in this research avoided flaunting their scantily clad bodies, a feature that is more common in posts of sportswomen from other regions.[56] Furthermore, the participants were from conservative countries from the

MENA region (Egypt, Saudi Arabia, Kuwait, United Arab Emirates, and Iran), which largely contributed to their not posting overly sexualized images of their sporting bodies. The participants demonstrated an awareness that they did not have to use sexy images to gain followers or sponsors. However, many found themselves entering careful deliberations about what and how to post. For some, such as Sarah and Dina, this evoked a 'double identity crisis' between the cultural expectations of their sporting codes and the cultural rules and norms of their communities.

Social media allows MENA sportswomen to share images and text, and to express and share parts of their identity often restricted by cultural, religious, and societal norms. Athletes who use digital media are able to counteract negative portrayals of their image commonly found in mass media representations.[57] This seems to be the case for MENA sportswomen who use social media to challenge dominant media portrayals of them as the 'oppressed other', which is often associated with Arab/Muslim sportswoman.

'I Will Not be a Martyr, it is Not My Battle to Fight': Preserving Family or Community Honor while Maintaining Online Sporting Identity

As previously stated, mainstream Western media tend to portray women from the MENA region as oppressed by cultural and religious norms.[58] Furthermore, when it comes to the coverage of sportswomen, media representations tend to be stereotyped and focused on aspects of their identity outside of sport.[59] However, social media provides opportunities for sportswomen to bypass the traditional media framing of their identities by giving them the power to choose which aspects of their identity they want to share,[60] allowing individuals to sustain relationships with family, friends, and strangers.[61]

For many of the sportswomen in this project, family and/or community relations were important. Each of the athletes interviewed spoke about supportive parents inspiring them to pursue their athletic endeavors, even in sports deemed culturally inappropriate. Some of the participants engage in sports dominated by men, and commented on the important roles played by their fathers in supporting their sporting pursuits. For example, Dina stated that 'a female mountaineer is rare, so the point of my focus on Instagram is trying to not just influence other girls.' Continuing, she explained that she uses her account to connect with other women in her country and region, while at the same time showcasing her athletic abilities to attract 'local sponsors' and 'promote the sport.' Shirin has a similar approach, and uses her

Instagram account to promote her sport—which falls in the category of action sports such as surfing, climbing, BMX, snowboarding, skateboarding, and parkour, and which is often ignored in her country. Additionally, stories of her accomplishments are rarely mentioned. To bring awareness to the sport, Shirin recently used social media to showcase her success by taking screenshots of her 'ranking'; she noted that when 'people saw the flag and my name', she received messages of support and new followers. More importantly, Shirin was able to share a different narrative about herself, her sport, and even her society with international followers.

Social media aids athletes who participate in lesser-known sports to increase awareness of the sport, which can be seen in the cases of Dina and Shirin.[62] However, another participant, Lamya, a 34-year-old action sports-woman and digital media influencer who runs her family's business, refuses to take part in any opportunity that would feature her as the first woman from Saudi Arabia to participate in her sport. She turned down multiple requests, and when asked why, she simply stated 'I will not be a martyr.' She listed her family as one of the reasons for not taking part. Lamya stated that sport 'is an important cause, and yes, it is something I need to fight for, but to me my family is more important.' She also said that she has nothing to 'prove' and prefers to focus on other aspects of her life, such as building her brand, which is not related to sports, but features her sporting lifestyle, and her family business. Lamya has no interest in 'hurting' her family and their 'reputation,' particularly her father who has 'worked hard' to develop his reputation in the industry. Importantly, she also said that she was wary of any 'negative' consequences on the family and the 'people around you.' She was hinting at a possible backlash from extended family members and even the wider community who might comment that a woman should not be participating in sport, or that it is not culturally or religiously appropriate for a woman to take part in sports at all, or those who might say things like 'you know these kids were not raised right and they do not represent this country.' Raha Moharrak, the first Saudi woman to summit Mount Everest, faced similar criticisms as well as online and offline 'disagreements' from family members and Saudis in general.[63] Family is an integral part of the MENA sportswomen's lives, especially when they have been supported (financially and/or emotionally) in their sporting pursuits. For this reason, they keep their family in mind when they post aspects of their sporting identities.

Conclusion

Social media is changing the ways that sports are consumed, discussed, and debated. The body of scholarship examining how athletes are using social media and adapting it for personal and professional use is growing quickly. Since the literature to date mostly focuses on Western sportswomen, this chapter adds to the discussion of how sportswomen are using social media by including voices of sportswomen from the Middle East. The available research shows how Western sportswomen use social media for self-branding, offering intimate details of their lifestyles, and often revealing images of their bodies.[64] In contrast, the women in this research carefully consider what and how they share with their audiences, applying different strategies to safely and effectively navigate the digital terrain. For the women in this study, issues of family and culture are central to their digital decision-making. When it comes to discussion of gender and sports in the region, much of the focus has been on the limited opportunities for women and girls, and the Olympic achievements of a select few.[65] By expanding the discussion to include digital platforms, this research allows for an understanding of the various ways sportswomen in the region are using their social media platforms for self-branding in a culturally considered manner. Additionally, this opens up an avenue for further research on the role of social media in influencing women's participation and opportunities in sport in the region, as well as more studies on non-Western sportswomen's use of social media.

6

THE WORLD CUP AND FREEDOM OF
EXPRESSION IN QATAR

Craig L. LaMay

Introduction

Much has been written about sporting mega-events and human rights in the countries that host them, but very little on how these events affect rights of expression and publication. The subject of this paper is the effect, if any, that sporting mega-events, and especially the 2022 FIFA World Cup, will have on Qatar's environment for free expression and journalistic independence. Qatar, an Arab Gulf state and a member of the six-nation Gulf Cooperation Council (GCC),[1] is both deeply traditional and aggressively modern, and has made sport a centerpiece of its long-term development strategy.[2] In 2015, for example, the country played host to fifty-five international sporting competitions, and an additional forty-three regional and local ones.[3] Qatar is also an absolute monarchy with a tightly controlled media sector. The country's media market consists almost entirely of state-owned or state-affiliated firms, and publishers require a license to operate; the only arguably independent news organ, the online and unlicensed *Doha News*, has been blocked in the country since late 2016.[4] The country's media laws, discussed below, all include criminal penalties for everything from copyright violations to defamation, a feature of a restrictive media system. A representative measure of Qatar's standing in the world is its ranking in the Reporters Sans Frontières (RSF) 2017 World Press Freedom Index, where it sits at 123 out of 180 countries—*down* from a high of 74 in 2003.[5]

At the same time, on matters of free expression, Qatar is arguably the most progressive member of the GCC. Most famously, it is home to a leading international television news operation, Al Jazeera, for which it is reviled by other Arab states, including Saudi Arabia and the United Arab Emirates—both of which, as of this writing, have demanded Al Jazeera be closed as one of thirteen conditions for ending a blockade of the country they instigated in June 2017. In response, Qatar has since hosted a major international conference on free expression and published the record of that conference;[6] its foreign minister has spoken publicly on free expression rights at Chatham House in the United Kingdom;[7] and the emir, Sheikh Tamim bin Hamad Al Thani, has appeared on a major US television news program ('60 Minutes') in which he emphasized the importance of media freedom to his legacy and the country's future.[8]

So which way do the winds blow? Assuming Qatar succeeds in hosting the 2022 World Cup—the continuing Saudi-led blockade means that the games would be played in a conflict zone, and the Saudi leadership is undergoing dramatic change, raising tensions in the wider region—what would the competition mean for Qatar's media environment? The World Cup is, with the Summer Olympics, one of the two biggest global media events, and hosting it will make Qatar a focus of intensive world media coverage. International journalists will want to report not only on the games, but on Qatar itself.

On the one hand, the record of other recent sporting mega-events argues that Qatar's World Cup will have no effect on the environment for independent media in the country. The 2008 Beijing Olympics, for example, changed China's media regime not a bit, despite assurances from Chinese authorities and the International Olympic Committee (IOC) that there would be changes. In a world where Western countries now often decline to host sporting mega-events, the more autocratic ones that are willing to host these tournaments have little incentive to care about the criticisms of outsiders. What realistic expectations does anyone have, for example, that Russia will improve its human rights performance—or liberalize its state-controlled media regime—as a result of hosting the World Cup in 2018?

Yet Qatar is not China or Russia. Much more than other states in the region, it has been relatively open to its critics, including international human rights NGOs (nongovernmental organizations). Qataris themselves feel free to discuss and voice their opinions about public affairs, among themselves if not publicly; 'Western' ideas about human rights and free expression are, if not accepted, acceptable for debate. Qatar's constitution has an explicit free speech provision. Finally—and importantly, given the focus of this paper—Qatar's modernization strategy rests on the four pillars of sport, education, media, and art, which are all fundamentally expressive enterprises.

Of these, none draws international media attention like sport. After completion of the 2018 Russia World Cup, Qatar is beginning to brand and promote the 2022 tournament, and the country will come under renewed pressure from international human rights groups and international news organizations to clarify its rules for media practice. In 2019, Qatar is host to the World Athletics Championships, a major event in the run-up to the 2020 Tokyo Olympics. Accredited news organizations will want to cover these events, but so will non-accredited and un-accredited media wanting to cover the competitions and the country itself. How will Qatar respond? Will international media enjoy greater freedoms than domestic media before and during the games? Will domestic media enjoy greater freedom to report than they do now? If reporting norms or laws do liberalize, what changes will last and what will be temporary?

The author predicts—cautiously, given the volatile mix of Gulf state politics and the business of world football—that Qatar will continue to liberalize its media laws if only because it has to. The existing media law, dating from 1979, is long obsolete; it makes no mention of electronic media of any kind, for example, and gives authority to government ministries that no longer exist. Despite the difficulties of doing independent reporting in Qatar, the overall direction of media freedom in the country is arguably positive at a time when in much of the rest of the world, including in the United States, it is arguably negative. The 2017 RSF Index that rates Qatar so poorly, for example, rates the United States at 43rd (and falling) behind several developing and non-Western countries like Surinam, Samoa, Namibia, Ghana, South Africa, and Burkina Faso.

Significant change in Qatar's media environment will take a generation or more and will proceed along lines that make sense to Qataris. To be fair, 'press freedom' has no universal meaning even among Western democracies. In any comparative discussion of press freedom, the problem is what to measure and how, and most measures are incomplete in the sense that they consider inputs—the structure of the press, how it is regulated, its place in the political system—and not outputs—how citizens actually understand and use the information they receive.[9] At the same time, international norms concerning restrictions on press freedom do exist.[10] At a minimum, media freedom is not possible where there is government or monopolistic control over the instruments of mass communication. Free media systems do not license journalists or imprison them for reporting and publishing content the government finds objectionable. Qatar, like all of the GCC countries, falls short on each of these basic measures.

One indication of the future of Qatar's media environment comes from the author's conversations with newspaper editors in the country.[11] The state of media law in the country is obviously important to journalism practice, but economic factors matter more. Because all domestic news media in Qatar are in some measure state-subsidized, they are, if not profitable businesses, secure ones. Qatar could dramatically liberalize its press laws tomorrow and the print media would have no economic incentive to change how or what they report, never mind to test the boundaries of government tolerance. It is as true in Doha as it is in New York or London that there is good money in bad journalism.

Qatar, the World Cup, and 'Soft Disempowerment'

A Federation Internationale de Football Association (FIFA) World Cup provides a host country 'exceptional opportunities to construct new, authorized, brand identities before their own citizens and global audiences.'[12] The combination of global media coverage and hoped-for legacies are among the defining characteristics of what social scientists call a mega-event,[13] and have been promoted as a form of what political scientist Joseph Nye calls 'soft power,' defined as 'the ability to get what you want through attraction rather than coercion or payments.'[14] For Qatar, sport tourism is one part of a soft power strategy that includes arts, education, and media,[15] but a World Cup is something else. The tournament is rivaled only by the summer Olympic Games as the world's most-watched television program, and Qatar's successful bid has brought the country both new attention and intense criticism.[16] Brannagan and Giulianotti call such negative consequences of hosting a sporting mega-event soft disempowerment, 'the loss of attractiveness or influence' that can result from international scrutiny.[17] The risk of soft disempowerment is that hosts might 'lose more than they can gain in terms of destination image.'[18]

In Qatar's case, soft disempowerment began almost immediately after the country was awarded the World Cup in December 2010. The international sporting press sneered at the country's pretensions to football status despite Qatar's enormous financial investments in European football, which have only increased since 2010.[19] In May 2011, news reports appeared claiming that Qatar had paid more than $1 million to African FIFA officials in return for their votes.[20] In 2015, FIFA announced that the 2022 tournament would be moved to the winter months to avoid Qatar's brutal summer heat, in direct conflict with the European football season.[21] Then, in November 2017, a witness in the criminal trial of three former FIFA officials in a US district court testified that Qatar paid an Argentinian football executive $1 million for his World Cup vote.[22]

Without question, much of the international press coverage of Qatar's football ambitions has been one-sided. Research shows that national media tend to cover sporting mega-events as members of the cultures in which they reside, and the Western press has consistently portrayed Qatar as a football interloper.[23] The British press, in particular, has been relentless in criticizing Qatar's suitability as a World Cup host, in some measure presumably because Britain was a losing bidder for the 2022 tournament.[24] As a later investigation by former US Department of Justice Attorney Michael Garcia showed, Britain was as willing as Qatar to provide inducements to FIFA officials when they demanded them.[25] Indeed, the Garcia report made clear that bribery infected FIFA's negotiations with *all* countries, simply because the process was so non-transparent. If there is a moral cancer in world football, Qatar is not its source. As of this writing, more than forty former FIFA officials have been indicted for fraud and other crimes by the US Department of Justice, two have been convicted in jury trials, and more than twenty others have pleaded guilty.[26]

Nonetheless, the international media portrayal of Qatar began to change after 2010. Previously, the country had been covered mostly favorably in Western media as an enlightened outpost of modernity in the Middle East. After the World Cup announcement, a new depiction of Qatar emerged as a conservative Muslim autocracy, indifferent and even hostile to democracy and the rule of law. Most significantly, Qatar has been vilified by international human rights organizations for its *kafala* labor system, so much so that, in 2015, FIFA commissioned a report by Harvard Professor John Ruggie to assess living and working conditions for Qatar's huge immigrant labor population.[27]

Most Western media portrayals of Qatar, including those by international human rights NGOs, are incomplete representations of a complex place. The award of the World Cup has advanced conversations within Qatar about sensitive subjects such as citizenship and naturalization, freedom of expression, and rule of law more generally. Journalist James Dorsey writes that Qatar has 'worked with human rights and trade union activists in shaping internationally accepted living and working standards for migrant workers who account for a majority of its populations', and 'it has allowed activists to do independent research and launch their hard-hitting critical reports at news conferences in Doha.'[28] At the same time, Qatar has made international news by arresting foreign journalists (from the United Kingdom and Germany) and domestic ones who have attempted to report on World Cup stadium construction.[29]

More widely, write two scholarly critics of FIFA, the Qatar World Cup award 'has had broad and permanent consequences for the international governance of sport.'[30] Where once protests around sporting mega-events were mostly state-based boycotts and domestic demonstrations, protests by transnational networks now focus on the 'international sport nongovernmental organizations (ISNGOs)' that own the rights to and profit from the tournaments, and range across 'an increasingly broad range of issues', such as human rights, poverty, and the environment.[31] Not just the IOC and FIFA, but other ISNGOs, have been accused of offenses against rights of labor, women, gay/lesbian/transgender athletes, children, indigenous peoples, and the poor, to name a few. One legal scholar has described sporting mega-event venues as 'law exclusion zones.'[32] Indeed, for all the criticism directed at Qatar, the problem of human rights in international sport begins with the failures of the ISNGOs that run that world.

Sporting Mega-Events and Human Rights

Governance of international sport resides overwhelmingly in the International Olympic Committee (IOC) and the International Federations (IF). The most important IF is FIFA, the governing body for football, the world's most popular sport. In their charters, both the IOC and FIFA use language that aligns closely with the International Covenant on Civil and Political Rights. The Olympic Charter is more explicit in this regard than FIFA's, noting that 'Olympism is a philosophy of life' that promotes 'respect for universal fundamental ethical principles.'[33] The charter states that 'the practice of sport is a human right' connected to 'the preservation of human dignity,' and that 'any form of discrimination with regard to a country or a person on grounds of race, religion, politics, gender or otherwise is incompatible' with the Olympic movement.[34] In 2014, the IOC entered a formal accord with the United Nations to align its charter values with the Universal Declaration of Human Rights.[35]

Similarly, articles 2, 3, and 4 of the FIFA statutes include language regarding 'humanitarian values,' and FIFA has a commendable history of human rights stands. In 1961, it was the first international sporting body to impose sanctions on South Africa. In 2001, FIFA's 'Buenos Aires Resolution' publicly committed the organization to antidiscrimination and launched its continuing 'Say No to Racism' campaign. FIFA has also made alliances with United Nations bodies, including the International Labor Organization and the UN High Commissioner for Refugees. In 2013, following a series of ugly racial incidents on and off the pitch, FIFA launched an Anti-Racism and Discrimination Taskforce that includes in its membership a representative of the UN Office of the High Commissioner for Human Rights.[36]

Today, the FIFA statutes explicitly prohibit 'discrimination of any kind against a country, private person or group of people on account of ... ethnic, national or social origin, gender, ... language, religion, political opinion' or any other reason.[37] In its mission statement, FIFA states that its core values are authenticity, unity, performance, and integrity. A key component of integrity, the statement says, is transparency.[38] The values are to support FIFA's three pillars: to develop the game, touch the world, and build a better future. The organization's commitment to social and human development, it says, is accomplished 'by strengthening the work of dozens of initiatives around the globe to support local communities in the areas of peacebuilding, health, social integration, education and more.'[39]

In February 2016, in response to the FIFA-commissioned Ruggie report that focused in significant part on Qatar's human rights record, FIFA added an additional article on human rights to its statutes.[40] Ruggie recommended that FIFA embed the United Nations Guiding Principles on Business and Human Rights into its own policies and practices, and that 'FIFA include human rights within its criteria for evaluating bids to host tournaments and should make them a substantive factor in host selection.'[41] The problem with this commitment is that sporting mega-events are increasingly located in illiberal or even authoritarian countries, in part because more democratic countries, and more developed ones, increasingly do not want them.[42] Where voters are given a chance to weigh in on a bid, they often reject it.[43] The result, in some cases, is that the only bidders left are illiberal states. For example, Beijing and Almaty were the only bids for the 2022 Winter Olympic Games after Munich, Oslo, Stockholm, and Krakow were forced out by voters. Beijing won, thus becoming the first city to host both a summer and winter Olympics.[44]

The appeal of sporting mega-events to illiberal states is presumably the international recognition and status that comes from hosting them. Economic reasons may also play a role, but there is wide agreement among economists that as a tool for economic growth, sporting mega-events are poor investments. With a few exceptions, they cost far more than they return; worse, they are often beset by charges of financial corruption and fraud.[45] But as vehicles for national promotion on an international stage, politicians understandably see the Olympics and the World Cup as singular opportunities, and, in that respect, their value is arguable but incalculable.[46] Among recent or scheduled sporting mega-events in illiberal countries are the 2014 Winter Olympics in Sochi, Russia; the 2015 European Games (athletics) in Baku, Azerbaijan; the 2015 International Association of Athletics Federations (IAAF) World Championships and the 2022 Winter Olympics, both in Beijing; the 2018 FIFA World Cup in Russia; and the 2019 IAAF World Championships and the 2022 FIFA World Cup, both in Qatar. What critics find alarming about these venue decisions is the signal they convey about the place of human rights in international sport,[47] especially when they come from the IOC and FIFA, which are singular among ISNGOs for their riches, their aspirational charters, their political power, and their global influence.[48]

Many critics, both in the academy and in sports media, go further to argue that the IOC and FIFA are themselves illiberal bodies.[49] Their leaders have on occasion made public statements that seem to confirm those criticisms. In 2013, famously, FIFA Secretary General Jerome Valke mused in front of a room full of reporters that 'less democracy is sometimes better for organizing a World Cup ... When you have a very strong head of state who can decide, as maybe Putin can do in 2018 ... that is easier for us organizers than a country such as Germany ... where you have to negotiate at different levels.'[50]

FIFA's public image has been especially battered. Arguably, the low moment came in May 2015, when agents from the US Federal Bureau of Investigation and the Swiss police rounded up fourteen FIFA-related figures in Zurich on US indictments for racketeering, fraud, and money laundering, alleging crimes dating to 1991.[51] Those indictments came almost five years after the December 2010 decision, taken in a single FIFA Congress, to award the 2018 and 2022 World Cups to Russia and Qatar, respectively. Shortly after that announcement, amidst allegations of bribery, FIFA expelled two executive committee members, one of them Mohamed bin Hammam, a Qatari and president of the Asian Football Confederation. Finally, new and broader accusations of corruption within FIFA emerged in 2016 with revelations from the Panama Papers, a leaked cache of more than 11 million documents from the law firm Mossack Fonseca.[52]

Sporting Mega-Events and Expressive Rights

In the growing international criticism of the IOC and FIFA, relatively little has focused on offenses against expressive rights, including those of journalists, by ISNGOs, host cities, and countries.[53] Especially because sporting mega-events are *by definition* media events, this seems odd, but there is economic logic to it: the organizers of sporting mega-events and the accredited media that cover them share a financial interest in the games' success. As a media product, sport is, above all, valuable commercial property, sporting mega-events especially so. In an otherwise fragmented media universe, sport, along with film, is the only content that still aggregates large audiences; unlike film, sport is almost always consumed live—and with younger audiences watching on multiple, simultaneous platforms—so it is uniquely valuable to sponsors and advertisers.

But the media world that made the IOC and FIFA rich and powerful has changed. Digital media have completely scrambled long-standing relationships between media firms, sports firms, athletes, and fans. The most significant change is that virtually all sports firms—from ISNGOs themselves to sports leagues and individual clubs—are now also media firms.[54] All have their own channels to which they wish to drive audiences, and so as a condition of access they will often impose on news organizations restrictions on the real-time posting of scores, photos, and videos.

Social media are especially disruptive. For sports firms, the challenge has been how to wade into this milieu without damaging existing relationships with more traditional media. Even as they attempt to control access to their valuable property and the exclusive rights of sponsors, broadcasters, and other licensees, they are awash in competition from fans, athletes, and bloggers who—in addition to posting their own stories, photos, and videos of competitions—will also appropriate and distribute licensed content on social media platforms like Facebook, YouTube, and Twitter. In that sharing environment, sports firms and their rights-holders have less control than ever over the narratives that surround their events, their products, and their brands.[55]

The difficulty that sports firms have in this media environment is trying to separate their legitimate concerns about the commercial value of their intellectual property from the legitimate purposes of journalism and social protest. Bylaw 48 of the IOC Charter, for example, states the IOC's commitment to media coverage that will 'promote the principles and values of Olympism'—a commitment that also binds the host city. It then goes on to forbid 'any athlete, coach, official', or other participant to 'act as a journalists, or reporters or in any other media capacity.'[56] Article 50 of the charter further prohibits anyone who enters an Olympic venue from doing, saying, or wearing anything that can be construed as advertising or publicity, or any 'kind of demonstration or political, religious or racial propaganda.'[57] From a commercial point of view, restrictions like these are understandable, but the problems with the language are nonetheless obvious for an organization that celebrates human rights, including expressive rights. They are also unrealistic: athletes at the Olympics and virtually all sporting events now routinely record their experiences there and post that material to their social media sites. Fans do the same.

In 2008, the IOC attempted to reconcile with this reality by issuing its first guidelines for 'social and digital media', in which it wishfully asserted that social media posts are a 'legitimate form of personal expression and not a form of journalism.'[58] In 2012, and again in 2016, the IOC guidelines noted that any participant or accredited person can post in a 'personal' blog or tweet in the 'first-person', which does not constitute journalism;[59] apparently, a posting becomes 'journalism' when it is posted in the third-person.[60] This is not how journalism works. A first-person posting by an athlete, even a personal one, is newsworthy precisely because of its unique point of view. And what about a third-person post by an athlete that is not about the sport event itself, but something tangential to it? And what about fundamental rights of conscience? What does the IOC charter mean for an athlete who wishes to use the world's focus on a mega-event to express personal views on a controversial subject?[61]

Presumably, the primary concern for sports rights-holders in the digital media ecosystem is not critical reporting, but the republishing and repurposing of their exclusive content on mobile platforms; the loss of value in that content from the posting of user-generated content; the loss of exclusive value to sponsors and damage to their brands; and outright ambush marketing.[62] A sports firm, like any other, is required to protect its intellectual property, an endeavor that can appear as (and sometimes is) bullying. Nor is the

IOC alone in trying to navigate the user-driven media environment. Popular sports from cricket to rugby have struggled to protect the financial value of their games, while also meeting the expectations of fans and sport journalists in digital space.[63]

For sporting mega-events like the Olympics or World Cup, however, the problem with restrictive media policies is that they undermine the larger message the sponsoring organizations say they want to convey, that sporting mega-events are not just sports events but social movements. If they are, citizens everywhere will want to cover and comment on them freely. That coverage will focus not just on the sport body, such as FIFA, but also on the hundreds of subcontractors in its supply chains. FIFA's 2015 Ruggie report on Qatar and Russia will further ensure that sporting mega-events will become a focus of human rights reporting. The report begins by questioning the human rights bona fides of both countries, and notes that all World Cup host governments have the 'primary obligation to respect, protect and fulfill human rights.'[64]

If so, it follows that the games and their hosts will increasingly also become the focus of media freedom advocates. Qatar 2022 will be a test for what is possible. The Russians may not care what the world thinks about them, but, for reasons of national pride, regional security, and international standing, the Qataris do.[65] Before and during the 2022 Cup, international media will want access to venues throughout the country, and to public officials, and will want to report freely. Importantly, non-sporting and unaccredited media will cover the 2022 World Cup precisely as Qatar has proposed them—as a measure of its standing in the world. How Qatar deals with these different media, how and whether it seeks to control the narratives that develop before and during the games, will be a test of its still unfolding ideas about press freedom and practice.

Qatar's Media Law and Practice, and the Consequences of Sport Diplomacy

By several objective measures, Qatar's media environment is progressive. It has one of the highest rates of internet use in the world—96 percent of households are connected—and one of the highest mobile phone penetration rates, at 80 percent.[66] The country is also home to a world-class journalism school, Northwestern University in Qatar, and to a growing journalism program at Qatar University. The Josoor Institute, a program of the government's Supreme Committee for Legacy and Delivery, offers seminars intended to inform and encourage professional reporting, including reporting related to the World Cup.[67] Doha is home as well to the Doha Center for Media Freedom, established in 2008 under the auspices of the Qatar Foundation to promote press freedom in the region. Article 47 of Qatar's 1971 Constitution guarantees freedom of expression and opinion,[68] and Qatar is pledged to respect the right to free expression under article 32 of the Arab Charter on Human Rights, to which it is a party. In addition, it is home to Al Jazeera, a major international news organization that, significantly, does virtually no domestic news coverage.

Indeed, it is in the domestic news environment where Qatar comes in for criticism. Two international media freedom indices, Freedom House and Reporters Sans Frontières, both rate Qatar as not free; in 2016, Qatar fell from ranking 104 to 117 out of 180 countries in the RSF index, then fell to ranking 123 in 2017.[69] In 2009, the director of the Doha Center for Media Freedom was critical of the government for not issuing visas to foreign journalists threatened in their own countries.[70] Later that year, he resigned after being held responsible for a visit by Danish newspaper editor Flemming Rose, who, in 2005, created controversy by publishing cartoons depicting the Prophet Muhammad in the *Jyllands-Posten* newspaper. Rose came to Doha as part of a UNESCO-sponsored conference at the center, but the event angered many Qataris in and out of government. In response, the country's Advisory Council passed a new media law in 2009 that provided criminal penalties for journalists who slander the emir, the religion, or the constitution of Qatar. That law was never implemented.[71] The Doha Centre for Media Freedom took on a new director, who was dismissed in 2013 after the organization published an overview of media laws within the GCC countries—a report that described all of them in essentially the same terms as Freedom House and RSF did.[72]

Though Article 47 of the Qatar constitution provides for freedom of expression, the critical qualifying phrase in the provision, as with media laws everywhere, says 'in accordance ... with law,' and Qatar has multiple restrictions in its media law, penal code, and cybercrime law that weigh heavily on speech and press freedoms. For print publications in Qatar, the law requires a license to operate. The license requires publishers to pay guarantees against any future fines,[73] and all licensees must be Qatari nationals.[74] Foreign journalists working in the country must be accredited by the Qatar Foreign Information Agency, sponsored by a local institution (like Al Jazeera) or by the Ministry of Culture, Arts and Heritage;[75] the great majority of journalists working in Qatar's media, including at Al Jazeera, are in fact non-Qataris.

The government can require corrections for news stories it finds false or misleading if they offend the 'public interest,' and a publication can be suspended for a maximum of three months if it publishes items contrary to the public interest.[76] Article 47 of the 1979 media law allows for prior restraints; publication of material that criticizes the emir or attributes statements to him without official permission are subject to criminal penalty under both the media law (Article 46) and the penal code. Finally, Article 47 includes a list of banned subjects that cannot be part of any publication: anything that incites or advocates the overthrow of the governing regime or offends it, or causes any damage to the 'supreme interests of the country'; anything that might harm the reputation of a person, his/her legacy, or commercial interests; anything that would give 'offense to public morals.' Violations include both fines and possible imprisonment.

Qatar has, for almost a decade, promised a new press law but none has been enacted. A draft revision was proposed in 2010, revised and proposed again in 2012, and has yet to come into effect.[77] The draft media law includes some significant reforms: it proposes to eliminate criminal libel and to prohibit officials from questioning journalists without a court order.[78] Though it abolishes criminal charges for criticizing the country's rulers, it still prohibits the publication of information that would 'throw relations between the state and the Arab and friendly states into confusion'—a clause that has been unofficially but effectively suspended with the beginning of the Saudi-led blockade—or that 'abuse the regime or offend the ruling family or cause serious harm to the national or higher interests of the state.'[79]

Criminal laws are suspect in any media system, and Qatar's penal code has several provisions affecting journalism. Article 34 criminalizes criticism of the emir. Articles 326 and 327 establish criminal penalties for defamation, with added penalties for defaming a 'public employee.' Article 331 provides criminal penalties for privacy violations, specifically, 'spreading news, photos or comments related to secrets of private life, or families, or individuals even if they were true.' Article 256 criminalizes blasphemy.[80] Finally, Qatar's 2014 Cybercrime law includes *additional* criminal penalties, both fines and jail time, for defamation made in public or private communications.[81]

Against all this, the only certain thing that can be said of Qatar's media environment is that its limitations are likely to become an issue when the world's media renew their focus on the country after the conclusion of the 2018 World Cup in Russia. Media coverage of a sporting mega-event has predictable phases and emphases. It begins with the award of the games (Qatar was awarded the FIFA 2022 World Cup in December 2010) and, as Qatar has learned, follows immediately with stories about the moral worthiness of the host.[82] News coverage then follows the years of preparation for the tournament, including the development of physical and administrative infrastructure, and gets most intense in the immediate few months before the competition begins. If the host can get over these hurdles, the rest is usually easier—the competitions themselves are covered overwhelmingly as entertainment by the accredited media that have a financial stake in their success, and few international news organizations stick around to see how the legacies work out.[83]

The media coverage of the long run-up to the tournaments is high-stakes business. It is the one thing a host country or city cannot control, and as the concept of 'soft disempowerment' suggests, it can be damaging, even fatal, to the host's goal of shining on the international stage. When China won the bid to host the 2008 Summer Olympics, for example, it did so after two previous unsuccessful attempts, and only twenty-four years after returning to the summer games as a participant in 1984.[84] For the Chinese, however, what was supposed to be an occasion for national triumph became one of international humiliation. In the months before the games began, human rights organizations focused on Tibet and other issues and branded the Beijing games as the 'Genocide Olympics' for China's support of the Sudanese government in Darfur—a theme widely reported in the international press. The torch relay was beset by protests, some of them violent, from the moment the flame left Athens. The protests provoked outraged reactions from the Chinese public.

What a host country can more easily control, of course, is news coverage *at* the event, *during* the games, when it can limit access to places and information.[85] In its bid for the 2008 games, for example, the Chinese government had agreed that all attendees at the games, including all journalists, would have unfettered access throughout the country and could report on anything they wanted.[86] Once the games began, however, Chinese authorities denied international journalists access to several internet sites such as Amnesty International, Radio Free Asia, and the BBC Chinese-language sites, or sites about Tiananmen Square, Tibet, and Taiwan.[87] Internet speeds were slowed down and virtual private network (VPN) applications were interrupted.[88] Reporters covering the Beijing Games had been assured they would have unlimited internet access, but an IOC official at the games told them otherwise: 'the regulatory changes we negotiated, ... and which required Chinese legislative changes were to do with reporting on the games. This didn't necessarily extend to free access and reporting on everything that relates to China.'[89] Then IOC President Jacques Rogge had promised repeatedly that foreign journalists would have full internet access, and indeed the IOC had awarded the games to Beijing on the expectation that it would make China more open. Only two weeks before the 2008 games began, Rogge had said, 'for the first time, foreign media will be able to report freely and publish their work freely in China. There will be no censorship on the Internet.'[90]

At the 2014 Winter Olympics in Sochi, domestic news organizations complained to the IOC of official censorship before and during the games. International reporters in Sochi told of police harassment and intimidation.[91] The environment for press freedom in Russia has deteriorated steadily since 2010, the year of its successful World Cup bid. Under Vladimir Putin, the country has recriminalized libel, introduced new restrictions on online media, banned 'gay propaganda', and cracked down on civil society groups through its foreign agent law. In its 2017 Index, RSF ranks Russia at 148, which is 25 positions *below* Qatar.

It is tempting to argue that if Qatar intended to liberalize its media environment, it would have done so by now. But international pressure related to the World Cup has thus far focused elsewhere—on Qatar's *kafala* labor system—and that is where the country's leadership has directed its attention. Moreover, Qatar has a reputation for acting with confounding independence, and often to the annoyance of its GCC partners. For example, not long after the blockade crisis began in June 2017, Qatar surprised everyone—and probably especially its GCC adversaries—by proposing changes to its residency laws that would give significant new rights to some expatriates who comprise almost 75 percent of the population.[92] Not long after, the emir issued a new law to protect the rights of domestic workers such as drivers, maids, and nannies.[93] Importantly, announcements such as these come with virtually no follow-up news reporting about a policy's implementation and practical effects, and Qatar has a history of announcing liberalization measures that come to nothing.[94] But the heart of the World Cup controversy has always been a demographic one, about the status and rights of migrants, and the blockade crisis has given Qatar an opportunity to experiment with social change. The proposed law and the enacted one are reminders that soft power, in addition to having an international audience, also has a *domestic* one, including powerful actors who have different ideologies and ambitions than the ruling branch of the royal family. In that environment, a political crisis—or a World Cup—can provide cover for social change.

Thus, while there is no way to know how Qatar's media environment may change in response to the media scrutiny surrounding the World Cup, if the

Cup comes then scrutiny *will* come. The world will watch and comment, and obviously so will Qataris, whose views about expressive freedom and official censorship are varied but also demonstrably changing, particularly among the young and college educated.[95] An anecdote makes the point. In June 2017, only a few days after the Saudi-led blockade began, a Northwestern alumnus wrote a letter to the student paper at the home campus in Evanston, Illinois, that was highly critical of Qatar and asked if it was time for the university 'to quit' the country, or whether 'Doha's dollars outweigh Evanston's ethics.'[96] He asked, rhetorically, how an American journalism school can be in a country without a free press. Several students at the Qatar campus wrote to take issue with the letter's author. A common theme in all the responses, as one student put it, was that 'American' journalism standards would not work in Qatar, but rather Qataris will create their own, which in time will break more boundaries and develop their own understanding of what it is to practice journalism and communication in Qatar.

When asked, my Qatari students are apt to be realistic rather than idealistic when they assess the future of media freedom in their country. Many believe it prudent to keep the law's licensing requirement for publications, even if they think licenses should be easier to get and harder to lose. Many are willing to retain criminal penalties for some speech offenses. Some of their ideas about liberalizing speech restrictions—to protect all religions against disparagement, for example, not just the monotheistic ones—can be puzzling to an outsider, but also understandable. For my students, cultural traditions are important, Qatari national identity is a work in progress, and regional politics cannot be ignored. Qataris will liberalize their media environment on their own terms.

But the pressure to change will be real. Qatar has immersed itself in an extraordinary confluence of factors: the right to host one of the world's biggest sporting and media events, intense scrutiny of the human rights performance of ISNGOs, and its own aspirations to be recognized as a modern and influential state.

7

TURKISH SPORTS

LOST IN POLITICS?

Cem Tınaz

Introduction

Despite being well established and continuously updated, sports policy has been a crucial matter for the Turkish Republic since the 1930s; to this day, the search for an appropriate long-term sports policy continues. The current government, run by the Justice and Development Party (AKP), has implemented a variety of sports-related policies since it began its tenure in 2002. Most of the AKP's initiatives have been related to elite sport. Policies include bidding for the Olympic Games; hosting over forty high-profile international sporting events between 2010 and 2017; offering monetary awards for professional athletic achievements; naturalization of foreign athletes; and the construction of football stadiums and other sports facilities. Motives behind the policies range from gaining international prestige for Turkey to promoting internationally successful elite athletes and increasing sports participation among different age groups. However, the statistics regarding sports participation reveal that attempts to stimulate grassroots development in order to increase sports participation have been largely insufficient and inconsistent.

In 2017, the Turkish Ministry of Sport spent approximately $155 million on the construction of new sport facilities, but their effectiveness and accessibility to the community is questionable since they were constructed primarily to accommodate elite athletes. The main sources of sports participation for ordinary Turkish people are nonprofit sports clubs, most of which are suffering financially. The so-called 'decentralized' sport federations are actually state-dependent, as most of their funding comes from the government. Turkish football, which is often the first sport that comes to the Turkish community's mind, has been able to solidify its firm standing in the larger European football industry as the sixth-largest market in terms of total revenue earned through recent business agreements. On the other hand, decreasing numbers of spectators, the burden of financial debt on professional teams, and a highly politicized management structure create a questionable future for the sport. Despite this, football remains the most popular sport in Turkey, meaning the central government continues to subsidize the sport. Additionally, local municipalities have become important institutions when it comes to offering various sports services to their communities.

Due to the growing social significance of sport and their potential to provide an outlet for implementation of the state's welfare ideology, sport and leisure became a legitimate area of public policy in developed countries in the 1960s and early to mid-1970s.[1] There is vast evidence in the literature that sport as a policy concern has gained greater salience as a government priority worldwide.[2] As a social product, sport is easily integrated into government projects. Penelope Kissoudi points out that there are some states in which sport is fully integrated into the political system; while in others, sport is organized by non-political bodies.[3] International sport, especially Olympic sport, is deeply integrated into most domestic political systems. There are often debates within governments regarding elite sport funding, building facilities, applications for hosting events, and the achievements or failures of elite athletes at the Olympic Games.

States promote sport to increase participation, and manage sport with the goal of establishing a regulation mechanism for sporting bodies and/or producing top athletes.[4] Additionally, governments fund the organization of world-class sporting events and cover the costs of sports facilities. The United Kingdom, Australia, and Canada have increased the levels of resources for sport, leading to improved performance by their elite athletes over the past decade.[5] Many countries are increasing funding for recruitment programs to scout talented youth and develop them into athletes. In addition to these countries, another group of emerging countries is increasingly interested in hosting international sport events. Examples include the 2008 Summer Olympic Games and the 2022 Winter Olympic Games in China; the 2010 FIFA World Cup in South Africa; the 2014 FIFA World Cup and the 2016 Summer Olympic Games in Brazil; and the 2022 FIFA World Cup in Qatar. As Danyel Reiche has indicated, emerging countries are aiming to gain international prestige, achieve national unity, and improve their countries' infrastructure through sports.[6] Despite the long-standing cliché that 'sports and politics should not mix',[7] the reality today is that politics and sport coexist to a considerable degree.

This chapter provides an overview of Turkey's sports policy during the years 2002–2018. I focus on this period because the country has been under the rule of the AKP party throughout, and the AKP's political ideologies have been consistent over the past two decades. The AKP has held power for longer than any party before it, going back to the 1950s when Turkey became a full democracy. The chapter will identify pathways for the state to achieve success in elite sports and to increase sports participation; it discusses the state's reasons for hosting international sport events; and, finally, it examines problems and deficiencies in national sport. In order to understand the current mismanagement in Turkish sports, I also discuss the state's motives for hosting international sport events. A substantial amount of money has been allocated to these events, which could be used for different areas of sports development.

For this research, I conducted nineteen semi-structured, in-depth, face-to-face interviews between 2012 and 2018 with former Turkish sports ministers and other sports authorities, including the CEO of Istanbul's 2020 Summer Olympics bid, the President of the Turkish National Olympic Committee, and the secretary general of the Turkish Tennis Federation. I transcribed interviews, analyzed data, and examined and summarized the results of this study. I conducted all interviews in Turkish, and the transcribed summaries were later translated into English. In addition, I reviewed academic literature, government files, news stories, and other reports for an evaluation of sports policy created by the Turkish government.

Government Policies through the Years

Since the establishment of the Turkish Republic, the government has utilized sports to display a positive image of Turkey as a developed country. The term 'sports' first appeared in the official government programs of Turkey in 1937. In 1938, through law no. 3530, the 'Law for Education of the Body', sports funding was given a legal basis and was implemented through government programs, budgets, decrees, and plans. This could be considered the Turkish government's first attempt at official policy formulation. During the 1940s and 1950s, the government focused primarily on three areas: opening advanced physical education institutes, training instructors in all kinds of sporting activities in schools and clubs, and initiating the establishment of sports fields. In 1961, for the first time, a sports minister was appointed to the cabinet, in which he served until 1965.[8] Prior to this period, sport had been considered a leisure activity, and the state was only responsible for maintaining material-technical conditions. However, after this period, it was also decided that efficient organizational attempts in the field of physical education should be accelerated; hence, sports fields and facilities accessible to youth in all provinces and districts of the country would be established.

In the early 1960s, the government began to prepare five-year development plans. By definition, these plans were prepared by the State Planning Organization; their purpose was both to guide the private sector and to order the public sector to aim for the economic and social objectives that in turn formed part of the development objectives set for all or specific regions of the country.[9] Sports became a feature of the second five-year plan in 1968. This plan involved a comprehensive analysis of the relations between the state and sports organizations as well as the conditions and problems of sports clubs and facilities.[10] In the third development plan, the government declared that it intended to build sporting facilities and stands for any entity that desired to participate in sports. Another intention was to provide funding for amateur sports, including track and field, wrestling, and gymnastics.[11] In the fourth development plan, the focus was on improving sport for all ages and building sports facilities to accommodate large numbers of spectators.[12] In 1982, the newly promulgated Constitution was the first to include a specific reference to sports; thus, sports were now protected under the Constitution. Articles 58 and 59 of the Constitution declared that 'the state shall take measures to promote the physical and mental health of Turkish citizens of all ages, encourage the spread of sports among the masses, and protect successful athletes.'[13] During the 1980s and 1990s, sports policy remained focused on increasing participation, building sports facilities, achieving success in elite sports, educating human resources for the sporting sector, and restructuring sports environments where necessary. However, the unstable political environment in Turkey in the period 1980–2000 left most of these sport-related goals unachieved.

In 2002, the Justice and Development Party (AKP) won the general election. After coming to power, the government made sports one of its investment priorities. Prior to that, the Turkish Republic faced considerable economic instability, which saw the Gross National Product fall to $148 billion in 2001 from $201.4 billion in 2000.[14] Despite considering sports an important part of the economy, the government found it difficult to invest in Turkish sports due to economic hardship. In the 1990s, Turkey became a candidate to host the Summer Olympic Games for the first time, and the AKP has continued to work on this desire to host the event. Though Turkey has not won its bids to host the Games, it has still hosted many top-tier sporting events in the country since 2000. Additionally, Turkey has offered various financial awards for its elite athletes and has built many sports facilities, demonstrating significant policy change.

Sports Structure and Commendable Actions in Turkish Sports

In recent decades, Turkey has made progress, albeit slow, in terms of sports development. Despite this progress, interviewees were aware that Turkey still lacked a well-established sporting culture in Turkey. Many projects have been created with the goal of fostering a richer, more vibrant sporting culture in Turkish communities, especially for the younger generation. In order to understand how the management system works in Turkish sports, it is useful to first examine the sporting structure.

Within the Turkish sporting framework, the following all play active roles: the Ministry of Youth and Sports, the Ministry of National Education, the General Directorate of Sports, the Directorate of Spor Toto, local administrations, the Turkish National Olympic Committee, the Turkish National Paralympic Committee, independent sports federations, sports clubs, and universities. These organizations are responsible for managing and executing sports services and activities. As Çolakoğlu and Erturan have concluded about Turkish sporting history,[15] there seems to have been constant change in terms of structure and authority over the years. Despite this constant change over the years, the government has maintained its role as the centralized directing organism of Turkish sports. From the introduction of a formal sports policy, to the recognition of sports as a national priority, to the encouragement of professionalism in sports, a total of eight structural changes in the sports governing organizations are evidence of the centralized power of the government in this regard.[16]

Figure 1 presents an organizational map for a better understanding of the current structure. The main aim of the mapping process is to recognize and identify all organizations within the sporting sector and their relationships with each other. The solid lines between the stakeholders represent direct relationships, while the dotted lines represent indirect relationships. As the map shows, there is a variety of organizations within the sporting sector in Turkey. The provision of sports services is the responsibility of some of these different organizations. In addition to the organizations listed on the map, there are sports marketing and management agencies that are for-profit and that provide supportive marketing, management, and communication services for individuals, clubs, and/or federations. As seen on the map, the sporting environment in Turkey is highly saturated. Governmental organizations like the Ministry of Sports and the General Directorate of Sports have a central role; the state regulates the system, identifies sports-related policies, provides funding for sports federations, builds most of the sporting facilities, and funds the international sport events hosted in Turkey. Thus, the sport

Figure 1: Mapping the Turkish Sporting Structure

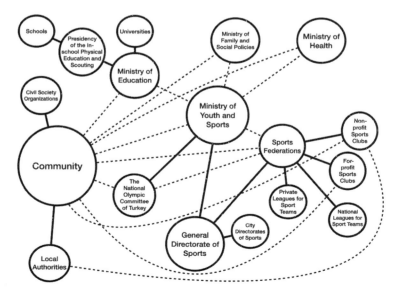

sector in Turkey is mostly state dependent. Since this map identifies the important relationships between organizations in the Turkish sporting sector, it will also be helpful to understand the ideology behind the country's sports policies and decisions.

Priorities in Turkish Sports Policy (2002–2013)

The AKP's first sports-related political action was to pass a law in 2004 for the decentralization (authorization) of sports federations, with the aim of decreasing political intervention in federations, instead giving full authorization to the federations to manage sports in the country. According to this law, general assemblies elect the autonomous federations of their bodies; they also approve budgets for the autonomous federations, and they hand responsibility to these federations for a range of decision-making within their own bodies.[17] Interestingly, all transactions and activities of autonomous federations are subject to the supervision of the Ministry, to which the General Directorate is affiliated. This law could have allowed federations to participate more in decision-making and to secure their own financial resources.[18] However, over the last few years, only a handful of federations have been able to generate their own income. The failure of the other federations could be a result of limited sports participation, limited media and sponsorship interest, and low numbers of spectators. These federations have remained dependent on government subsidies and therefore have been unable to become fully autonomous in terms of management.

Former Sports Minister Mehmet Ali Şahin explained the government's second subsequent step as follows: 'as an extension to the policy for sport funding, the law on sponsorship was adopted in 2004. As a result of this law, Turkey was able to increase sponsorship investments and that has provided additional funding to sports.'[19] According to this new law, companies that sponsor Turkish sports can deduct their expenses from their tax payments. With the introduction of this law, the future scope of youth and sports activities increased due to increased investment from sponsors, which happened after the re-regulation of taxes for the sponsoring companies.

The third important step, taken when Mehmet Ali Şahin was minister (2002–2007), was the establishment of Iddaa, a sports betting company regulated by the government as part of the National Lottery Administrations (Spor Toto), which is a public institution affiliated with the Ministry of Youth and Sports, but also a separate legal entity, as stated in Article 1 of Law no. 7258.[20] Iddaa acts as a monopoly since private sports betting companies are not allowed to operate in Turkey. Since its introduction, wide acceptance and high interest from the public has made Iddaa one of the most important financial resources for Turkish professional sport. Between 2004 and 2009 Iddaa generated more than $4 billion in revenue and delivered over $350 million to football clubs.[21] After its attempts to place sports funding on a sure financial basis, the government focused on developing its own bureaucratic system for sports management. In 2011, at the end of former Sport Minister Faruk Özak's term (2009–2011), the ministerial approach changed from being state-minded to sport-minded. Özak has stated that 'operations are now less bureaucratic, and this change was highly necessary. Additionally, sports clubs are subject to the "law of associations." We should also change this structure. If that is achieved, clubs will be able to find new revenue sources and/or manage themselves more efficiently.'[22]

During Özak's ministry, a law for the prevention of violence and match-fixing in sports (Law no. 6222) was also adopted.[23] The purpose of this law is to prevent irregularities at sporting venues and in their surroundings before, during, and after competition; wherever fans are permanently or temporarily resident or present; and on their departure and arrival routes to games.[24] Under the law, various types of security and protective measures have been issued. Measures include effective arrangements for the removal of individuals involved in violent behavior from sporting venues and introduction of a new electronic ticketing system. Along with issuing tickets, the aim of the e-ticket system is the detection, removal, and control of individuals engaging in violent behavior. Another aim is prevention of ticket sales on the black market, which arguably has still not been achieved. This law has a particular focus on football since over 90 percent of violent behavior in sport occurs in football stadiums.[25] Despite creating a new control system, this law has faced severe backlash. Because football games were widely used as forums in which to protest against the government, this law has resulted in a decline in the number of spectators at football games, since many fans have refused to be recorded, controlled, and potentially blacklisted by the government.

In Turkey until the late 1990s, the main sources of elite sport development were through sports clubs. However, compared to other European countries, such as France, Germany, and Spain, Turkey's total number of sport clubs was extremely low.[26] For example, Turkey had 14,009 sports clubs, while France had 164,137, Spain had 94,511, and Germany had 91,000. In order to improve the number of clubs and their level of competitiveness, after the AKP party took power, elite sports development became the state's financial responsibility; yet, many sports clubs still faced financial difficulties.[27] Since 2004, non-profit sport clubs in Turkey have been managed according to the 'law of associations' (Law no. 5253),[28] which was passed to cover regulations for all nonprofit associations in general, with nonprofit sports clubs included. The law has obvious disadvantages, however. For one, it is highly bureaucratic: managers or presidents are not nearly as independent in their financial and managerial decisions as they would be in private companies. Arguably, amending this law could have seen clubs become more efficient in finding new revenue sources and/or management strategies.

In 2013, the Turkish government released the 'National Youth and Sport Policy Paper', which examined the government's current sport and youth-related policies and strategies. According to the paper, the main aims of sports policies were:

- To encourage people of all ages to participate in sporting activities, ensuring that healthy generations are raised;
- To enable sports facilities for amateur sports;
- To introduce a new education system with support of the Ministry of Education to ensure that physical education and sports lessons are part of the curriculum;
- To identify and educate young talented children and train and support them to become successful elite athletes on the international scene;
- To establish analysis centers as part of the fight against doping, and to inform athletes about the harmful effects of drug usage;
- To take necessary precautions to prevent violence and unethical behavior in sports;
- To develop projects for the participation of disabled citizens in sport, to make sports facilities suitable for the use of disabled people, and to support disabled sportspeople and their families;
- To organize Olympic Games, Paralympic Games, and other prestigious international sporting events in Turkey.[29]

According to this paper, the government believed that early talent identification was crucial for achieving success in elite sports, and claimed that it was very important for children and young people with high levels of sporting talent to be identified. For this reason, it was necessary to carry out comprehensive and consistent scientific studies on young people old enough to take up a sport in order to identify, and to educate, those who were determined to reach the highest levels of performance. Although children begin sports at different ages, depending on the sport, the government insisted that exposing children to sports earlier on would be essential if they were to acquire basic sporting skills at a young age, as well as to prepare them for a career at the elite level. For the development of elite sports, the following strategies were considered:

1. Increasing the quality of experts and qualified technical staff;
2. Offering awards for achievements and the development of incentive programs;
3. Fostering and developing elite athletes;
4. Performing a general sport talent scout across the country and preparing a map of sporting potential.

The government aimed to provide professionals such as coaches, nutritionists, conditioners, masseurs, sports physicians, and sports psychologists, so that elite athletes could achieve success in international competitions through working with experts. In addition, providing financial aid, equipment, and facilities for athletes during training was also considered important.

In Turkey, rewards for high-performance athletes participating in both national and international sporting tournaments were first introduced in 1986 with the Law on the Organization and Duties of the General Directorate of Sports (Law no. 3289). Despite there being no stipulation regarding the amount or type of rewards, authorities emphasized the necessity of giving both nonfinancial and financial aid. Based on this law, in the year 2000, the government issued regulations for the value of rewards and announced them to the public.[30] In accordance with this regulation, medalists in the Olympic Games, World Championships, and European Championships received gold coins as prizes. An Olympic gold medalist could receive a reward of 750 gold coins, equivalent to a six-figure cash prize in Euros. However, after scrutinizing the prize proceedings in 2013, I found that athletes who received cash prizes due to their successes in the championships were not as successful in subsequent competitions, suggesting that athletes lost motivation to maintain their high performance in subsequent competitions.

To support this argument, I analyzed Turkey's performance in the Olympic Games between 2002 and 2012; only two Turkish athletes won more than one medal at the Olympic Games in that period. Besides this, doping incidents made officials reexamine the effect of such rewards and prizes. The law also declared that prizes awarded to athletes would be taken back by the authorities if athletes were later found to have used drugs. Nevertheless, fur-

Table 1: Number of gold coins awarded to medalists

	Gold*		Silver		Bronze	
	Before 2013	After 2013	Before 2013	After 2013	Before 2013	After 2013
Olympic	2000 (470,000 €)	1000 (235,000 €)	1500 (352,500 €)	600 (141,000 €)	1000 (235,000 €)	300 (70,500 €)
World Championships	1000 (235,000 €)	500 (117,500 €)	750 (176,250 €)	300 (70,500 €)	500 (117,500 €)	150 (35,250 €)
European Championships	500 (117,500 €)	300 (70,500 €)	350 (35,250 €)	150 (35,250 €)	200 (47,000 €)	75 (17,625 €)

* One gold coin equals €235 as of 2 December 2016.

ther increases in the numbers of doping incidents in Turkish elite sports forced the authorities to redesign the reward system in 2013 (under the same law), resulting in the Ministry of Youth and Sports announcing two major changes. Firstly, the coins were given to the medalist in installments over time, rather than as a lump sum. In addition, the coins were doubled for athletes winning the medal for a second time.[31] Secondly, the amount of the reward was halved, such that the prize for a gold medal changed from 2,000 gold coins to 1,000 gold coins for the Olympic Games. The changes in the amount of gold coins are depicted in Table 1.

The rewards offered by the government were not sufficient in Turkey, considering the effort and time put into training by the athletes. In an interview, athletics manager Önder Özbilen explicitly noted that elite athletes, despite representing Turkey at the Olympic level, were having financial difficulties due to the government's negligence.[32] Additionally, the system did not provide any meaningful incentive for trainers and clubs. For many athletes, it was almost impossible to continue their professional sporting career without getting financial support from their clubs, especially in sports like athletics, judo, fencing, and rowing. However, in some sports, like football, basketball, and volleyball where Turkish teams are internationally recognized, there is hope for a financially stable future.

The strategic plan of the Ministry of Youth and Sports states that one of its goals is to improve the reward system as an incentive for high performance in sports by 2019.[33] The reward system is seen as a major tool with which the Turkish government can motivate high-performance athletes to succeed. Job opportunities have also been created within governmental departments for those athletes who have important achievements to their name or demonstrated promise.[34] Not only is recruitment a clever step to ensure athletes' futures, it can also motivate young competitors. Following a possible elite or professional sporting career, the prospect of finding a well-respected position within the government may further entice young people to achieve success in sport.

All interviewees for this research were aware of the importance of different levels of sport participation. When it comes to increasing sports participation, school sports are crucial. Although many ministers were aware of the importance of school sports as a recruitment source for elite sports, integration of the two has still not taken place. As the authorities have indicated, a strong relationship between the sporting and educational systems has yet to be established. The president of the Turkish National Olympic Committee, Uğur Erdener, mentions another important aspect of the problem in the following terms:

We should have proper criteria for evaluating the success of not only athletes but also our sports institutions. If we are only medals-oriented, then we will probably miss some important values. For example, in some branches of sport, athletes might not win any medals at the Olympic Games, but that does not necessarily mean that this sport's governing federation is unsuccessful. They might have planned for the next games, made investments in the next generation, or focused on facility development ... instead of winning medals. We should consider these different areas of success carefully, not only focus on the medals won.[35]

As mentioned, school sports policy is one of the most problematic areas of sports development in Turkey. Basic physical education courses for pre-primary education are needed, studies on education through play at the primary school level should be conducted, and education specific to different sports should be provided. When it comes to physical education lessons, debates are ongoing regarding the duration of lessons at the primary, intermediate, and high school levels. During the late 1990s, the duration of lessons was increased to two hours per week. It then decreased to one hour per week and, during the late 2000s, increased again to two hours. In addition, the number of lessons per week and their content has been a contentious issue. Repeated curriculum changes are not a surprise. During the ministries of Şahin (2002–2007) and Başesgioğlu (2007–2009), free-of-charge sports schools were opened for youngsters wanting to take up sports. Özak adopted a project called 'Construct, Donate and Cut Your Tax Expenses' in order to build more sporting facilities in schools. Perhaps the most important and effective projects, however, were those run by the Turkish Olympic Committee, whose president Uğur Erdener stated:

We are running a project in primary schools called 'Oli.' So far, our instructors have educated 650,000 students. We are planning to teach 1.5 million within the next year. Our goal is to teach students the importance of Olympic sporting culture during early childhood. We are making the effort to reach a broader community in Turkey, in case Istanbul is chosen as the host city for the Games.[36]

At that stage, the support of the Olympic sponsors had greater salience. According to Erdener, some of the Olympic sponsors showed an interest in supporting such social projects. A supportive system in which young, talented athletes can simultaneously achieve educational success and sporting success is yet to be developed. The Turkish education system evaluates students through a centralized examination system, which focuses on their academic ability. Before even turning eighteen, the students have to go through a number of these competitive exams. With continuous pressure from their parents to study hard, potential athletes face a dilemma: whether to continue competitive sports and neglect their studies or to pursue higher education and quit competitive sports.

Updates on Turkish Sports and Politics Post-2014

In 2013, after losing its fifth bid to host the Olympic Games, things took a turn for Turkey. The government faced a setback in its ongoing ambition to host the Olympic Games. In addition to a lack of victories for Turkish sports teams, this led to a change of attitude on the part of the government. Government spending on sports was cut as the budget was reallocated and spending priorities reconsidered. The aim of this section is not to highlight the difficulties faced by Turkish sports after 2014, but to acknowledge mismanagement and misjudgments; to draw attention to political involvement in Turkish sport; and to focus on an objective, success in elite sports, common to both sports teams and sports administrators. The hunt for a long-term policy continues.

The number of Olympic medals won is widely considered by many sports policies to be the most important criterion of success. The government and wider society, however, fail to realize that sports teams are part of a much larger administrative structure, which is essential to ensure a sustainable support system for sport as a whole and teams within it. In other words, sports participation rates, fan experience, and sports clubs' financial health all matter just as much as team championships and athlete successes. As the history of Turkish sport confirms, the simple desire to win competitions does not translate into effective, sustainable, and long-term success. Yet the government's focus remains on winning games and trophies.

The timing of federation elections also seems to be related to this focus. All sports federations in Turkey, with the exception of the Turkish Football Federation, conduct their elections once every four years. Scheduling the elections in such a manner permits evaluation of the federation presidents and boards based on the successes achieved in their respective sports at the Olympic Games. At the 2016 Rio de Janeiro Games, Turkish athletes won eight medals (one gold, three silver, and four bronze) in four sports; in terms of number of medals won, these Games were more successful for Turkey than the 2008 Beijing Games and the 2012 London Games. However, the Wrestling Federation won five of these medals, with the Taekwondo Federation winning one, and two others were won for Turkey by naturalized athletes. The 2016 Games, therefore, saw only two Turkish sports federations (taekwondo and wrestling) achieve success if the criterion used is winning medals.[37] Meanwhile, when it comes to the Winter Olympics, there have so far been no achievements of note.

After the Rio de Janeiro Games, between September 2016 and January 2017, fifty-six federations held their elections. Thirty-five former presidents were reelected as presidents of their federations, with twenty-one federations electing new presidents. Of the federations with athletes competing at the 2016 Games, seventeen presidents retained their positions while twelve were replaced. Interestingly, thirty-three of these fifty-six federations had only one presidential candidate. Subsequently, a lack of alternative candidates led to these presidents being reelected. The continuation in office of unsuccessful presidents and its possible effects on sporting success needs further research. One possible reason for this situation is government intervention: federation board members and presidents who have good relations with the government may be able to keep their status despite their management failures and lack of on-field successes. Another interesting detail to mention is that in 2016, for the first time in Turkey's history, three female presidents were elected.[38] Despite these changes, the representation of females managing sport is still very low; of the 724 board members representing fifty-two sports federations, only twenty-four are female.

A changing economic climate and political tensions in the Middle East also forced the government to reconsider its expenses. The government's new funding model reveals the bias towards elite sport in Turkey. Due to lack of financial resources, the government has mainly funded the Olympic sports federations. Up until 2017, the AKP government has offered generous support for many sports federations, though Spor Toto continues to be the biggest funder of sports in Turkey. The following table shows the amount of funding allocated to sports by Spor Toto.[39]

Table 2: Funds allocated by Spor Toto to sports federations between 2004 and 2017

Construction of facilities	2,148,925,997.35 TL
Sponsorships in respective sports	390,108,261.71 TL
League or event naming rights	
Football	2,453,532,918.58 TL
Basketball	573,223,819.41 TL
Volleyball	219,180,507.74 TL
Handball	73,815,596.96 TL
Individual athletes	23,446,059.89 TL

The government sports funding system, as mentioned earlier, has been reformed once again. According to the secretary general of the Turkish Tennis Federation, the government currently makes funds available according to the success potential of athletes at the Olympic Games.[40] Under the current system, there are three different budgets available for sports federations: the Directorate of Sports budget, the Spor Toto budget, and the Special Projects budget. The Directorate of Sports budget is only available for federations managing Olympic-material athletes; the Spor Toto budget is available for the general expenses of sports operations; and the Special Projects budget is available to federations involved in sports development projects, such as 'sport-for-all,' or school sports competitions, and only if approved by the Committee of the Ministry of Sports, which is responsible for budget allocation.

In recent times, there has been one important additional budgetary consideration for the Ministry of Sports as well as the federations: the inclusion of refugees residing in Turkey in sporting activities. As of March 2017, there were 2,957,454 registered Syrians in Turkey,[41] and the Ministry of Sports has been organizing a variety of social, arts, and sports-related projects to engage them. Additionally, numerous sport clubs apply for grants offered by the European Union in order to organize and fund different kinds of sports-related activities for refugees.

Recently, municipalities have become important institutions in Turkey for the provision of sports-related projects and services,[42] and the Law of Municipalities (No. 5393) bestows the following sports-related responsibilities upon these municipalities:

- Municipalities give, when necessary, sports equipment to young people in order to encourage sports; provide sports equipment and cash aid to amateur sports clubs; provide necessary support; organize all kinds of amateur sporting events for athletes as well as technical staff who have demonstrated success in national and international competitions; and coaches may receive prizes with approval of the city council.
- Mutual cooperation with municipalities elsewhere in Turkey or municipalities in foreign countries (subject to permission from the Ministry of Interior) can be established to carry out activities and projects in fields such as culture, art, and sports in order to improve economic and social bilateral relations.[43]

Although many municipalities around Turkey provide the services and projects mentioned above, controversially, many are using their resources for professional sports instead of creating recreational sport opportunities.

TURKISH SPORTS

Importance of Hosting International Sporting Events

Hosting international sporting events has become an important topic in Turkey. In this regard, considerable budgets have been set by the state for sports organizations to cover the expenses of hosting these prestigious events. Examples of sporting events organized in Turkey over the last decade include the Istanbul Grand Prix Formula 1 (2005–2011), Universiade Summer Games 2005 and Winter Games 2011, UEFA Champions League Final 2005, and the UEFA Cup Final 2009. Between 2010 and 2013, Turkey hosted more international sport events than it ever had before in one three-year span. As the government continued to demonstrate its commitment and capacity to host during the Olympic bidding process, the country set a new personal record for itself. Even though the bid was lost, Turkey continued to host international sporting events. Some of the important sporting events that Turkey hosted between 2010 and 2017 are listed below.

Table 3: International Sport Events Organized in Turkey 2010–2017

	Year	Event	Location
1	2010	International Basketball Federation (FIBA) World Championship	Istanbul, Ankara, Izmir, Kayseri
2	2010	Karate World Clubs Cup	Istanbul
3	2010	Formula 1 (F1) Turkish Grand Prix	Istanbul
4	2010	2010 World Weightlifting Championships	Antalya
5	2011	TEB BNP Paribas Women's Tennis Association (WTA) Championships	Istanbul
6	2011	European Amateur Boxing Championships	Ankara
7	2011	Fédération Internationale de Volleyball (FIVB) Volleyball Girls' U18 World Championship	Ankara
8	2011	European Youth Summer Olympic Festival	Trabzon
9	2011	World Wrestling Championships	Istanbul
10	2011	Winter Universiade	Erzurum
11	2011	European Judo Championships	Istanbul
12	2011	F1 Turkish Grand Prix	Istanbul
13	2011	Karate World Clubs Cup	Istanbul
14	2012	TEB BNP Paribas WTA Championships	Istanbul
15	2012	European Weightlifting Championships	Antalya
16	2012	European Sports Capital	Istanbul

17	2012	International Association of Athletics Federations (IAAF) World Indoor Championships	Istanbul
18	2012	FIBA Euroleague Women Final Eight	Istanbul
19	2012	Euroleague Final Four	Istanbul
20	2012	Fédération Internationale de Natation (FINA) World Swimming Championships (25 m)	Istanbul
21	2013	Fédération Internationale de Football Association (FIFA) U-20 World Cup	Istanbul, Trabzon, Rize, Bursa, Kayseri, Antalya, Gaziantep
22	2013	Mediterranean Games	Mersin
23	2013	Confédération Européenne de Volleyball (CEV) Women's Champions League Final Four	Istanbul
24	2013	TEB BNP Paribas WTA Championships	Istanbul
25	2013	FIVB Volleyball Men's U21 World Championship	Ankara, Izmir
26	2013	World Archery Championships	Antalya
27	2013	FIBA EuroChallenge Final Four	Izmir
28	2014	FIBA World Championship for Women	Istanbul, Ankara
29	2014	FIBA Europe Under-18 Championship	Konya
30	2014	Turkish Airlines Ladies Open (Golf)	Antalya
31	2014	World Rhythmic Gymnastics Championships	Izmir
32	2015	FIVB Volleyball Women's U23 World Championship	Ankara
33	2015	FIBA EuroChallenge Final Four	Trabzon
34	2016	FIBA Europe Under-18 Championship	Samsun
35	2016	FIBA Euroleague Women Final Four	Istanbul
36	2017	FIBA EuroBasket	Istanbul
37	2017	Euroleague Final Four	Istanbul
38	2017	Summer Deaflympics	Samsun
39	2017	European Youth Olympic Winter Festival	Erzurum
40	1963–Present	Presidential Cycling Tour of Turkey (2UWC Class)	Multiple locations in Turkey
41	1979–Present	Istanbul Marathon (Gold Label)	Istanbul

The following sentiment has always been the primary motive of the previous Olympic bids: 'If we can host the Olympic Games, this changes the international reputation of Turkey and the attitudes of the Turkish population regarding sport.'[44] Interviewees for this research also shared their opinions that prominent sporting events hosted in Turkey have positive local as well as international effects. The aim of hosting prominent sport events, they contend, is to contribute to the brand value of Turkey through successfully organized sporting events, consistent with the views of Whitson and Horne, Waitt, and Essex and Chalkey.[45]

Sporting authorities interviewed also outlined the following key objectives in hosting these events:

- increasing Turkish youth sporting participation;
- improving Turkish elite athletes' performance;
- improving the sporting image of Turkey;
- gains in internal and external prestige.[46]

At the national level, hosting the Olympic Games is a good opportunity to stimulate trade activity and to boost the host nation's economy in various ways. South Korea used the opportunity of hosting the 1988 Olympic Games to draw attention to its rapidly expanding industrial economy;[47] as a result, the country saw an increase in tourism and foreign investments. Media coverage plays a key role here, as a positive portrayal attracts audiences from the international community. Another important dimension is that host cities have the opportunity to rebuild their infrastructure, improve their transportation networks, and upgrade their visitors' accommodation, if needed. Arguably, however, there are also disadvantages and large expenses associated with hosting big events like the Olympic Games. As Latouche and Searle have suggested, mega-sporting events can be especially burdensome for host cities.[48] Zimbalist links mega-sporting events to 'white elephants', a prestigious but costly gift in early Eastern cultures—similar to hosting mega-sport events, 'white elephants' came with certain financial obligations.[49]

One of the most important benefits of hosting international sport events in Turkey accrues to the tourism sector. With more than thirty million annual foreign visitors, tourism has a major impact on Turkey's economy. Hosting international sporting events creates a global community by bringing together fans and lovers of sports from different parts of the world. Media coverage of international sporting events being held in Turkey broadcasts the country's contribution to the world of sports, creating a positive image and global reputation for the country. This media-tourism model is common to other mega-events, as highlighted in the literature.[50] Turkey's youth population (15–24 years old) is around thirteen million, and that means a large active work force.[51] As Özak has stated,[52] the Olympic Games would create new job opportunities. Arguably, the Olympic Games have been a missing part of the world-famous, mega-city image of Istanbul.

Problems and Deficiencies of Sport in Turkey

Despite efforts and investments made on the part of the government, sports development in Turkey has been slow. Low numbers of participants; insignificant increases in young active-sport participants and numbers of sport clubs; and inconsistent levels of achievement in elite sports support this observation. The number of active athletes is low in comparison to the total population. The actual numbers support this thesis; in contrast to the total population of seventy-five million, there are 3,841,600 licensed athletes in total.[53] However, this number does not reflect the reality of active sports participation. Although there are 222,795 licensed basketball players, according to the Turkish Basketball Federation, the number of actively participating basketball players in all competitions is only 50,444.[54] Similarly, there are 30,663 licensed tennis players, but the Turkish Tennis Federation states that the number of these athletes who participate in competitions is actually only 4,863.[55] Despite the many efforts to bring education and sport together and to use sport as a tool for education, the two have never been fully integrated. The Turkish education system has faced many radical changes over the last twenty-five years, and most of these changes have arisen due to the political priorities of various ruling parties.[56]

In addition to these deficiencies, former Sports Minister Özak has observed that 'there is a lack of accessibility to sport at schools. Although we do offer sports classes, most of them remain ineffective when it comes to gaining new participants in sports.'[57] In big cities like Istanbul, Ankara, and Adana most schools suffer from insufficient sports facilities, while rural areas, despite the availability of land, have insufficient financial resources to create sports facilities. This has created an inconvenient and discouraging environment for active participation in sports at the school level.

In many developed countries, participation in elite sports is greatly dependent on active school sport programs.[58] In Turkey, however, due to the lack of development and support for sport in the education system, there is a deficiency in talent identification and grooming. Turkish sports development depends mainly on sports clubs; with restricted resources, most sports clubs and their managers are only able to educate, train, and develop athletes at later stages of development from a pool that is self-assembling at the earlier stages. Only minimal developmental opportunities are available at the grassroots level. There is a dire need to invest in scouting and approaching potential athletes, instead of waiting for athletes to identify themselves. There is no centralized talent identification system that can integrate prospective athletes from a larger pool of younger participants into the competitive elite sport system. Professionalization of sport in Turkey still needs to be developed. In this light, Uğur Erdener describes the profile of Turkish sports administrators thus:

> In the past, we had sports administrators who were able to speak a couple of foreign languages and had relevant experience in the sports field. If we compare these people with the current administrators, it is obvious that the current Turkish sports model is aiming to protect the status quo, instead of supporting better, more experienced, and more effective people who can contribute more to the international reputation of Turkey.[59]

Here arise questions about the quality of education in sports administration departments across Turkey, and possibly about the employee selection criteria of sports administrators. In order to make sports administrators responsible for athlete development and club duties, their professional and social skills need diversification. They need to understand the dynamics of the various departments in the sports management world in order to create a sustainable productive system that utilizes the potential of its athletes, whilst improving the economic situation of the clubs.

Without question, football is the most popular sport in Turkey, as it is in many European countries. Indeed, two other former Sports Ministers, Başesgioğlu and Şahin, state that many people consider football to be the only important sport in Turkey, one that therefore deserves full attention and support.[60] Football has long been a fan favorite in Turkey, attracting many followers and is often used as a tool by politicians to gain the votes of loyal club fans. Since the establishment of the Turkish Republic, the ruling authorities, including the army when it came to power, have used football as a political tactic to build public support. Additionally, football clubs also use politics to gain extra benefits like more funding and better infrastructure. This relationship between football and politics has existed throughout Turkish history. Because of the political, social, and economic advantages of supporting football, the AKP government is putting tremendous effort and money into the construction of new football stadiums, hoping to increase the number of spectators. In a country that has seen football spectatorship suffer, the motives for these investments require further academic investigation.

The government is currently funding construction of thirty football stadiums around the country, the total budget for which is around $1 billion.[61] However, many of these stadiums are located far away from city centers, which could be part of the government's attempt to modify rural areas by expanding city limits. When it comes to these urbanization attempts, the Turkish government has lessons to learn from its previous experiences. At the beginning of the 2000s, the government used a similar strategy and selected an underdeveloped rural area for Istanbul's Formula 1 track. After thirteen years of construction, the area had turned into a functional suburb with accessible transportation, schools, universities, houses, and shopping malls. However, the Formula 1 track is suffering since it has not hosted any prominent race since 2011. Instead, the track has recently provided services as a test-drive venue for global car companies, a parking lot for a rent-a-car company, and a driving school. As an iconic international event, the development of the Formula 1 track created a positive global image for Turkish sports during the years that it was actively used, and also helped to urbanize the area and to add to the economy of the country. However, after the end of its prime racing days, the track failed to live up to its primary purpose, resulting in the government improvising secondary uses for the track. The government achieved economic success but lost the focus on sport.

Conclusions

Since the establishment of the Turkish Republic, the government has been at the helm of a centralized control system for Turkish sports. In the past, the government adopted an interventionist approach towards sports policy. Through the establishment of new governing organizations, the government formalized sports policy; provided various kinds of sports activities; educated individuals for the sports industry; promoted sports to Turkish citizens; and built sports facilities in different parts of the country. However, economic instability prevented the government from achieving their sports policy-related goals. This economic instability was addressed when the AKP party came to power in 2002, and is one of the reasons that it has been winning elections ever since. Regaining economic stability enabled the AKP party to invest more in sport than previous governments. Despite this investment, however, most of the sports-related goals remain unachieved.

As a country that lacked a sporting culture, Turkey required intensive attention to its sports system, which required a long-term sustainable strategy such as subsidizing the sports sector and providing it with proficient management. Consisting of over fifty so-called 'decentralized' sports federations, the Turkish sports sector suffered losses in its attempt to generate its own financial resources. Ineffective management, insufficient participation rates, and poor oversight have all contributed to this failure. Taking stock of the situation, the government made subsequent attempts to increase sports participation, build new facilities, and host international sports. These moves were, however, more of a political tactic than a constructive sports policy. Creating a results-oriented mentality amongst athletes, efforts to increase sports participation saw a rewards policy emerge, one focusing on elite athletes while overlooking unsuccessful ones. The government's inability to integrate sports into the education system created a dilemma for potential athletes, despite their desire for active sport participation.

A top-down bureaucratic system emerged that was ineffective in its management of Turkish sports. Once comparable with the sporting elites of Europe, Turkey soon found itself on the margins of the elite international sporting community. Although economic growth has been considerable, and the government has improved infrastructure and facilities, there still needs to be a long-term sports policy. Using a holistic approach, sports should be a goal in themselves, not a tool for political and economic gains. As Masterman has stated, 'the short-term impacts of these policies require considerable thought and planning if they are to be developed into long-term and positive legacies.'[62] With a wide network of stakeholders responsible for the sporting system, it is essential to optimize and appoint efficient staff for specific roles. To engage Turkey's large youth population of thirteen million, and to support their participation in sport, it is essential that the government deliver sports to the young generation, developing a growing sport culture with strategies that follow up on initial initiatives.[63]

8

DEVELOPING A NATIONAL ELITE SPORT POLICY IN AN ARAB COUNTRY

THE CASE OF LEBANON

Nadim Nassif

Introduction

Winning in international sport competitions goes beyond the collection of trophies. It is a matter of national pride, a contest to show the superiority of one country over others. In what became a famous quote, George Orwell defined international sports as 'a war minus the shooting.'[1] According to Pierre Colomb, winning in sports is essential to reflect the strength of a nation,[2] and because it costs much less than military war, all countries can use it, regardless of their size, influence, or power. Although a debatable practice,[3] scholars usually refer to the Olympic medal table when measuring the performance of a country in international competitions.[4] The competition among nations for the maximum number of medals, what Reiche has labeled the 'Gold War',[5] started at the beginning of the twentieth century. Because of this, the various governments of different countries across the globe started to develop national elite sport policies specifically aimed at achieving success at major international competitions, particularly the Olympics.[6]

Lebanon can be considered an underachiever in this quest. Since 1948, the year the country first participated in the Olympics, Lebanon has only won four medals. One could perhaps blame this shortcoming on the country's civil war that shook Lebanon to its core from 1975 to 1990. But since the 1992 Games, which took place two years after the end of the conflict, only eleven athletes have been able to qualify.[7] Six of them were either naturalized or were Lebanese athletes from the diaspora; none won a medal.[8] In the same period, Estonia, Georgia, and Jamaica, with smaller populations and lower Gross Domestic Products (GDP), were able to win twenty,[9] thirty-two,[10] and fifty-eight medals,[11] respectively.

This paper will not explore whether achieving results in international tournaments is beneficial for a country's sustainable development and social well-being; rather, it focuses on the factors that might, in theory, lead to success. I discuss the macro- and micro-level factors contributing to success, analyze why they are not present in Lebanon, and, finally, propose an elite sport policy for the country.

Factors for a Country's Success in Elite Sport

The global acknowledgment of the medal table arises from the fact that the Olympic Games are the most universal, multidisciplinary competition in the world. Evidence for this fact is the participation of 205 National Olympic Committees in the 2016 Rio de Janeiro Olympic Games. Due to the universality and media coverage of this event, most governments have decided to invest substantial funds in the sports that are part of the Olympic program.[12]

The Olympic medal table is a ranking model that computes the gold, silver, and bronze medals obtained by the different countries in the different sporting events for every edition of the Summer and Winter Olympic Games. A gold medal has superior value over any number of silver medals, and a silver medal has superior value over any number of bronze medals. In the event of two countries obtaining the same number of gold medals, the country with more silver medals is better ranked. Likewise, in the case where two countries obtain the same number of gold and silver medals, the country with more bronze medals will be better ranked.

Scholars working on the identification of the factors behind success in international sport generally use the number of medals won at the Olympics as a starting point of their analyses. Several authors have suggested analyzing a country's political,[13] economic,[14] and demographic situation at a macro level,[15] as a means to understand its performance. Other models like SPLISS (Sport Policies Leading to International Sport Success),[16] developed by De Bosscher, and WISE (Women, Institutionalization, Specialization, Early Learning),[17] developed by Reiche, have advocated that more specific factors at the meso and micro levels should also be considered in a comprehensive model of a country's success.

Macro-Level Factors

Political Factors

Seeking national pride, international prestige, or establishing public interest in sport are indispensable in implementing a successful elite sport policy. Grix and Carmichael claim that governments seek to win in sports for international prestige, to create a 'feel-good factor' among the population, and to increase participation. This strategy will consequently lead to a healthier nation.[18] During the Cold War, the Soviet Union's massive investment in Olympic sports was driven by its will 'to demonstrate the superiority of Soviet-style communism over US-style capitalism.'[19]

Using sports as a political message was also the case for Egypt. The country's involvement in international competitions in the 1950s was a means for this newly emerging regional power to demonstrate its rejection of Western imperialism and colonialism.[20] In Iran, the gold medal won at the 1956 Melbourne Olympic Games by wrestler Gholamreza Takhti, who was politically connected to the National Iranian Front, was a symbol of opposition to the shah and British imperialism.[21]

Newly independent countries, such as Namibia,[22] Morocco, Algeria, Tunisia, Senegal, Benin, Congo, and Cameroon, also expanded national sports programs to gain international political recognition.[23] The same applies to world powers such as France. At the 1960 Olympic Games held in Rome, for the first time in its history France won no gold medals and finished in the twenty-fifth position, the worst record in its Olympic history. This failure caught the attention of French President General de Gaulle, who noted that a country with the historical 'weight' of France should succeed in sports, since such success indicates the strength of a country.[24] In 1961, De Gaulle appointed former elite mountaineer Maurice Herzog to spearhead a series of reforms involving construction of sporting facilities all over France. By also making physical education a compulsory subject in the French educational curriculum, Herzog secured a large number of participants who could train free of charge in all sports in villages, towns, and cities throughout France. This establishment of elite sport centers in all the French territories included those overseas, which followed suit.[25] These centers allowed the best French athletes, scouted by national federations, to live in a place where they could engage in intensive training while keeping up with their studies. These measures allowed France to become one of the leaders at the Olympics, finishing in the top ten in the last nine Summer editions, the last one being in 2016.

Economic Factors

Novikov and Maximenko have stated that successes at international competitions are defined by the socioeconomic development of a country.[26] Similarly, the importance of wealth has been raised by Kiviaho and Makela,[27] and also by Rathke and Woitek who consider that money,[28] combined with a large population, determines the success of countries in sports. Many studies, including those by Den Butter and van der Tak,[29] Johnson and Ali,[30] Hon-Kwong and Suen,[31] Van Tuyckom and Joreskog,[32] and Andreff,[33] have supported the idea that GDP, which is the result of wealth and population, is the major factor behind success in sports. According to Kuper and Sterken,[34] and Moosa and Smith,[35] the number of athletes and expenditure on healthcare are the strongest variables for success. For Tcha and Pershin, 'a country wins medals in a more diversified range of sports if its wealth increases or if it is a socialist country.'[36]

Demographic Factors

For Bernard and Busse, however, demography is not a major factor. They showed that China, India, Indonesia, and Bangladesh, which accounted for 43 percent of the global population at the time, only won 6 percent of the total medals at the 1996 Summer Olympics in Atlanta. They explained that 'first, countries cannot send athletes in proportion to their population for each event, for example, in team competitions, where each country is determined by the IOC in negotiation with the country's Olympic committee. As a result, not all the Olympic caliber athletes from a large country are able to participate.'[37] Den Butter and van der Tak had a similar theory:

A country with two times as many inhabitants as another country is not expected to win two times as many Olympic medals. Or in the economists' jargon: the 'production' of Olympic medals is apparently subject to diseconomies of scale with respect to population. This may partly be caused by the fact that each country is only allowed to delegate a limited number of participants per sporting event.[38]

Houlihan and Zheng have highlighted the importance of population by showing that at the 2012 London Summer Olympics, the 50 percent of countries with the lowest populations won only 11 percent of the medals.[39]

Cultural Factors

Sport being part of the culture of a country can also be an asset to attract private sponsors. Indeed, sponsors usually intervene in a sport that can offer visibility to their brand.[40] In the United States of America, the country that has collected the highest number of medals in Olympic history in elite sport,[41] youth participate massively in school, church, and municipal sport competitions. They are also enthusiastic followers of professional sporting competitions.[42] High numbers of fans attract private investors who will in turn fund sporting development.

Meso- and Micro-Level Factors

To achieve international success, the establishment of a national sport policy must take into consideration the political, economic, demographic, and cultural factors. Green has reviewed the emergence of sport as a sector of public policy from 1960 to 2002.[43] By taking the example of England, he has focused his studies on the development of elite sport policy in the mid-1990s. Houlihan formulated a framework for analysis of a public sport policy that starts at a meso level with the advocacy coalition model.[44] The SPLISS and WISE models are then used to identify the main characteristics of setting up an elite sport policy.

SPLISS Model

The SPLISS network, created in 2003 and led by De Bosscher, develops and shares expertise in elite sport policy in cooperation with policymakers, National Olympic Committees, international sports organizations, and researchers worldwide.[45] Its goal is to create a framework for analysis related to successful elite sport policy. SPLISS released its first results in 2008, and was followed up by the second results in 2015 with the participation of researchers and policymakers from fifteen countries. The SPLISS model is based on nine pillars of elite sport success, which are divided into three phases: input, throughput, and output.[46] The input phase consists of the first pillar: financial support. The second phase, the throughput, is made up of the eight other pillars:

- Governance, organization, and structure of elite sport policies;
- Participation in sports;
- Talent identification and development system;
- Athletic and post-career support;
- Training facilities;
- Coaching and coach development;
- (Inter-)national competition; and
- Scientific research.

The third and last phase, output, is concerned with the degree to which an organization has achieved its goal. In the case of the Olympics, output is related to the success or failure to win medals. According to De Bosscher et al., establishing a successful elite sport policy goes beyond the output of winning medals.[47] It is a virtuous circle shaped by the outcome countries look for, which is motivated by a national agenda.

The WISE Formula

Reiche identified four elements that he deems significantly more relevant, and brings them together to form the WISE formula:[48]

Figure 1: Outcome searched by the establishment of successful elite sport policies[49]

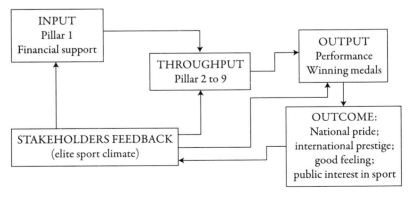

- Promotion of women (W) in sport: developing women's elite sport will strongly enhance the potential of a country to win medals;[50]
- Institutionalization (I) of the promotion of Olympic sports: setting up a centralized governmental sports system that offers the proper structure for athletes to develop their skills is crucial to obtain results;[51]
- Specialization (S) in medal-promising sports: focusing on sports where there are higher chances of winning medals is a commonly used method for countries to achieve success;[52]
- Early (E) learning in sports has been newly added to the Olympic program and gives countries opting for this strategy an advantage over rivals.[53]

Analyzing Success in Elite Sport using the Elite Sport Ranking of the International Society of Sports Sciences in the Arab World (I3SAW)

The Olympic medal table, which only rewards the top three placed competitors, can only include a limited number of countries. In fact, in the last Olympic cycle (2014 Winter Olympics and 2016 Summer Olympics), despite having a record number of countries winning medals, only eighty-seven countries were ranked. In order to address this issue, Nassif proposed a new ranking methodology that allows the 206 countries that have National Olympic Committees to be included:[54]

- A weighted points system that replaces the three-medal Olympic system;
- The introduction of universality and popularity coefficients for each sport; and
- A computation model that attributes to each country its share of points in at least one sport, and, consequently, its ranking in the 'global sporting arms race' based on the total number of points, which a country would have garnered in all sports.[55]

The I3SAW ranking, therefore, makes it possible for all national sport authorities to gain an idea of their ranking in international sport competitions. It also offers different results from the Olympic medal table, rewarding some countries (such as Spain, Argentina, and Brazil) that have been successful in universal and popular sports (such as football, basketball, and volleyball), and appropriately scaling those that mainly won medals in minor sports. Indeed, Norway wins most of its medals in winter sports where, compared with summer sports, a much smaller number of countries participate.

Table 1: Comparisons between the top 20 in the combined 2012–2014 Winter and Summer Olympic medal table and the 2014 I3SAW elite sport ranking

Rank	2012–2014 Olympic medal table	2014 I3SAW elite sport ranking
1	USA	USA
2	China	Russia
3	Russia	Germany
4	Great Britain	China
5	Germany	France
6	South Korea	Japan
7	France	Great Britain
8	Netherlands	Australia
9	*Norway*	South Korea
10	Canada	Italy
11	Japan	**Spain**
12	Italy	**Brazil**
13	*Switzerland*	**Argentina**
14	Hungary	**Mexico**
15	Australia	Netherlands
16	Ukraine	Canada
17	*Belarus*	**New Zealand**
18	*Kazakhstan*	Poland
19	*Czech Republic*	Hungary
20	Poland	Ukraine

In Table 1, it can be observed that the countries in bold ranked in the top 20 in the I3SAW elite sport ranking are unranked in the top 20 of the Olympic medal table. Meanwhile, the countries in italics ranked in the top 20 of the Olympic medal table are unranked in the top 20 of the I3SAW elite sport ranking. Five countries present in the Olympic medal table top 20 were absent in the I3SAW ranking, and vice versa.

A similar comparison is shown in Table 2 between the top 20 in the combined 2014–2016 Winter and Summer Olympic medal table and the 2016 I3SAW elite sport ranking. Six countries present in the Olympic medal table top 20 were absent in the I3SAW ranking, and vice versa.

By ranking all the countries, the goal is to provide a holistic comparative approach to determine a framework of analysis for the factors behind success in elite sport. For this purpose, the correlations of the 2014, 2015, and 2016 versions of this ranking with population,[56] GDP, and scientific research output rankings for the same years were measured. This comparative study has been undertaken for the following reasons:

Table 2: Comparisons between the top 20 in the combined 2014–2016 Winter and Summer Olympic medal table and the 2016 I3SAW elite sport ranking

Rank	2014–2016 Olympic medal table	2016 I3SAW elite sport ranking
1	USA	USA
2	Russia	France
3	China	Great Britain
4	Great Britain	Germany
5	Germany	Russia
6	Netherlands	China
7	Canada	Japan
8	France	Australia
9	Japan	South Korea
10	South Korea	Italy
11	*Norway*	**Argentina**
12	*Switzerland*	Brazil
13	Australia	Spain
14	*Hungary*	Canada
15	Italy	Netherlands
16	Brazil	**New Zealand**
17	Spain	**Sweden**
18	*Belarus*	**Mexico**
19	*Jamaica*	**Czech Republic**
20	*Kenya*	**Denmark**

– Population and GDP rankings will show the impact of demography and wealth, which were two of the macro-level factors identified by researchers in the field.[57] Those two rankings have been taken from the CIA World Factbook;[58]

– Research output ranking will be examined, because the establishment and optimization of meso- and micro-factors (governance, participation, talent identification, athlete support, training facilities, coaching development, scientific research, competition organization, promotion of women, institutionalization, sports specialization, and early learning), which were identified by De Bosscher et al.,[59] and Reiche,[60] cannot be achieved without extensive knowledge of sports management, sports marketing, sports communication, sports law, sports physiology, sports psychology, and sports coaching. The research output ranking was taken from the website Scimago Journal & Country Rank,[61] which is a publicly available portal that includes the journals and country scientific indicators developed from the information contained in the *Scopus* website, a database gathering all the papers that have been accepted for publication.

There will be no comparative study between sporting performance and any indicator related to hard or soft political power, such as the Composite Index of National Capability (CINC),[62] or Comprehensive National Power (CNP),[63] both because they already include economic strength as one of their variables, and because the political factor is related to a decision taken to succeed in sport, not to measurements like wealth and population that have a direct impact on the countries' performances.

The following were the results of the calculations of correlations between the I3SAW ranking and the ones of the population, GDP, and research output for the years 2014, 2015, and 2016:

Table 3: Results of the correlations between the I3SAW, population, GDP, and research rankings for the years 2014, 2015, and 2016

Correlation sports ranking 2014 / population ranking 2014	0.39
Correlation sports ranking 2014 / GDP ranking 2014	0.78
Correlation sports ranking 2014 / research output ranking 2014	0.82
Correlation sports ranking 2015 / population ranking 2015	0.35
Correlation sports ranking 2015 / GDP ranking 2015	0.76
Correlation sports ranking 2015 / research output ranking 2015	0.81
Correlation sports ranking 2016 / population ranking 2016	0.34
Correlation sports ranking 2016 / GDP ranking 2016	0.76
Correlation sports ranking 2016 / research output ranking 2016	0.81

Table 3 shows that the correlation between a large population and good sports results is weak; the correlation between a high GDP and good sporting results is strong; and that the correlation between a high research output and good sport results is very strong. Following these calculations, we can conclude therefore that having a large population is not an asset. For the countries that have more than thirty million inhabitants, the correlation is even less than 0.2, which is very weak.

Synthesis of the Factors Determining Countries' Successes in Elite Sport

As mentioned earlier, Houlihan and Zheng stated that population is important based on the fact that in the 2012 Olympics, the 50 percent of countries with the lowest populations won only 11 percent of the medals.[64] While recording the performance of these small states, the scholars did not undertake an analysis of the more populous countries. Andrew and Busse highlighted that China, India, Indonesia, and Bangladesh, which have 43 percent of the world's population, only collected 6 percent of the total number of medals in the 1996 Atlanta Games.[65] Andrew and Busse and Den Butter and van der Tak explained that the limited quota of athletes awarded to each country considerably reduces the importance that size of population can have.[66] By also looking at the correlations between the I3SAW ranking and population for three consecutive years, we can see that population has a much reduced impact.

While the importance of demography is undermined, there is question as to the important contribution made by wealth, scientific knowledge, and the expertise needed to implement elite sport policies at meso and micro levels, components of which were measured by De Bosscher et al. and Reiche.[67] Thus, at a macro level, we can see that political interest and wealth are the major factors behind a country's success in the Olympics. With their holistic approach, De Bosscher et al. and Reiche have given a detailed framework that has identified the meso- and micro-factors. For De Bosscher et al., the base of the pyramid of success is made up of financial support, organizational structure, and the number of participants. The next level is the existence of a support system, including scouting and support for athletes, provision of training facilities, coaching programs, and organization of national and international competitions. For Reiche, it is the combination of the implementation of a governmental system that offers the proper support for athletes and the choice of sports that offer more chance of success. After synthesizing macro-, meso-, and micro-factors, we can say, therefore, that succeeding in sports starts first with political interest and economic power. It is then followed by financing, which depends on a country's wealth, and the establishment of a structure that offers the optimal conditions for athletes to succeed.

Implementing an Elite Sport Policy in Lebanon

The Case of Lebanon

The Lebanese sport movement started officially in 1933 with the founding of the Lebanese Football Federation.[68] In 1935, the Lebanese Football Federation became a member of the International Federation of Association Football (FIFA).[69] Between 1943, the year of the country's independence, and 1948, several Lebanese federations were created: wrestling, boxing, weightlifting, basketball, volleyball, swimming, skiing, athletics, cycling.[70] In 1947, Gabriel Gemayel, elected IOC member in 1952, founded the Lebanese

Olympic Committee.[71] Since 1948, Lebanon has participated in every Olympic Summer edition except 1956, when it boycotted the games to protest against the French and British expedition in the Suez Channel after the invasion of the Sinai by Israel.[72] Although Gemayel's project was to put Lebanon on the global map, the country has only managed to win four medals in seventy years.[73] In fact, elite sport in Lebanon has never been a priority for the government, and this is one of the main reasons behind the country's difficulties in achieving success in international competitions. Comparing Lebanon today to Estonia, Georgia, and Jamaica, confirms that political interest, defined by the prioritization of sports by the government, is the first stepping-stone in a country's climb to success at the Olympic Games. As a macro-level factor, it has more importance than a country's wealth. Indeed, in 2015, Lebanon had a GDP of US$83 billion, more than three times that of Jamaica (US$24.65 billion) and more than twice that of Estonia (US$37.55 billion) and Georgia (US$39.3 billion). Lebanese government expenditures in 2015 were US$13.53 billion, more than three times the amount spent by the governments of Jamaica (US$3.941 billion) and Georgia (US$4.142 billion), and one and a half times higher than Estonia (US$8.975 billion).

When it comes to sport, however, the annual budget allocated by the Lebanese government to the Ministry of Sport is US$2 million.[74] That is 200 times lower than that of Jamaica (US$400 million),[75] 175 times lower than that of Estonia (US$350 million),[76] and ten times lower than that of Georgia (US$20 million).[77] Lebanon's budget for sport only represents 0.015 percent of the country's expenditure, while Jamaica's expenditure is 10 percent, Estonia's expenditure is 3.9 percent, and Georgia's expenditure is 0.5 percent.

Although less wealthy than Lebanon, sports in those three countries actually receive much higher governmental financial support, which is, as De Bosscher et al. note, the first and most indispensable pillar of success, one that optimizes the efficiency of the other eight pillars.[78] The output of these pillars, winning medals, demonstrates this fact: Lebanon has not won any medals since 1992. On the other hand, Estonia, Georgia, and Jamaica have won twenty, thirty-two, and fifty-eight medals, respectively, since that year. In the 2014, 2015, and 2016 I3SAW rankings, Lebanon was respectively ranked 95th, 97th, and 114th. For the same years, and in the same order, Estonia was ranked 58th, 57th, and 58th; Georgia 65th, 62nd, and 62nd; and Jamaica 63rd, 43rd, and 56th.

In Jamaica, sport is more than a matter of national pride. For Olivia Grange, Jamaican Minister of Culture, Gender, Entertainment and Sport, success in elite sport will significantly impact GDP growth. She said that the Jamaican government is committed to 'move sport front and centre of economic growth.'[79] By promoting the 'Jamaican brand' through Jamaica House—a marketing initiative promoting the popularity and success of superstar athletes like Usain Bolt—in the 2017 World Athletics Championship in London, Grange intended to exploit opportunities to promote Jamaican culture and tourism and to 'hopefully bring in new business.'[80]

The failure of Lebanon to win medals in the Olympics or to achieve a high ranking in international sport is thus related to the limited importance placed on sport in the agenda of the Lebanese government. This state of affairs does not provide sufficient financial support that will allow the stakeholders of the sporting movement to adopt the necessary strategies to succeed. As stated previously, governments invest in elite sport to seek national identity, pride, international prestige, diplomatic recognition, feel-good factors, and public interest in sport.[81] Why, despite having greater financial means than Jamaica, is the Lebanese government not investing in elite sport? To answer this question, it is important to examine the Lebanese political system and its vision of sport, because as the literature on sport and politics has shown, understanding the national sport program of a country cannot be undertaken without looking into its national ideology.[82]

The successive foreign powers that occupied Lebanon and the eighteen different religious communities that coexist in the country created a republic that is constantly threatened by a fragile balance of power.[83] To establish a republic where the main characteristic would be a fair division of powers among the various communities, each was allotted a quota in the government related to their size in the Lebanese population.[84] Lebanese politicians had thought that this compromise—the multi-confessional political system—was essential to secure political stability. But despite these measures, tensions remained and have led to several major conflicts, the most devastating of which was the civil war that tore the country apart between 1975 and 1990.

The influence of religious communities goes beyond the text of the Constitution. Political 'bargaining' happens after every legislative election (every four years) regarding the 'distribution' of the different ministries. The search for a power balance among the different communities fails very often, and instead turns into a struggle for power that regularly leads to the 'freezing' of government activities. This struggle for confessional overrepresentation is systematically reproduced in the different sectors of Lebanese society, whether in the areas of media, health, education, or sport.[85] The struggle for political overrepresentation in Lebanese sports is at the expense of developing a transparent and functional national sport structure. Sport, like other governmental institutions, reflects Lebanese political reality. Membership in the Lebanese sports federation is often associated with under-the-table arrangements made by various politicians,[86] and the stakeholders of the sporting movement are subject to political parties' struggle for overrepresentation, which is the key characteristic of the country's political system. This concern to win an internal political battle has overshadowed the will to succeed in international competitions.[87] This is one of the main reasons behind the derisory budget allocated to elite sport, and the subsequent absence of macro-, meso-, and micro-level strategies that could lead athletes to success. As of 2017, there are no policies being implemented by the Lebanese Ministry of Youth and Sports (LMYS) and the Lebanese Olympic Committee (LOC) regarding short-, medium-, or long-term strategies targeting success at the Olympics.

According to Reiche,[88] Lebanon encounters the same difficulties as other developing countries in implementing elite sport policies. They lack government funding and depend mainly on the support of the International Olympic Committee. When Mazen Ramadan was head of the 2016 Lebanese Olympic Delegation,[89] a 'Ministry of Youth and Sport Strategy 2010–2020' was released, but never implemented. This document included the following proposals: the creation of a National Sports Academy for the training of elite athletes; and the identification of sports where Lebanon could perform at an international level. These two strategies can be associated with two of the components of a successful elite sport policy according to Reiche's framework:

- Institutionalization (I) of the promotion of Olympic sports by setting up a centralized governmental sports system that offers the proper structure for athletes to develop their skills.[90]
- Specialization (S) in medal-promising sports.[91]

The 'Ministry of Youth and Sport Strategy 2010–2020' was never implemented. For Ramadan, developing elite sport is not a priority for the Lebanese government.[92] In the absence of government support, one has to look to private or sponsor funding to finance athletes. Sponsors usually intervene in a sport that can offer visibility to their brand.[93] This is very problematic in the Lebanese context considering the small fan base and consequently limited television exposure.[94] Competitive sport is not deeply embedded in Lebanese culture, especially when it comes to the low number of fans and participants,[95] which is the opposite of the situation of the United States, as mentioned above.[96] Sport being part of the national culture is a major asset for two components of a successful elite sport policy: financial support provided by sponsors (pillar 1 of the SPLISS model); and participation (pillar 3 of the SPLISS model), which is necessary in order to have a sufficiently large pool of athletes from which to select the most talented who will represent a country in international competitions. In Lebanon, people's interest in elite sport does not compensate for the government's lack of interest. Aside from the small number of fans, the other reason behind sponsors' lack of motivation is related to the lack of transparency in the Lebanese federations and associations, discussed below.

Perspectives for Development

Without national political interest, success is impossible. By examining the Lebanese sport funding model, we can identify the stakeholders who might effect the changes needed for the improvement of elite sport results. In 2000, the 247 Decree saw the establishment of the Lebanese Ministry of Youth and Sports (LMYS), and a Parliamentary Committee of Youth and Sport (PCYS) was created to vote on the budget of the LMYS.[97] In collaboration with the government, the PCYS participates in the preparation and approval phases of the budget allocated to sport. Once the government gives its approval, funds are sent to the LMYS to proceed with the implementation phase. Generating public funds starts, therefore, with lobbying the PCYS and approval of the Government. Without these actions, the LMYS and LOC will not be able to undertake any relevant plan and would have to count on the private sector. The latter was, and still is, generally hesitant to invest money because of the corruption prevalent in the national federations, which are members of the LOC and are responsible for developing their sport at a national level.[98]

Indeed, if we look at what happens during the implementation phase of LMYS funding (itself quite meager), it is clear that sport in Lebanon also suffers from an absence of audit and evaluation. According to LMYS officials, an annual report indicating which federations and sports associations deserve financial aid, based on their performance, is submitted to the LMYS. When it comes to the implementation phase, however, they 'most of the time' receive 'phone calls' from high-profile politicians requesting a share of the funding for their 'friendly' associations and federations, even if they are totally inactive.[99] During a parliamentary session in 2010, deputy Member of Parliament Simon Abi Ramia demanded that every sport association and federation submit a financial report for the year 2010.[100] Similarly, in April 2011, the late Antoine Chartier, former president of the LOC, also asked the thirty-two federations recognized by the LOC to submit a financial report for the year 2010.[101] Both Chartier and Abi Ramia's requests received no response because of the 'political backing' that national sport federations receive from political parties.[102]

Developing a national elite sport policy in Lebanon at a macro level should, therefore, be achieved with the following steps:

- Lobbying from the PCYS to increase Lebanese government funding. This funding can be done directly or through local communities. This will be helped if major decisions towards the development of elite sport were taken by high-level government officials, like the one of former French President Charles De Gaulle initiated after the poor performance of the French Olympic team at the 1960 Rome Olympic Games.[103]
- Establishing strict auditing measures to control the actions of the national federations in order to attract private investors, which can be a substitute for the government's lack of funding or as a complement to it should the government decide to increase its budget for sport.

Good governance in the national federations is also essential if efficient actions are to be undertaken on the meso and micro levels. For Jihad Salame, candidate for the position of Minister of Youth and Sports, administrative corruption in Lebanese sport is a 'plague.'[104] He was referring to the phenomenon of people occupying key positions based on their political affiliations, rather than on their skills and capacities. The meso- and micro-level strategies proposed by Reiche and De Bosscher et al. must be implemented by the national federations.[105] These include the organization of sports policies, increasing sporting participation, establishment of a talent identification system, support for athletic careers, development of coaching programs, organization of national and international competitions, promotion of women, development of sports-related scientific research, and promotion of experts in sports policy, management, coaching, and in the different fields of sports sciences.

Therefore, establishing a successful elite sport policy in Lebanon requires implementing measures that will go from top to bottom. It has to start with a political decision taken by the government to invest funds in order to succeed in international competitions. This has to be followed by a system of good governance undertaken by the LMYS and the LOC and must involve financial auditing. It must finally be completed with a plan at the meso and micro levels targeting an increase in competitive sports participation for both genders, development of a scouting and support system for elite athletes, and scientific coaching programs. These actions are necessary for Lebanese athletes to have an opportunity to improve their performance on the world stage.

Conclusion

This chapter has identified a state-supported national sports program as a key factor in any country's success in elite sport—one that is driven by a political ideology striving towards international recognition through triumph in elite sport. This is a prerequisite for the funding and proper policies that must be implemented. The complexity of the Lebanese political system creates a situation whereby the stakeholders of the Lebanese sporting movement adopt strategies targeting political overrepresentation and neglect adequate policies for success in international competitions. A successful elite sports policy should start with a change in the country's political ideology. Lebanon does not have the wealth to be a leader in the 'global sporting arms race,' but if elite sport were to be more valued, and therefore better funded, the results can be immensely improved. These developments will also be strengthened by a more committed expertise in sport management and in quality coaching programs, which will improve if the government undertakes transparency and good governance reforms.

The will to succeed on the world's sporting stage is more than a century old and yet the science dedicated to pinpointing a holistic explanation of the factors behind a country's success in sport is relatively new, with the first SPLISS network created in 2003 and the first congress of elite sport policy taking place in November 2013 in Antwerp.[106] This paper does not pretend to give a 'miracle success formula' for sport in Lebanon; rather, its main aim is to identify some general concepts leading to success.

9

LEGACIES OF MEGA-SPORTING EVENTS IN DEVELOPING COUNTRIES

A CASE STUDY OF LEBANON

Danyel Reiche

Introduction

Governments all over the world justify spending public money on mega-sporting events by claiming there are a multitude of benefits for the host community. A common argument is that mega-sporting events would give tremendous exposure to host countries and increase their influence in global politics.[1] Apart from improving a country's international prestige, mega-sporting events are considered to be a valuable tool for fostering national pride and unity, and, particularly relevant for emerging countries, for development.[2] This chapter discusses the extent to which these anticipated benefits apply to Lebanon. Internationally known for its 1975–1990 civil war, did hosting mega-sporting events positively impact the tiny Mediterranean nation-state?

After the Lebanese civil war, the multi-religious country hosted four mega-sporting events: two multi-sport events—the Pan-Arab Games in 1997 and the Francophone Games in 2009—and two continental championships in football and basketball—the Asian Football Confederation (AFC) Asian Cup in 2000 and the International Basketball Federation (FIBA) Asia Cup in 2017. The events illustrate the different identities of Lebanon as an Arab, Asian, and Francophone country. With reference to the 1959 Mediterranean Games in Beirut, which are not studied in detail in this chapter, one could also add the Mediterranean identity of the Lebanese people.

This research is relevant because the academic literature on mega-sporting events neglects the role of small, developing countries as hosts. While there is a rich body of academic literature on mega-sporting events, most of this work focuses on the FIFA World Cup and the Olympic Games, events that are mainly hosted by large, developed countries such as the United States, Japan, and the United Kingdom.[3] A recent trend is for these events to be hosted by emerging countries such as Brazil (FIFA World Cup 2014, Summer Olympic Games 2016), China (Summer Olympic Games 2008, Winter Olympic Games 2022), and South Africa (FIFA World Cup 2010) that have large populations and maintain leading roles in regional politics. An exception to this trend is Qatar, a small country with a population of about 2.7 million people (a vast majority of which are not citizens of the country) that will host the FIFA World Cup 2022. However, Qatar is economically very strong and the per-capita income in the Gulf country is one of the highest in the world. The author has argued in a previous publication that hosting the FIFA World Cup 2022 and other mega-sporting events is a soft power tool for Qatar that also serves national security purposes.[4]

Only twenty-four countries have ever hosted the Summer or Winter Olympics in the entire history of the Games (1896–2018). The remaining 182 National Olympic Committees (NOCs) that were recognized by the International Olympic Committee (IOC) in February 2018 have never hosted the Olympics.[5] While some emerging countries such as South Africa and India may be hosts in the future, a vast majority of countries will most likely never be able to host the Games due to their economy, geography, climate, or other factors.[6] The FIFA Men's World Cup has been hosted by even fewer countries than the Summer and Winter Olympic Games. In 2018, Russia became the seventeenth, and in 2022 Qatar will be the eighteenth, country to host the FIFA World Cup, a tournament that began in 1930. This means that only 8.53 percent of the 211 FIFA members (as of February 2018) have ever hosted the Men's World Cup.[7]

By mainly focusing on the FIFA World Cup and the Olympic Games, events that are classified by Horne as 'Tier 1 sports-mega events',[8] research neglects two important characteristics of mega-sporting events: first, a vast majority of mega-sporting events are continental and regional games ('Tier 2' and 'Tier 3' events in Horne's terminology) and, second, not all hosts are large, developed nation-states. Horne argues that 'lower order mega-events can act as "springboards" for cities to go on to bid to host first order mega-events.'[9] This might apply to a large country like India that hosted the 2010 Commonwealth Games and that may one day host the FIFA World Cup or the Summer Olympics. However, many Tier 2 and Tier 3 events are hosted by small, developing countries that are often considered part of the global periphery—for them, continental and regional games are the most they can achieve as a host country of mega-sporting events.

This research is a case study of experiences with hosting mega-sporting events in developing countries. The article follows a comparative approach by analyzing the legacies of four mega-sporting events hosted by Lebanon: the Pan-Arab Games in 1997; the AFC Asian Cup in 2000; the Francophone Games in 2009; and the FIBA Asian Cup in 2017. The comparative approach examines the similarities and differences of the four events, identifying patterns in Lebanon's previous experiences in hosting mega-sporting events and, in broader conclusions at the end of the chapter, determining if it is beneficial for a small, developing country to bid for mega-sporting events in the future. The Lebanon case-study findings are applicable to other developing countries, and contribute to a broader understanding of the topic of developing countries hosting mega-sporting events. While there may be some characteristics unique to Lebanon, such as hosting sporting events in the context of rebuilding the country after the civil war, many findings of this work also apply to other developing countries that have hosted mega-sporting events.

Governments and representatives of sport governing bodies often use the term 'legacy' to justify what are often costly bids for mega-sporting events. But what exactly does legacy mean, and how can the term be operationalized? What variables should be examined when investigating the legacy of mega-sporting events in a developing country like Lebanon? For Cornelissen, hosts of mega-sporting events aim 'to showcase economic achievements, to signal diplomatic stature or to project, in the absence of other forms of international influence, soft power.'[10] Nye coined the term 'soft power', defined as the 'ability to get what you want through attraction rather than coercion or payments. ... When you can get others to admire your ideals and to want what you want, you do not have to spend as much on sticks and carrots to move them in your direction. Seduction is always more effective than coercion.'[11] What is relevant for the case of a small, developing country like Lebanon is Nye's belief that 'soft power is available to all countries, and many invest in ways to use soft-power resources to "punch above their weight" in international politics. ... Even if they do not have the overall power resources to match the largest countries, smaller or less powerful countries still can present challenges greater than their military size would imply.'[12]

For Horne, 'symbolic politics—the promotional politics of promotional culture via public diplomacy, "soft power" and/or propaganda—are fundamental features of the contemporary politics of sports mega-events. Whether competing with other cities or nations to host an event, winning the right to do so, or actually hosting an event, the potential for symbolic power plays, or pitfalls, are real.'[13] Harris, Skillen, and McDowell argue that 'fostering a temporary "feel-good factor" is the most that many mega-sporting events can ever achieve.'[14] Horne emphasizes that the outcome of hosting mega-sporting events may not always be positive for the image of a country: 'All such exercises in promotional politics—nation branding, city branding, image alteration—run the danger of heightening reputational risk to the bidders (and eventual hosts) involved.'[15] An example is the case of Qatar, and the critical discussions in the international media on the situation of migrant workers in the country.[16]

The analysis of the legacies of the Pan-Arab Games in 1997, the AFC Asian Cup in 2000, the Francophone Games in 2009, and the FIBA Asian Cup in 2017 is divided into two parts, following Horne's differentiation between tangible and intangible legacies of mega-sporting events. Tangible legacies refer to 'substantial and long standing changes to the urban infrastructure', while 'intangible legacies of sports mega-events refer predominantly to popular memories, evocations and analyses of specific moments and incidents associated with an event.'[17]

There is a dearth of academic literature on the four events discussed in this article. There are two articles on the Pan-Arab Games, one of which also discusses the 1997 Games in Beirut, while the other highlights earlier games including the 1957 Pan-Arab Games in Beirut.[18] There is one general article on the history of the AFC Asian Cup with a special emphasis on the 2015 edition in Australia that does not discuss the tournament hosted by Lebanon in 2000.[19] There is no published work on the Francophone Games or the FIBA Asia Cup. Because of this limited body of academic literature on the four mega-sporting events hosted by Lebanon after the civil war, a review of press articles (secondary sources) as well as collection of primary data through interviews are important sources for the empirical part of this research, as elaborated below.

In analyzing Lebanon's intangible legacies from the four events, there is an internal and external promotional discourse that must be taken into consideration. Lebanon is a 'mosaic society' with eighteen state-registered religious sects.[20] The internal discourse considers the enthusiasm of the Lebanese people around the four events. Were the sporting events well attended? Were the local athletes successful? Did they contribute to what the aforementioned academic literature calls a 'feel-good factor' and a sense of national pride? Since few international tourists travelled to the four mega-sporting events, opting instead to follow the events in the media, this makes the media key in measuring the perception of the events outside Lebanon because soft power depends, according to Nye, on the recipient.[21] But even within Lebanon, most people followed the events in the media and did not attend events. I have therefore reviewed press articles published prior to, during, and after the events. Which issues were highlighted in the local and international media about the four events? Were reports in the international media positive for Lebanon's prestige, or did they mainly highlight negative issues, such as problems with the organization of the events or the political instability within the country? In short, did the press articles positively or negatively affect Lebanon's image?

After elaborating on the intangible legacies, I explore the tangible legacies of the Pan-Arab Games in 1997, the AFC Asian Cup in 2000, the Francophone Games in 2009, and the FIBA Asian Cup in 2017. While it is not possible to evaluate the long-term effects of the relatively recent FIBA Asian championship in 2017, more reliable statements can be made about the other three events that took place in 1997, 2000, and 2009. How much did Lebanon benefit from the Pan-Arab Games in 1997, the AFC Asian Cup in 2000, and the Francophone Games in 2009? Did these events lead to substantial long-lasting change in Lebanon by improving the sports sector and helping the country overall? Or are the legacies primarily negative, such as unused and unmaintained purpose-built stadiums and facilities?

Methodology

One research limitation is the lack of surveys available that gauge how the public perceived hosting the four mega-sporting events. However, apart from reviewing the academic literature and press articles, I collected primary data by interviewing key stakeholders in the Lebanese sports sector that have been involved in one or more of the four events. The objective of the interviews was to learn about the respondents' views on the tangible as well as intangible legacies of the Pan-Arab Games in 1997, the AFC Asian Cup in 2000, the Francophone Games in 2009, and the FIBA Asian Cup in 2017. I conducted eight in-depth, semi-structured interviews with Lebanese stakeholders. The chosen format of asking a series of open-ended questions had the advantages of allowing more fluid interactions with respondents and of providing a multi-perspective understanding of the topic by not limiting respondents to a fixed set of answers.[22] Furthermore, as a professor in Lebanon since 2008, I have directly experienced the unit under study, regularly interacted with sports officials, attended several basketball and football games at the 2009 Francophone Games, as well as football matches of Lebanese clubs or the Lebanese national men's team in stadiums that were built for the 1997 Pan-Arab Games and the 2000 AFC Asian Cup.

The interviews were held in person, with the exception of one interview conducted via telephone. Some sources were interviewed on more than one occasion. The interviewees are as follows: 1) a member of the Lebanese National Olympic Committee (NOC); 2) the president of the Lebanese Basketball Federation; 3) a senior editor of *Al Hayat* newspaper, who also served as media officer for the AFC Asian Cup in 2000 and as president of the Lebanese Cycling Federation in the 1997 Pan-Arab Games; 4) the president of Lebanon's largest and most successful sports club, Mont La Salle (the sports club venue that hosted the fencing, karate, taekwondo, and table tennis events at the 1997 Pan-Arab Games), and a member of the organizing committees for the 1997 Pan-Arab Games and the 2000 AFC Cup; 5) a professor from the Lebanese University Antonine who wrote a dissertation on Lebanon's football history from 1907–2007, a period of time that included the 1997 Pan-Arab Games and the 2000 AFC Asian Cup; 6) and another professor from the Lebanese University Antonine who wrote a dissertation on the 2009 Francophone Games where she served as executive director of the organizing committee; 7) a professor from the Notre Dame University Lebanon who specializes in Lebanese sports and has published on corruption in the domestic sports sector, an aspect relevant for discussing the legacy of the four mega-sporting events hosted by Lebanon; 8) and a staff member from the Ministry of Finance who gave her perspective in order to better understand the government's sport budget, information that is not publicly available.

Intangible Legacies

The Lebanese government and particularly Rafiq Hariri, prime minister from 1992–1998 and 2000–2004, supported the bids for the 1997 Pan-Arab Games, the 2000 AFC Asian Cup, and the 2009 Francophone Games as a symbol of rebuilding the country and post-war recovery. The initial idea was to host the three mega-sporting events within a brief period of time. However, Lebanon's first two bids for the Francophone Games in 2001 and 2005 were unsuccessful. Unlike the events in 1997, 2000, and 2009, the government was not behind the bid for the FIBA Asia Cup 2017; the initiative came solely from the basketball federation. However, the government eventually supported the event. After a meeting with the head of the Lebanese Basketball Federation, President Aoun stated, 'All the required support will be provided to ensure the success of this championship, which will be widely covered by media to convey Lebanon's bright side to the exterior.'[23]

Before the civil war, Lebanon hosted two major regional sporting events: the Pan-Arab Games in 1957 and the Mediterranean Games in 1959. The first mega-sporting event in Lebanon after the civil war was the Pan-Arab Games 1997, which was 'established by the League of Arab Nations in 1953 as a means of expressing cultural unity between Arab peoples across nation-state boundaries.'[24] According to Silva and Gerber, 'the Arab Games offered an opportunity to temporarily overcome the borders of the individual Arab countries set by the colonial powers after World War I.'[25] However, the Pan-Arab Games in 1997 in Beirut did not only unite Arab countries but also reflected 'the tensions within the pan-Arab project.'[26] The Iraqi team was banned from participation, which became one of the most reported issues of the 1997 Pan-Arab Games. Pressured by Kuwait and Saudi Arabia, two countries that provided financial assistance to Lebanon for rebuilding the country after the civil war, Lebanon decided not to issue visas to the ninety-seven Iraqi athletes who had already travelled to the Syrian–Lebanese border and who, ultimately, had to return home. The British newspaper *The Independent* quoted the head of the Kuwait Olympic Committee saying, 'if Iraq's teams even turned up, Kuwait's 277 athletes would march around the track at the opening ceremony waving photographs of the 600 Kuwaiti prisoners kidnapped by Iraq and never released after the liberation of the emirate in 1991.'[27] As a consequence of the boycott, Iraq announced it would freeze business ties with Lebanon.[28] Another incident at the 1997 Pan-Arab Games that reflected tensions among Arab countries was fan violence by Syrian spectators after their national men's football team lost to Jordan in the final of the tournament. According to an article in the *Jerusalem Post*, 'some 30,000 Syrians destroyed an estimated 400 seats and hurled rubbish and empty bottles at the players while Syrian players beat and kicked Lebanese photographers, witnesses said.'[29]

This was not the first time that politics had interfered in the Pan-Arab Games. When Lebanon hosted the event in 1957, well before the civil war, Egypt abstained from the Games. From a political perspective, Egypt's absence could also indicate that the different paths of Lebanon and Egypt to interact and trade with the international community might have prevented the participation of Egypt. Because Western countries refused to sell arms to Egypt, President Nasser turned to the Communist bloc. In September 1955, he announced that Egypt would obtain arms from Czechoslovakia. Lebanon, on the other hand, turned to the United States in 1957 because President Camille Chamoun believed that Nasser was a direct threat to Lebanon's independence.[30]

Further, Lebanon refused to invite Israel to the Mediterranean Games in 1959. The Lebanese Organizing Committee argued that an invitation to Israel would not be possible because of the daily incidents at the Lebanese–Israeli border, resistance from all Arab countries, and security concerns for Israeli athletes in Lebanon.[31] This incident is relevant to better understand why Lebanon has only hosted regional and continental events, and never global sporting events. 'It is the policy of all international sporting federations that the host country of world championships and other international competitions must issue entry visas for participants, regardless of their country of belonging or personal characteristics such as religion, race, gender, etc.'[32]

Unlike both the Pan-Arab Games in 1957 and 1997 and the Mediterranean Games 1959, the AFC Asian Cup 2000, the Francophone Games 2009, and the FIBA Asian Cup 2017 did not face any political boycotts. The AFC Asian Cup is a continental competition that was founded in 1956 and held every four years. According to Rowe, the AFC Asian Cup has an 'identity as both a regional and global sporting event',[33] because it involves the 'world game' of association football, because Asia is of increasing importance to global sport, and because it 'attracts interest from Asian diasporas and, ironically, from fans who track Europe-based elite club footballers.'[34]

The Francophone Games are a multi-sporting event for mostly French-speaking countries—Lebanon was under French mandate from 1923–1946. French schools and universities and the popularity of the French language, particularly among Christians, are a heritage of more than two decades of French control over Lebanon (and Syria). The Francophone Games were established in 1989, and the 2009 Games in Beirut were the sixth edition of the event. Lebanon's bids for hosting the Francophone Games 2001 and 2005 were unsuccessful. In 2001, the Games took place in the Canadian province of Quebec and, in 2005, in the West African country Niger, before Lebanon's bid was finally successful and the Games were staged in Beirut in the fall of 2009. While it took much effort to get the Francophone Games awarded to Beirut, Lebanon was more successful in the cases of the AFC Asian Cup, the Pan-Arab Games, and the FIBA Asia Cup.

The 1996 Pan-Arab Games were originally awarded to Lebanon, but due to 'Operation Grapes of Wrath,' a sixteen-day Israeli campaign against Lebanon in April 1996, as well as the lack of funds and unfinished facilities, the event was postponed by one year to 1997. Typically, there is not much competition in bidding processes for the Pan-Arab Games. Megheirkouni believes this is due to the weakness of the Arab economies—with the exception of Gulf countries—the lack of stability, and 'the absence of consensus on political issues such as Syria, Yemen, Libya, and Iraq.'[35] As a result of the Arab uprisings and the war in Syria, there have been no Pan-Arab Games since the 2011 edition in Doha.

Lebanon also did not face competition for hosting the FIBA Asian championship. The primary reason for the lack of interest from other countries is due to the fact that, unlike previous editions, the event did not serve as a qualification event for the FIBA World Cup or the Olympic Games. 'Nobody wanted this event' was an often-used phrase during interviews for this chapter. Being awarded the AFC Asian Cup and the Francophone Games is much more difficult than hosting the Pan-Arab Games and the FIBA Asia Cup. Winning the right to host the AFC Asian Cup 2000 was a significant soft power success for Lebanon. The country won the bid against the Asian powerhouse China. This is 'the biggest event our country will ever host,' said the Lebanese sports minister enthusiastically in response to the good news.[36] Prior to the AFC Asian Cup 2000, however, many articles were published in the international media raising concerns that the facilities would not be ready in time. Headlines read, 'Lebanon is not ready to host Asian Cup,'[37] and culminated in an 'Ultimatum to Lebanon' two months prior to the tournament with discussions on transferring the event to another country. To help ease tensions, the Lebanese president had to publicly announce that all work would be completed in time.[38]

The four mega-sporting events, and particularly their opening ceremonies, gave members of the Lebanese government the opportunity to make positive statements about Lebanon that were reported in the domestic and international media. At the opening ceremony of the Pan-Arab Games 1997, the Lebanese President Elias El-Harawi said that 'the decision of the Arab countries to hold the games in Lebanon affirmed their trust in the country's achievements.' He also stated, 'from Lebanon we say to the world, the Lebanese have returned to their heritage and unity, they have returned to build a Lebanon for heroes, youth and peace.'[39] President Aoun also used the word 'trust' when making a public statement prior to the 2017 FIBA Asia Cup, stating that the event 'proved the international trust in Lebanon, and in security and stability in the country.'[40] At the opening ceremony of the 2009 Francophone Games, Lebanese President Michel Sleiman emphasized Lebanon's diversity and tolerance: 'Today's event underlines that Beirut is the mother of dialogue. [It is a city] that embraces West and East. ... This event emphasizes Lebanon's presence in the Arab world as a democratic state that brings together all people.'[41] Similarly, Lebanese Education Minister Bahia Hariri said that the Lebanese people should 'be proud that their country is back on the world map.'[42] What supported the sentiment of being 'back on the map' was the presence of prominent members of foreign governments and sports governing bodies at the events. Juan Antonio Samaranch, President of the International Olympic Committee from 1980–2001, visited Lebanon for the Pan-Arab Games; Sepp Blatter, FIFA President from 1998–2015, attended the AFC Asian Cup; and the National News Agency reported that French Prime Minister François Fillon and approximately forty cabinet members from participating countries were present at the 2009 Francophone Games opening ceremony.

During mega-sporting events, countries are in the spotlight of the international media. *The Observer*, the Sunday newspaper of the British daily *The Guardian*, published an enthusiastic article about Lebanon prior to the AFC Asian Cup. Author Matthew Beard wrote that 'Lebanon has undergone a remarkable recovery from the ravages of a fifteen-year civil war. And in the sporting arena, too, this once benighted country is now making impressive progress.' Beard concluded that the Asian Cup 'offers this beautiful country the chance to establish itself again on the tourist map through sport.'[43] It is important to mention that this article was published before the continental football championship began. During the event, the media shed light on the low number of spectators attending the matches. Apart from the first two out of three Lebanese national team matches and the final between Japan and Saudi Arabia (which Japan won), no match attracted more than 10,000 fans.

Asian Football Confederation General Secretary Dato Velappan said 'these were not stadiums but cemeteries.'[44] The FIBA Asia 2017 championship did not attract spectators either; only Lebanese national team matches were well attended. While the 1997 Pan-Arab Games were, according to Nassif, 'a significant success because, for the first time since the end of the war, the Lebanese people took notice of the existence of its sport movement',[45] the low attendance again became a much-discussed topic at the 2009 Francophone Games. Despite free tickets, only 20,000 spectators attended the opening ceremony. I attended several football and basketball matches, all of which attracted only a few hundred spectators. Three days after the Games in Beirut had ended, Patrick Galey authored an article titled 'Why people only chose to see the worst in the Francophone Games' in Lebanon's English newspaper *The Daily Star*, in which he concluded: 'It is indeed a triumph for organizers that the games were held on time, in full, and without major security incidents. It is just a shame that more people didn't choose to witness them.'[46]

According to a study cited in *The Daily Star* 'the coverage was mostly limited to the official media sponsor of the games, Future TV, while Manar TV didn't show any interest in the event.'[47] This reflects the sectarian fractions within Lebanese society that is politically divided into two blocs, March 8 (pro-Iranian) and March 14 (pro-Western and supported by Saudi Arabia). The TV station Al-Manar is affiliated with Hezbollah, an Islamist political party supported by Iran that belongs to the March 8 bloc. Future TV, founded by former Prime Minister Rafiq Hariri, is affiliated with his political party, the Future Movement, which belongs to the March 14 bloc. The pro-Western stance of the March 14 bloc explains the support of Future TV for the Francophone Games that were initiated by France, a leading Western power. While not all Lebanese consider themselves as Francophone, an Arab identity is prevalent among Muslims as well as Christians. Christian sport clubs such as Mont La Salle, for instance, hosted events at the 1997 Pan-Arab Games.

The low attendance may be related to the lack of sporting success among domestic athletes. An exception was the 1997 Pan-Arab Games when Lebanon won seventy-six medals and finished eighth in the medal count. However, when Lebanon hosted the Pan-Arab Games forty years earlier in 1957, it was the most successful country—a fact that can also be explained by Egypt's absence, as mentioned previously.[48] At the AFC Cup in 2000, Lebanon did not win a match and did not advance beyond the group stage. At the 2009 Francophone Games, Lebanon won only four medals: two in sports, and two in cultural events, which are not part of the Olympics, the

Asian Cup, or the Pan-Arab Games.[49] Winning the FIBA Asia Cup 2017 was one of the main motivations for hosting the event according to the president of the Lebanese Basketball Federation. However, Lebanon made it only as far as the quarter-finals, where it lost to Iran.

Another contributing factor to poor attendance was that the best athletes did not compete. Henry, Amara, and Mansour Al-Tauqi note that 'recently some countries have preferred to abstain from participation in the Pan-Arab Games in order to prepare or participate in other international sporting events which they consider to be more important.'[50] They provide the example of Egypt withdrawing its men's national football team—the most successful in Africa—from the 1997 Games in Lebanon as well as from the 1999 Pan-Arab Games in Jordan, incidents that 'illustrate a decrease in the importance and the significance of the games.'[51]

At the 2009 Francophone Games, no matches for men's teams were scheduled in basketball, the most popular sport in Lebanon after football. There were two groups of national women's teams, and the best two teams in each group made it to the semi-final. However, the Lebanese women finished third in their group and did not qualify for the semi-final, tempering Lebanese excitement. In football, only national men's teams competed. The under-20 national teams represented the participating countries. Football stars from the French League 1, for example, were missing from the tournament. The Lebanese national team did not win a match and was eliminated at the group stage.

Similarly, at the 2017 FIBA Asian Cup, some countries did not send their best players. For example, none of the Australian NBA players were present at the tournament in Lebanon because the continental basketball championship was not a qualifying event for the Olympic Games or for the FIBA World Cup.[52] A naturalized Philippines basketball player, Andray Blatche, famous for playing nine years in the NBA for the Washington Wizards and Brooklyn Nets before moving to China, cancelled his participation in the FIBA Asian Cup in Lebanon because of security concerns.[53]

Tangible Legacies

A major achievement of the mega-sporting events hosted by Lebanon after the civil war was the rebuilding of the Sports City Stadium in Beirut, which served as a venue for the opening ceremonies at the 1997 Pan-Arab Games, the 2000 AFC Asian Cup (and most matches during the tournament), as well as the 2009 Francophone Games. It was inaugurated at the 1957 Pan-Arab

Games, but was destroyed during the Israeli invasion in 1982. When it was rebuilt for the 1997 Pan-Arab Games, Prime Minister Rafiq Hariri emphasized the symbolic importance of the reconstruction, noting that it 'marked the day when construction won over destruction and peace over war, adding Israel turned the Sports City into a cemetery but it has become a place for unity, peace, and Arab solidarity.'[54] Similarly, when Lebanon hosted the AFC Asian Cup, the vice president of the Asian Football Confederation stated, 'Our main objective from [sic] holding the tournament here was to help Lebanon build high-standard football arenas. We're very satisfied with what this beautiful country has achieved.'[55] Further, AFC Secretary General Peter Velappan said, 'Lebanon has two new stadiums in Tripoli and Sidon. The Sport City is back again to life. All these things among others are the legacies of the Asian Cup.'[56]

While these statements are all very positive, those interviewed for this research were less enthusiastic about the outcome of mega-sporting events in Lebanon. 'The only positive thing is we managed to organize the events without any major problems', one researcher said.[57] 'There is no lasting legacy', a representative from a sport's governing body noted.[58] 'We are repeating the same mistakes', added an interviewee involved in organizing the 1997 and 2000 events.[59] Some reasons for the negative perception cited in the interviews are: the heavy financial burden for Lebanon; 'white elephants', a term that refers to unused facilities after mega-sporting events; the lack of maintenance of the facilities; and corruption.

Regarding the Pan-Arab Games in Lebanon in 1997, Henry, Amara, and Mansour Al-Tauqi further conclude that 'the project merely represented costly items of little merit at this stage in Lebanon's reconstruction program.'[60] When Lebanon was awarded the right to host the Pan-Arab Games, the 1994 conference of sports ministers of the Arab League member-states promised to provide the necessary finances, 'but only Saudi Arabia, which donated $20 million, and Kuwait, which extended $6.35 million, have honored their obligations. The rest of the $75 million costs incurred so far has been footed by the Lebanese government.'[61] While Saudi Arabia and Kuwait helped Lebanon financially in 2000, the main donors in 2009 were France, which donated $10 million, and Canada, which donated $1 million.[62] French institutions in Lebanon also helped in organizing the cultural events that are part of the Francophone Games. 'Without French help we could not have hosted the Games', stated the former director of the Francophone Games during an interview.[63] However, the external financial help did not pay all bills. Interviews held during the summer of 2017 revealed that numerous fees, such as for hotel rooms to accommodate athletes and officials, had not been paid eight years after the event, making the Francophone Games an economic burden for some Lebanese businesspeople.

There was no external financial support for the FIBA Asian Cup 2017. The Lebanese Basketball Federation even had to pay a $1.7 million royalty fee to FIBA Asia, explained the president of the federation in an interview for this research.[64] The Lebanese government helped with financial support of $1 million, and the municipality refurbished the existing Nohad Nawfal Sports Complex in Zouq Mkayel that hosted all matches. The 8,000-seat complex was used for the FIBA Asian Cup and serves as the home site for the Tadamon Zouk basketball team.

Unlike Sports City and the stadium in Zaida, the Olympic Stadium in the Northern Lebanese city Tripoli is a 'white elephant.' Built for the 2000 AFC Asian Cup, the Olympic Stadium is one of three venues built for the tournament, including Sports City in Beirut and Saida International Stadium. During an interview in summer 2017, the spokesperson for the Lebanese Football Federation stated that 'there have been only about 25 matches in the stadium since the AFC Asian Cup in 2000.'[65] The local football club Tripoli SC plays in a different stadium, the Tripoli Municipal Stadium. Apart from the main problem that no local club regularly uses the venue, the facility is in poor condition. A media article prior to the 2000 Asian Cup read: 'the poor state of the Tripoli pitch has the AFC worried.'[66] According to a researcher specialized in Lebanese football history interviewed for this work, the stadium never fulfilled AFC norms and has problems due to its poor location directly by the sea producing poor soil quality. 'Experts had recommended a different location,' he said.[67] The stadium in Zaida is also located directly by the Mediterranean Sea, a contributing factor to rust. According to Rowe, when mega-sporting events are prepared, there is a 'relationship between stadium design and global communication.'[68] Often, the main criteria for new stadiums is that the location promises spectacular images on television, as it does in Saida and Tripoli, to boost tourism instead of putting most of the focus on the long-term use of the facility. The issue is comparable to the FIFA World Cup 2010 stadium in Cape Town, South Africa, which is hardly used and remains a 'national burden.'[69]

A common narrative among policymakers is that Lebanon lacks the resources to maintain its sports facilities. However, according to the Ministry of Finance, the draft budget law for 2017 includes 350 million LBP

($228,000) for maintenance of the Olympic Stadium in Tripoli and 1.31 billion LBP ($850,000) for Sports City in Beirut.[70] Given the poor state of both stadiums, many interviewees questioned whether the money is actually used for maintenance. I attended several matches in Sports City and remember it as an extremely dirty venue in very poor shape. For example, it was possible to detach the seat, which can lead to injuries in the stadium if spectators throw their seats at other attendees in acts of violence.

A member of Lebanon's NOC also recounted that when he was overseeing a cleaning prior to an event at Sports City in 2013, flags from the 2009 Francophone Games were found years later, even though it was likely that several cleaning bills were issued between 2009 and 2013. Consequently, when asked about the legacy of mega-sporting events in Lebanon, many responses referred to corruption. 'The money goes not to the right person', said one interviewee.[71] Another representative from a sport's governing body said, 'in other countries people might steal 10 or 20 percent of the money. But 100 percent, like here?' He concluded that Lebanon should not host any mega-sporting events 'because such events are just used to create funds to steal money.'[72] A researcher concurred by saying that 'big projects in Lebanon take place for personal gain, not the public good.'[73] The former director of the Francophone Games said, 'I asked France not to transfer money because it would disappear and requested to rather send us equipment.'[74] These statements reflect the pervasiveness of corruption in Lebanon. In the 2016 Corruption Perceptions Index issued by Transparency International, Lebanon is ranked 136 out of 176 listed countries.[75]

In an interview with a researcher, it was suggested that Lebanon should not host any mega-sporting events before a proper auditing system was introduced that clearly shows how public money is distributed. He also noted that there are fictitious sports clubs in Lebanon: 'they don't do anything but get financial help.'[76] Other stakeholders interviewed refer to Lebanon's sporting failure at the hosted events and suggested to first invest in athletic development before bidding for events. 'We don't learn from our mistakes', said an interviewee involved in the organization of the 1997 Pan-Arab Games and the 2000 AFC Asian Cup;[77] a representative from a sport's governing body also involved in both the 1997 and 2000 events said, 'there is no long-term thinking in Lebanon';[78] a researcher further noted: 'we do not have in Lebanon a process to form human resources for maintenance and how to manage sports infrastructure';[79] and another researcher stated, 'most people in the Lebanese sports sector are not competent and do not have any sports management background.'[80] In order to address these problems, in his research on mega-sporting events, Horne suggests engaging in a properly funded legacy management program that is able to continue for some years after the event.[81]

Conclusion

By hosting the Pan-Arab Games in 1997, the AFC Asian Cup in 2000, the Francophone Games in 2009, and the FIBA Asian Cup in 2017, sport has become a symbol of Lebanon's post-war recovery and for rebuilding the country. Rebuilding the Sports City Stadium in Beirut, destroyed by Israeli bombs during the civil war, was of major symbolic importance in that it showcased Lebanon's economic and political achievements in post-war reconstruction. Winning the bid for the AFC Asian Cup 2000 against Asian powerhouse China was a remarkable success for Lebanon. Members from foreign governments and presidents from sports governing bodies such as the IOC and FIFA visited Lebanon for the events, making these an effective soft power tool for the small country. Lebanon proved that it is capable of organizing major events and, as one member of the government framed it, is 'back on the world map.' The events gave Lebanon regional (Pan-Arab Games), continental (AFC Asian Cup, FIBA Asian Cup), and partly global (Francophone Games, AFC Asian Cup) exposure. Members of the Lebanese government used the opening ceremonies as an opportunity to portray to the world that the Mediterranean nation-state is a diverse, democratic, and tolerant country.

However, some articles published in the domestic and international press prior to and during the events were less favorable toward the host country. Negative media coverage began prior to the events, with many reports expressing concerns that the facilities would not be ready in time. During the tournaments, many articles in the media pointed out the low number of spectators attending the matches, even comparing the stadiums to cemeteries. Poorly attended events are attributed not only to the absence of many international stars competing, but also to the lack of sporting success of local athletes that prevented a temporary 'feel-good factor' and sense of national pride in a divided country.

While the idea behind the Pan-Arab Games is to make a statement for Arab unity, banning Iraq from participation and spectator violence in the football final between Jordan and Syria in 1997 showcased tensions within the Arab world that became even worse in the two decades following the event. The main failure of the 1997 Pan-Arab Games, the 2000 AFC Asian Cup, and the

2009 Francophone Games is the absence of a legacy management program that deals with the post-event use of the facilities. While the venue of the 2017 FIBA Asian Cup will be utilized by a local basketball team, the International Olympic Stadium in Tripoli is a 'white elephant' that has hardly been used since the AFC Asian Cup in 2000. Maintenance budgets have become tools for stealing money while the facilities are dirty and rusty, reflecting the serious problem of corruption in Lebanon.

Overall, there is a mixed picture when assessing Lebanon's experiences of hosting mega-sporting events, with some short-term image gains but few indications of long-term benefits for the country. During FIBA Asia 2017, Lebanon's President Aoun said 'that his country is willing to host any regional or international sports tournaments,'[82] but I believe that Lebanon should take a more critical stand and give priority to youth and grassroots sports programs before hosting other mega-sporting events. If Lebanon does host other mega-sporting events, it should consider co-hosting them with other countries to limit the risks.

There are some broader conclusions from the case study that also apply to other host countries of 'Tier 2' and 'Tier 3' mega-sporting events, particularly those that are small and underdeveloped like Lebanon. Governments from around the world tend to focus on the potential gains and to ignore the risks of hosting mega-sporting events. In nondemocratic countries, there is typically no critical discourse around the bidding processes. While hosting 'Tier 2' and 'Tier 3' mega-sporting events may have some short-term promotional benefits for the country, the case of Lebanon shows the difficulties in generating enthusiasm beyond the competitions, the lack of strategies for the post-event use of facilities, and the financial burden on the government for building and maintaining stadiums and sports halls. In addition, if a country is poorly rated in corruption indices, there is a good chance that financing for mega-sporting events will be pilfered.

One could argue that small, developing countries, such as Lebanon, which struggle to provide their populations with basic needs, should not host mega-sporting events. However, a proposed alternative is co-hosting future events with other countries. Just eleven days after FIBA Asia 2017 in Lebanon concluded, the continental championship in European basketball started and set an excellent example for the future of 'Tier 2' and 'Tier 3' mega-sporting events. EuroBasket 2017 was hosted by four countries: Finland, Israel, Romania, and Turkey. Two years earlier, EuroBasket 2015 was the first European basketball championship that was hosted by more than one country: matches took place in Croatia, France, Germany, and Latvia. While Lebanon hosted the AFC Asian Cup in 2000 by itself, the continental football championship in Europe, the UEFA European Championship, was co-hosted by Austria and Switzerland in 2008—countries with similar populations to Lebanon, and by Poland and Ukraine in 2012. These examples demonstrate that multinational hosting is gaining popularity. Co-hosting may increase local community acceptance, an important feat given the growing skepticism toward hosting large-scale sporting events, as the results of referendums on hosting mega-sporting events as well as protests in many countries demonstrate. Apart from reducing costs and avoiding 'white elephants', joint bids also enhance cooperation between countries, a positive effect particularly for troubled regions such as the Middle East.

10

THE BUSINESS OF SPORTS IN THE
GULF COOPERATION COUNCIL MEMBER STATES

Simon Chadwick

Introduction

Over the last decade, there has been a dramatic shift eastwards (towards Asia) in sport's global powerbase. This is evident across Asia, for example, in the growing number of major mega-events being hosted by Asian countries, the proliferation of investors located there, and the number of commercial deals being instigated and funded by Asian corporations and governments. As such, it is becoming increasingly apparent that the twenty-first century will be characterized by the predominance of Asia's influence on international and global sport.

Although several countries in East and Central Asia have made a strategic commitment to building sustainable sport industries, China and Kazakhstan being two such countries, it is within the Middle East that much of the recent activity has originated. More specifically, countries of the Gulf Cooperation Council (GCC) have been a driving force in promoting the economic, indus-trial, and commercial development of sport—regionally, internationally, and globally. Indeed, there is ample evidence of this, ranging from the acquisition of sports assets such as football clubs (for example, English Premier League club Manchester City by Abu Dhabi's Sheikh Mansour bin Zayed Al Nahyan) and the staging of sports mega-events (such as Bahrain and Abu Dhabi's staging of the Formula 1 Grand Prix), through to the creation of extensive sponsorship portfolios (like Emirates Airlines' multiple deals with top European football clubs such as Real Madrid and AC Milan) and government-level commitments being made to the industrial development of sport (for instance, via Qatar's 2030 National Vision and the country's accompanying sports strategy).

The business of sport has therefore become important for individual GCC countries, for the GCC collectively, and for the world of sport in general. It is contributing to national planning, especially as GCC countries look towards diversifying their economies beyond a dependence upon oil and gas. Yet the role of sport is extending beyond this to embrace goals such as job creation, establishing competitive advantage, enhancing national image, improving international relations, fostering social cohesion, and promoting health and active lifestyles.

Such is the breadth, pace, and intensity of growth and change in GCC sport that a closer examination of its industrial and business features is therefore warranted. This chapter begins with a brief examination of the GCC, specifically its economic profile, and then goes on to analyze the sport industry within the GCC. Initially, several common features of the industry are examined: economy and industry; soft power and diplomacy; nation branding and national identity; health and well-being; and sociocultural factors. The chapter then moves on to provide a statistical profile of sport in the region, highlighting a range of data focused on each GCC country's interest in sport, participation in sport, commercial revenues, and economic contribution of sport. Thereafter, key issues pertaining to sport in the region are explored. Specifically, these are: consumption; risk and security; regional tensions; resource management; economic and state pressures; and general observations, which broadly includes reference to specific GCC sports, such as camel racing. The final section of the chapter draws conclusions in the context of the above, the essence of which is that although the business of sport across the GCC is growing, it remains relatively small in global terms and faces a number of challenges to its continuing development.

Sport and the GCC

The GCC is a regional political and economic alliance consisting of six members: Bahrain, Kuwait, Oman, Qatar, Saudi Arabia, and the United Arab

Emirates. Four of the countries (Bahrain, Qatar, Saudi Arabia, and the United Arab Emirates) have formulated industrial visions (typically up to 2030), and created accompanying strategies to realize these visions. These national visions specifically address the overdependence of each country on oil and/or gas and, therefore, reflect a view of what the countries want their post-oil futures to look like. At the same time, there is a pervading sense of the need to productively utilize the revenues currently being derived from mineral resource deposits. While the likes of Abu Dhabi have targeted tourism as a major pillar of its strategy for moving the country towards its industrial vision, Qatar and Saudi Arabia specifically reference the significance of sport.

In 2016, Saudi Arabia announced its vision for sport, acknowledging that opportunities for playing sports in the country have historically been limited, but that sport is an important part of an active, healthy lifestyle among its population. Indeed, the vision statement explains that the country aims to foster 'widespread and regular participation in sports and athletic activities, working in partnership with the private sector to establish additional dedicated facilities and programmes ... we aspire to excel in sports and be among the leaders in selected sports regionally and globally.'[1] As part of this process, the following are identified as being particularly important:

• Grassroots development of sports and sporting infrastructure
• Development of women's sport
• Privatization and promotion of football and other sports clubs
• Commercializing trademarks and logos

By comparison, the nature and scale of Qatar's vision for sport appears to be significantly more ambitious than other GCC countries, given its nature and scale, which extends across sports and outside the country's borders. Qatar's sport sector strategy generally highlights the following as being important goals:

• Greater community participation in sports and physical activity
• Improved and integrated planning for community and elite sports facilities
• Increased and improved sports talent development, management, and performance.[2]

Yet a more broadly encompassing view appears to characterize the sport industry in Asia, particularly in the GCC. Not least is the way in which the model of sport appears to be predominantly state-led, but with active support for the development of an accompanying commercial sector. Indeed, the visions for sport adopted by Qatar and Saudi Arabia are entirely consistent with such a model. However, this emergent Asian model does not conceive of sport simply as a form of physical or social activity. Rather, sport is advocated as a means of driving activity and affecting cognitive and behavioral change in various ways, specifically by promoting economy and industry; soft power and diplomacy; nation branding and national identity; health and well-being; and sociocultural factors.

Economy and Industry

Sport is increasingly viewed as a source of employment, tax contributions, and export earnings, as well as a source of competitive advantage and differentiation.[3] As such, a growing number of Asian governments have been taking a strongly interventionist approach to the development of their sport industries. This stands in stark contrast to the role of the state in sport elsewhere in the world. The United States does not even have a sports ministry, while in countries such as Great Britain and Germany a liberal approach to sport has been adopted in which government fulfills more of an oversight role in the development of their respective sports industries.

However, across the GCC the position is significantly different, with governments strategically and proactively engaging in both the creation of industrial infrastructure and the pursuit of revenue-generating investment opportunities. In the case of Qatar, the country has vigorously pursued a strategy of sports mega-event bidding that has resulted in it hosting football's World Cup in 2022, the International Association of Athletics Federations (IAAF) World Championships in 2019, cycling's world road race championship in 2016, and the men's handball world championship in 2015. This has already had an economic impact in Qatar, for example in the way it has led to the creation of infrastructure.[4] In addition, the country has been investing in organizations that have been designed to build distinctive national competences. Some examples of this include the International Centre for Sports Security, which specializes in providing sport safety, security, and integrity services; and Aspetar, a specialist orthopaedic and sports medicine facility. Qatar and its business leaders have also invested heavily in overseas sports properties, with the intention of generating new revenue flows, but also with a view to building the country's profile and presence across the world of sport. One of the most notable organizations in this sphere has been Qatar Sports Investments (QSI). Among its portfolio of assets are French Ligue 1 football club Paris Saint-Germain; Burrda Sport apparel company; and the Doha Golf and Spa Resort.

It should also be noted that the economic development of sport in the GCC is consistent with a characterization of its members as rentier economies. This entails countries—in the context of sport, most notably including Qatar and Abu Dhabi—generating rents externally by manipulating global political and/or economic environments.[5] As Reiche notes,[6] in addition to economic benefits, this may have further advantages in terms of fostering soft power, improved national security, industrial diversification, and the development of a healthy society.

Soft Power and Diplomacy

There has been a growing recognition that sport can make a significant contribution to the pursuit of soft power and diplomatic goals.[7] Indeed, it is acknowledged that some countries within the GCC have become hugely adept at utilizing sport for these purposes.[8] Nye's original work on soft power accentuates the role of appeal and attraction as a means through which to influence the perceptions and behaviors of others.[9] Committing to the development of sport plays into such a narrative in the way that it enables countries to make a statement about the values they hold, their desire to engage with other nations, and their capacity to successfully plan and deliver events. Furthermore, sport can be a means through which to access important resources or to gain preferential access to investment opportunities.[10]

A convergence of sport, commerce, and soft power in the GCC can be clearly seen in sponsorship strategies of the region's major airlines. The airlines are state-owned, relatively young, and have had to establish market presence and build market share at a time when carriers from elsewhere in the world, particularly in Europe, have been privatized. Sports sponsorship has therefore been a way for Emirates Airlines (EA), Etihad Airways, Qatar Airways, and Gulf Air to generate consumer awareness of their services, influence their brand preferences, and affect consumption choices. In many ways, this has been a classic example of soft-power execution, creating favorable perceptions of the nations, their companies, and the activities in which they engage, not least through sport.

EA particularly stands out, especially as it was only established in 1985. Yet within thirty years it has become one of the world's biggest carriers. There are several reasons for this, not least the deliberate positioning of Dubai as an international transit hub. However, the prominent role that its portfolio of sponsorships has played in the airline's development is significant. In key territories, EA has signed high-profile deals with some of the world's leading football clubs. The organization's deal with the English Premier League's Arsenal was initially notable for its duration (ten years) and because it combined shirt sponsorship and stadium naming rights deals. Thereafter, shirt sponsorship deals—with Spain's Real Madrid, Italy's AC Milan, France's Paris Saint-Germain, and Germany's Hamburger SV—has meant that EA has had a long-standing presence in the top five European leagues. Reinforcing its presence even further, the airline is also involved in tennis, horse racing, cricket, golf, rugby, and motorsport sponsorships.

Nation Branding

To an extent, issues of identity and branding are related to soft power and diplomacy, although they are nevertheless sufficiently distinct to warrant further discussion.[11] This body of work indicates that nation brands are multifaceted, involving the use of visual symbols, slogans, or straplines as the means of establishing and maintaining market position, thereby helping to build competitive advantage. In so doing, the brand contributes to the creation and projection of a national identity.[12] The contribution that sport can play in enabling and promoting national brands and identities has therefore been widely accepted, both globally and specifically within the GCC.[13]

Branding plays a particularly important role in the GCC; perhaps excepting Saudi Arabia, the international profile and stature of the GCC's member nations has been relatively weak. In part this has been due to their physical size and geographic location. It has also probably been attributable to their twentieth-century histories; for instance, the likes of UAE and Qatar were either colonized or under the protection of the British and, so, are relatively new—and newly independent—nations that have been seeking to establish a postcolonial image and identity. Furthermore, in seeking a post-carbon fuel legacy, sport provides an opportunity for GCC nations to become known as something other than oil and gas producers.

Across the GCC, sport has therefore become an important focus for wider industrial developments as well as being an important part of identity-creating and brand-building activities. The latter has taken place at two levels: sport as a feature of GCC countries' brands, and the GCC as a sport destination. As Nielsen has identified,[14] sport has become a core constituent in the branding activities of the GCC. It is now a feature of the region's identity, denoting the likes of Abu Dhabi and Qatar as being major sources of outward investment funding into sports properties. For instance, the Bahraini royal family's Mumtalakat investment company owns 50 percent of McLaren Group. This is consistent with Bahrain's commitment to staging a Formula 1 (F1) Grand Prix, as well as its sponsorship of the sport via its national airline Gulf Air (GA). In turn, GA actively positions and brands itself as a motorsport airline, its planes often carrying official F1 livery.

Abu Dhabi is also an F1 race host, additionally being home to the Ferrari World theme park, while Qatar retains a desire to host an F1 Grand Prix. Contractual difficulties may preclude this happening, though Qatar neverthe-less alternatively plays host to an international motor rally and a motorcycling grand prix. The GCC has thus rapidly become a sporting event destination, a brand identity that its various nations have deliberately sought to build. Alongside this, the GCC countries are now seeking to establish the region as a sport tourism destination, a goal that forms the basis of, for example, the Qatar Tourism Authority's strategy.[15]

Health and Well-Being

The economic and industrial effects of sport extend beyond the generation of direct financial flows; as such, sport is not simply an investment opportunity. Sport as a form of physical activity that should be promoted among populations has long been accepted, especially for the improvements in personal and public lifestyles and health it can bring.[16] These issues are particularly concerning for GCC countries, as cardiovascular disease and diabetes are both serious problems facing the region.[17] Such illnesses often reflect sedentary lifestyles and poor diet, hence a major commitment to promoting physical activity is one way of mitigat-ing and preventing their effects. This has the additional benefit of offsetting healthcare costs as a fitter population is less likely to use a country's medical system.[18] Healthier populations are also likely to be more productive.[19]

Similarly, sport can have an impact on psychological well-being,[20] another health matter that is somewhat problematic in some GCC countries.[21] Linked to this, physical activity, as well as sporting success, is increasingly being acknowledged as an important source of happiness.[22] Happiness is thought to deliver a range of benefits, including an improved sense of well-being and self-esteem and a stronger sense of communal and national identity.[23] In light of the above observations regarding national identity, the feel-good factor induced by various forms of sport is therefore one that some GCC members have been very keen to achieve.

One of only five countries in the world—the others being India, Iran, Japan, and Malaysia—and the only one from the GCC, Qatar hosts an annual national sports day each February. The public holiday aims 'to educate people on the importance of physical activity and help develop and promote a culture of healthy living in the Qatari society,' and seeks to 'develop a physically and psychologically active and healthy society where individuals can build their capabilities and interact with their social environment.'[24] What is particularly notable about this day of sport is that it is consistent with Qatar's 2030 National Vision, specifically its human development pillar.

Statistical Profile of the GCC Sport Industry

Although it is increasingly well established that sport can be a major driver of economic and commercial activity, the exact size of the global sport industry remains unclear. In one respect, this may be because of definitional issues regarding what constitutes the sport industry. While some measures of industry size focus specifically on activities relating to, dependent upon, or generated by competitive sports, other measures incorporate various aspects of the health and fitness industries. As such, estimates of global industry size vary greatly; at the top end, one study has identified that the industry may be worth $1.5 trillion.[25] Another estimate values the global sports industry at $750 million;[26] and another puts the figure at around $145 million.[27]

Given issues pertaining to the accurate measurement of industry size, it is therefore unsurprising that measures of sport industry size in the Middle East and North Africa (MENA) and the GCC are either nonexistent or methodologically questionable. Furthermore, in previous studies of the global sport industry, the GCC and MENA regions have often been embedded within regional classifications adopted by the research organization's business units. Hence, in a 2011 study of the global sports market,[28] a measure for Europe, the Middle East, and Africa (EMEA) identified that sport in the region would be worth $43 billion by 2015, accounting for 35 percent of a total market worth of $145 billion. A later estimate of global sport economy size indicated that its annual value could be worth as much as $650 billion.[29] However, once more EMEA was used as the area of measurement; the study established that spending in the sport economy was annually increasing by three times more than other overall expenditure across the region.

In the first study of its kind, the Josoor Institute undertook research aimed at identifying the specific nature and scale of the sport industry in the Middle East.[30] This revealed that sport in the GCC is likely to be worth around $6.5 billion, employing around 68,500 people; further details of which are shown in Table 1.

Table 1: Sport industry size and employment in the GCC

Country	Sport industry size (US $)	Employment
Bahrain	162 million	1,000
Kuwait	524 million	1,500
Oman	302 million	N.A.
Qatar	1.3 billion	6,000
Saudi Arabia	2.5 billion	50,000
United Arab Emirates	1.7 billion	10,000
Total	6.5 billion	68,500

The Josoor research clearly indicates that the sport industry is both a major source of economic activity in the GCC and a significant provider of employment. However, in global terms, the GCC's sport industry remains rather small, probably accounting for less than 5 percent of total global industry size. Furthermore, there are considerable variations in the industry across GCC countries; the industry in Saudi Arabia is clearly mature and apparently well-established, whereas in Bahrain and Oman there would appear to be investment and development potential. In summary, notwithstanding the sums of money now being spent on sport by the likes of the United Arab Emirates and Qatar, the region remains some way short of being a major global sport industry player.

Key Issues Facing Sport in the GCC

The importance of sport to the economic activities of GCC countries is undoubted. After nearly two decades of investment in sport, the region is increasingly viewed across the world as an important player in the global sport industry. Nevertheless, there are several issues that warrant further consideration, both for their implications domestically within individual GCC countries and for their impact upon other countries. While it is acknowledged that each GCC country may encounter specific local issues, in general, the main issues can be summarized thus: consumption; risk and security; regional tensions; resource management; economic and state pressures; and general observations. Each of these issues is now considered in detail.

Consumption

The GCC's appetite for sport is undoubted, the national visions of respective countries evidencing a strong predisposition towards consuming it. As participants, the region's population appears to be especially keen football players and swimmers. The former is consistent with the popularity of football in many countries around the world, while the latter possibly reflects the nature of local climatic conditions that are generally conducive to outdoor swimming. Participant needs have created interesting commercial opportunities, not least in terms of the demand for sportswear and equipment. One company that has taken advantage of this is Burrda, a Qatar-based sports clothing company.

Football is avidly followed in each country of the GCC by both spectators and fans. In a study by Deloitte conducted in the GCC region,[31] 73 percent of fans surveyed indicated that football was very important to them, while 89 percent said they watched football whenever they could. However, although the Deloitte study focused specifically on football, some of the observations made in its report provide telling insights into the general consumption of sport across the region. In many respects, these pose some important issues for the GCC's sport industry and those who manage organizations within it.

GCC fans would appear to have split loyalties when they consume sport, which is the source of some concern in the context of fan engagement. People often lead something of a polarized existence, as they will simultaneously be fans of both a local and an international team or athlete. This is the source of troubling fan-engagement issues across the GCC as fans will often flock to watch games involving the likes of Real Madrid and Bayern Munich, but will refrain from watching local or regional teams. Indeed, although clubs such as Saudi Arabia's Al Ahli can attract attendances of 60,000 men or more, average attendance across the country's professional league is around 7,000 men, and may sometimes even be as low as 2,000. As a result, getting people into sports venues can often be a major challenge in the GCC, with some participants in the research suggesting that events should even pay people as an inducement for them to attend a game.

Deloitte identifies the importance of television and social media as one reason for the weak attendance at games. Indeed, the organization has established that satellite and digital television subscriptions constitute the largest category of expenditure among football fans. Alongside this, the company's research has also shown that GCC sports fans are significant consumers of over-the-top content; that is, the likes of visual materials uploaded onto the internet and accessed via platforms such as YouTube, Facebook, and apps. In entrepreneurial terms, this suggests some interesting industrial and investment opportunities for sport organizations in the region, although it also implies that fan engagement across the GCC will continue to be a major challenge. The difficulty in getting people into stadiums and sports venues is therefore acknowledged as an impediment to the growth of sport in the GCC, especially when combined with some of the climatic difficulties associated with summer months that are not conducive to staging outdoor sports competitions.[32]

Engagement and attendance issues pose other problems too, notably their effects on the match-day experience. In the Deloitte research, atmosphere at games was specifically identified as an issue across the GCC, which is in turn believed to undermine consumer perceptions of product quality. Exacerbating this problem, there also appear to be concerns about the standard of sports venues across the region. In countries where disposable incomes can be among the highest in the world, matched by consequent consumer expectations about quality, this is a serious matter that must be addressed by the region's sport industry.

Risk and Security

Qatar's formation of the International Centre for Sport Security (ICSS), and its intention to promote the integrity and security of sport, may have reflected a perceived need to address some of global sport's most pressing problems. Furthermore, it could be viewed as a shrewd strategy intended to create competitive advantage for Qatar in a field where a range of existing sports organizations have struggled to address some profound challenges such as match fixing and money laundering. Equally, the ICSS may reflect the hugely contentious World Cup bidding process in 2010, when Qatar won the right to host the 2022 tournament, and could even be viewed as a positive legacy of what remains, for some people, a controversial hosting decision. Matters of risk and security nevertheless have a special pertinence in the GCC, strategically and in operational terms.

There are regional instabilities within the GCC and proximate to it that provide an important backdrop against which the regional and global sport industries must operate. Notably, this pertains to terrorist threats and the impact that specific organizations may have on the region. Particularly, ISIS has claimed on several occasions that it will seek to disrupt, for example, the 2022 World Cup in Qatar.[33] Whether such a threat ultimately manifests itself will remain a moot point for the time being; however, the perceived threat is such that terrorism will continue to impact upon the staging of events in the GCC, as well as the region's broader investment portfolio. As terrorist incidents in Paris and Manchester have demonstrated in recent years, sports and entertainment venues constitute a target for violent attack. This means that the likes of football matches, motor races, and sports mega-events held in the region will all require robust risk assessment, security, and contingency planning measures in place to mitigate whatever threat malicious individuals might pose.

Security should not, however, be conceived of purely in terms of threat to life or to physical infrastructure. A major issue facing the region over the last decade has been the threat of sea piracy, a problem that is now being jointly addressed across the GCC.[34] Piracy nevertheless remains an issue and constitutes a legitimate threat to sport in several ways. The construction of venues, particularly in countries like Bahrain and Qatar, relies upon the import of concrete and steel. This makes such countries especially susceptible to piracy, exposing them to the possibility of disruption to event planning, organization, and delivery.

There are also issues of natural resource security, most significantly water security. This is commonly identified as a major challenge facing the region, and is something that is exacerbated by the staging of sports events.[35] One estimate indicates that upwards of one million people will enter Qatar during the 2022 World Cup, the implications of which should be considered in the context of the normal, 'static' population of 2.7 million. In such circumstances, the importance of water is evident in its provision for drinking purposes but also for sanitation and for efficiently managing sports venues; for example, watering pitches. A further consideration for sport is that a principle source of water in the region is through desalination, which is polluting and can threaten environmental security. Managing this threat is a particularly important challenge for sport, as many of the GCC countries that have adopted national visions have made a commitment to protecting the natural environment. Alongside water, given that GCC nations buy significant amounts of food from overseas, food security is also a challenge about which sports organizers must remain vigilant.

Given the levels of investment being made in sport by the likes of Dubai and Abu Dhabi, economic security is an important issue too. At its most fundamental, this use of sport as a means through which to diversify the economies of carbon revenue dependency dictates that their sports investments must ultimately yield a tangible financial return. While threats to this form of security could come from, for example, a terrorist attack, poor investment decision-making, market turbulence, and geopolitical instability are other potential sources of threat.

Regional Tensions

When Bahrain first reached an agreement to stage an F1 Grand Prix from 2004 onwards, it insisted upon inserting a contractual clause that would prohibit any more than one other country in the Gulf region hosting a race.[36] In 2009, Abu Dhabi subsequently became the second GCC country to host an F1 event, which effectively precluded the likes of Qatar and Saudi Arabia ever hosting a race. This proved to be the source of some consternation, particularly for the Qataris. Indeed, in 2015, rumors surfaced that Qatar was seeking to buy Formula One outright, with a view to staging a race through the streets of Doha.[37] When, in 2017, F1's ownership passed into the hands of the American corporation Liberty Media, Qatar's route into the sport presumably ended— at least for the time being.

Even so, the protective nature of Bahrain's deal with F1 aptly illustrates the somewhat fractious nature of sport in the GCC, something that reflects the nature of wider relations between member nations. Following a 2014 diplomatic confrontation between Bahrain, Saudi Arabia, and Qatar, it was perhaps no surprise that during the summer of 2017 a more serious and escalating problem emerged in which Qatar was effectively isolated from its GCC neighbors. Notwithstanding the reasons for this and the subsequent outcomes of what became an escalating dispute, the spat had major consequences for sport in the region.

In one incident, Saudi Arabian football club Al Ahli instantly terminated its contract with shirt sponsor Qatar Airways. In a related but separate development, the Asian Football Confederation decided to move a Champions League game between Al Ahli and Iran's Persepolis from Doha to a neutral venue, fearing the implications of staging such a game in either country. At the same time, in the UAE, people and organizations making positive references to Qatar were threatened with imprisonment, a move that led sports stores to cover sponsor logos on sports shirts displayed in the windows of retail outlets.[38]

Sport in the GCC has therefore become an instrument of power, a focal point for asserting regional power, and a pawn in the diplomatic battles that periodically grip the region. There has long been resentment among some nations in the region towards Qatar's Al Jazeera, which, among other such measures, resulted in the channel and other Qatari media outlets being blocked amid the 2017 diplomatic crisis.[39] The channel has long been accused of propagating a distinctly Qatari view of the world, effectively underpinning the soft-power influence and national branding opportunities that broadcasting provides. However, BeIn Sport, Al Jazeera's sports broadcasting division, has also been criticized by some GCC countries for its aggressive growth strategy, which has seen the company successfully outbid many of its rivals, including Abu Dhabi's Yas Sports and Dubai Sports.

Regional tensions pose a real and ongoing threat to the GCC's sport industry. At the very least the region's problems inflict reputational damage, an observation brought forth by calls from across the world to move the 2022 World Cup away from the region. But it also causes tangible damage to economic activity within and outside the region. In one case, at games in France involving Qatari-owned Paris Saint-Germain, rival fans have often held up banners referencing the country's alleged links to terrorism.[40] In another case, flights into and out of Doha have been severely disrupted by transport bans since 2017. While this may have appeared petty to some, such moves during major sporting events in the region (not least the 2022 World Cup) would have implications for their successful staging, as well as subsequent bids to host other events.

Resource Management

In general terms, resources are typically conceived of as including land, labor, and entrepreneurship. In terms of land, the biggest challenges for sport in the region would seem to be in developing facilities in harsh climatic conditions. Still, there have already been several key developments in sports facilities, including the creation of motor-racing circuits on Yas Island in Abu Dhabi, at Sakhir in Bahrain, and at Lusail in Qatar. However, the construction of such venues has raised several issues, to which there have already been some references in this chapter. Capacity utilization, both during and after an event, remains an issue that links closely to fan engagement, and also to the way in which venues are financed, designed, built, and operated. Indeed, the general relevance of creating mixed-use, accessible sports infrastructure would seem to be an important consideration for sport in the GCC.

Climatic conditions have not thus far been examined in detail in this chapter. It is important to reference climate as a feature of the sports operating environment, particularly as summertime in the GCC represents a major constraint on the scheduling and staging of sporting events. Indeed, Qatar's successful bid to host the 2022 football World Cup has seen it moved from its usual June slot in the international football calendar to December, when the country's climate is more temperate. This move has antagonized some of football's most influential stakeholders, notably the European football leagues, thereby somewhat diminishing the brand-building effects that Qatar was seeking to achieve through its staging of the event. In addition, the eventual switch to December has challenged existing governance and organizational structures across international football which, again, has apparently caused some resentment.[41] The effects of local climate must therefore be an important consideration in the formulation and execution of sports strategies in the region.

Climate and heat are two of the factors that have also drawn the further attention of critics, who observe how they have contributed to difficult working conditions for people employed in the region. In turn, this is bound into a much bigger issue pertaining to the acquisition and management of immigrant labor.[42] While the 2022 World Cup has served as a rallying point for organizations such as Amnesty International and the International Labour Organisation to question the nature of worker rights, and the *kafala* labor system in general has been put in the spotlight following the construction of sporting infrastructure across the GCC.[43] Essentially, *kafala* requires migrants to have an in-country sponsor that becomes responsible for workers' visa and legal status once they enter the country. Observers stress that this creates opportunities for labor exploitation; the confiscation of passports, and the provision of poor living and working conditions often being the most obvious problems with the system.[44]

The importance of labor as a resource is accentuated in the industrial visions of GCC countries, some of which have identified human capital development as one of the intended outcomes of a commitment to investing in sport. Through its 'Challenge 22' initiative,[45] Qatar has been seeking to identify and fund talented, young entrepreneurs who can create new businesses that will contribute to building a sustainable sport industry in the country, both pre- and post-2022. Through other initiatives, such as the Josoor Institute, Qatar is also seeking to ensure that one legacy of hosting the country's World Cup is the education and training of sports industry professionals. This is consistent not only with Doha's vision of human capital development, but also of a broader regional perspective—that sport is a means through which countries can enhance their national labor competences.

It has not been within the scope of this chapter to specifically consider issues of on-field sporting performance among the GCC's athletes. However, the acquisition and retention of elite professional sportspeople does raise a further labor issue. Athlete harvesting and naturalization have become common in some GCC countries, practices that have resulted in widespread criticism in the international media. Together, harvesting and naturalization effectively entail the identification, recruitment, and reward of athletes whose places of birth and nationalities may be different to what they ultimately become when they agree to represent one of the GCC nations. African countries are often the source of such labor, although European and South American nations have sometimes been a source too. Typically, highly skilled sportspeople in these countries are targeted and offered a passport and highly lucrative remuneration packages in return for changing their national allegiances. The Qatar national handball team, which reached the sport's world championship final in 2015, is an example of this; the team attracted a considerable amount of negative publicity in light of this.[46]

Organizations such as the Fédération Internationale de Football Association (FIFA) have commented that harvesting and naturalization are not within the spirit of their rules,[47] although other federations including some in athletics and handball have adopted a rather more lax stance on them. This suggests there may eventually be attempts in the future to more closely scrutinize or even ban these practices. Until such time as that happens, the pursuit of elite-level success in sport will result in a continuation of harvesting and naturalization. This is likely to pose a range of ongoing issues, including upholding national identity and reputational damage in the view of nations that perceive the practices to be unfair, illegal, or immoral.

Economic and State Pressures

The GCC region in general is often significantly exposed to price movements in carbon fuel markets. The source of wealth that has enabled the likes of Qatar and the UAE to engage in well-resourced and proactive sport industry strategies has, at the same time, become something of a constraint. In recent years, an oversupply of oil has led to significant falls in its price resulting in a fiscally challenging period for the GCC nations. Members have responded by instigating various measures that have brought about relative austerity which, in turn, has impacted upon sport. The notable effect of these measures has been evident in Qatar, which is thought to have reduced its World Cup budget by between 40 and 50 percent in 2017.[48] At the same time, some events, including the Tour of Qatar professional cycling race, were cancelled, with organizers citing financial pressures as the cause of this move.

One of the ways in which GCC countries have been attempting to offset their vulnerability to fluctuations in carbon fuel prices has been to invest their wealth in revenue-generating assets overseas, several examples of which have already been mentioned. However, such investments have not been immune from the countries' exposure to the vagaries of the oil markets. Indeed, in a recent study of overseas football acquisitions between 2014 and 2017,[49] only Qatar appeared in the global top-20 (in twelfth place), with no other GCC countries on the list. Yet with the added pressure of the 2017 diplomatic stand-off also likely to have affected the economic welfare of both the region and sport, the importance of such overseas sporting investments seems to have become even more important.

While private capital has begun to emerge as a source of funding for activities in the sport industry, the paternalistic nature of the economic models employed across the GCC continues to dominate. Notwithstanding the broader relative merits and deficiencies of the state's role in sport, the GCC's public-sector dominance of the field has created some significant economic pressures that countries have needed to address. For instance, in Saudi Arabia, the Council of Economic and Development Affairs announced in 2016 that it would privatize its state-owned professional football clubs.[50] The motivation for such a move was the desire to release clubs from bureaucratic state control, thereby creating opportunities to secure private-sector revenues from sources such as new stadium developments and the more effective sale of media rights.

In somewhat similar moves, the Dubai government recently decreed the merger of three clubs—Shabab, Al Ahli, and Dubai Club—into one entity: Shabab Al Ahli Dubai Club. According to Dubai's government, the main motive underpinning the merger is a desire to build a football team capable of competing with rivals at continental and global levels. Having just won a 2016/17 domestic league and cup double, Qatar's Lekhwiya Club rapidly disappeared as it merged with league rival El Jaish to become a new club, Al Duhail. It has been predicted that the move will create 'a new superpower in Qatari football that has the potential to compete for the AFC Champions League and maybe one day bring Asia's most valuable club trophy to Qatar.'[51] The same thing happened early in 2017 in Sharjah, where a resolution merging

Al Shaab Club and Al Sharjah Club into a single entity—Sharjah Cultural Club—was issued.[52]

Other Sports

Throughout this chapter, the discussion about sport in the GCC has essentially been framed largely in terms of state intervention, bidding for mega-events, and a focus on what are effectively global sports, such as football and motorsport. It is nevertheless important to acknowledge that several sports are deeply rooted in the region, while others reflect cultural heritage in the GCC's member nations, with equine sports perhaps being the most notable among these.

Equine sports in the region can have a strongly domestic focus, but are also a point of engagement with other parts of the world. In the UAE, desert endurance races of up to 150 miles attract the entry of some 2,000 active endurance horses drawn from an Emirates Equestrian Federation register of almost ninety stables.[53] The UAE also has extensive interests in horseracing elsewhere; Sheikh Mohammed bin Rashid al Maktoum is a major investor in Britain's horseracing sector, where he owns the Darley breeding and Godolphin racing operations. Maktoum also owns breeding and training operations in Ireland, France, Australia, the United States, and Japan. Qatar has also been investing heavily in the sport, via investment and sponsorship deals with British courses at Ascot and Goodwood.

Figures pertaining to interest and participation in sport presented above provide little indication that sports in the region, other than those listed, are popular. However, falconry, camel racing, and horse racing are sports deeply embedded in the culture and traditions of GCC countries. Among some sections of the community, especially those more affluent members of society as well as those keen to preserve history, there remains a consequent willingness to continue following and spending in these sports. However, as Deloitte noted, the economic impact in terms of jobs created and income generated is limited.[54] Outward investments into the overseas equine sector are nevertheless believed to have a strong impact, albeit in places such as Great Britain. It is nevertheless acknowledged that such investments serve as the basis for nation branding, destination-marketing, and tourism generation.[55]

Conclusions

Over the last two decades, sport in the GCC has grown and matured to such an extent that it is now an important focal point for domestic, international, and global sports industry activity. Inside the region, sport forms the basis for government strategy, economic and industrial development, sociocultural aspiration, and political influence. Outside the region, the GCC has become a source of investment funds and commercial revenues, such as from sponsorship, as and is being widely recognized as a group of countries committed to the development of sport. As such, the GCC has rapidly become embedded within regional, international, and global sport networks. A key feature of the GCC's sport industry is the role played by the state. Whereas governments elsewhere in the world, notably in Western Europe and North America, have adopted a laissez faire approach to sports industry development, GCC governments have deliberately and strategically adopted sport as a focus for national development. Furthermore, their strategies have sought to utilize sport as a means through which to pursue a range of other goals, from soft-power projection through to the promotion of social cohesion.

The way in which GCC countries have envisioned their sporting futures has been ambitious, sometimes on an epic scale. This has often been accompanied by meticulous planning, with many of the world's leading sports planners, event managers, and other relevant experts hired to assist Gulf countries in creating strategies designed to realize their visions for sport. Nevertheless, challenges remain for the GCC, particularly in the way these strategies are implemented, managed, and developed. Grand vision is one thing, successful implementation is another.

The GCC's drive towards its sporting goals is taking place within a broader regional context in which there is significant turbulence. In particular, conflicts such as that in Syria, allied to political instability in countries including Libya, simultaneously distinguish the GCC region as being rather more stable, while at the same time embroiling it in a network of wider political and religious challenges. These issues manifested in 2017, when Qatar became the focus of a standoff between GCC countries, which then drew in other regional powers such as Turkey and Iran. Not only did this undermine a consensus that sport is somehow a unifying force for good, it also called into question the sports industry strategies being pursued by countries within the GCC. This highlights the sensitivity of the environment within which the business of sport operates across the GCC. Equally, economic issues continue to confront sport in the region, not least because of the pressures faced by this collection of carbon fuel-dependent nations. Fiscal challenges have become an important feature of everyday life, but also in sport. Indeed, it will be interesting to monitor how, for example, the emergence of new tax systems in the region affect the business of sport.

The tax systems will inevitably raise questions about the role of the state in GCC countries—sport is dominated by the notion of 'big state' across the region—as well as the objectives states are seeking to achieve with their new tax regimes. For sport, this arguably poses a more fundamental question: what role will the state continue to play in sport business development? Continuing support for sport by the GCC's governments has helped sustain the industry's growth over the last decade, although one must question how long this will continue. One suspects that in the decade up to 2030, governments will reevaluate their commitment to sport. Presumably this will result in governments reaffirming their commitment to sport; otherwise, they may seek to retrench from existing strategy, perhaps even adopting a more overt private sector strategy for sport. For each of these potential outcomes, the private sector's role in sport looms large. To date, the private sector has played a role that has been secondary to a GCC government's role. In the period between now and 2030, the private sector in sport will need to grow, mature, and replace the state as the industry's central focus. This will require sport in the GCC nations to wean itself off a reliance on state funding and strategy formulation. Whether the private sector will become strong and robust enough will remain, for the time being at least, a moot point.

Otherwise, there remain some significant challenges for the sport industry in countries across the GCC. Notwithstanding the potential for ongoing regional fractiousness, the relative global immaturity of the region's sport industry remains an issue, along with some stark differences in industry size and sophistication between GCC countries. This implies several issues, including the need for countries such as Bahrain and Oman to pursue similar strategies to those of their regional neighbors if they are to remain competitive. There is a sense too that if GCC countries are to globally compete in sport, they may need to collaborate to do so. Clearly, this suggests some fairly profound issues, many of which are currently in focus due to the ongoing regional crisis.

For GCC countries currently engaged in executing sport industry strategies, there are other, equally pressing issues. For example, Qatar's aggressive investment in sport has attracted widespread criticism, ranging from allegations that the country has engaged in corrupt activity to secure event hosting rights through to the way in which the country has skewed player transfer values in football—Brazilian international Neymar's transfer to Paris Saint-Germain being a notable example. In addition, concerns remain that Qatar, and other states in the region, are investing in sport without there actually being an established, underpinning culture to sustain the industry. In Qatar's case, its ostentatious hosting of the 2015 World Handball Championship led to the construction of expensive stadia, which are now significantly underutilized. The GCC has to contend with this major issue of sustainability in sport.

Qatar is not, however, alone in sharing such problems; for example, the UAE is now attracting criticism from some quarters for the way in which it treats immigrant laborers and denies basic human rights to some sections of its community. Indeed, English Premier League club Manchester City's recent successes have been condemned as being bought with funding from such a nation. Meanwhile in Saudi Arabia, following recent domestic political upheaval, the country's sports strategy is now in a state of disarray. Indeed, it is believed that several elements—notably the planned privatization of its professional clubs—have been halted pending a resolution to problems involving senior figures in the country.

There are other common issues that each GCC state must also seek to address—issues related to climate, gender, and global acceptance being the most notable challenges. Given summertime temperatures of 45 degrees Celsius and above, allied to extreme levels of humidity, climate will always be an impediment to the staging of major sporting events in the GCC. This implies that GCC states must either look towards creative solutions for staging events, or pursue strategies that are driven less by the desire to host competitions and tournaments. As the Qatari football World Cup experience shows, the world of sport often refuses to countenance challenges to its existing order. Similarly, given prevailing perceptions elsewhere in the world, there are likely to remain broader suspicions about some GCC states' influence of, and presence in, world sport.

The coming decade should therefore be an intriguing one for the GCC's business of sport. There are tremendous opportunities ahead, though some crucial challenges remain. The region's sport is a mega-project on a grand scale which—if successfully developed in a way that is consistent with country visions—will surely see the region and the GCC members ascend to a much more prominent position in the global sports landscape. Alternatively, failure to fulfill strategies or accomplish visions may have serious ramifications for the post-carbon fuel legacies of the GCC's six member nations.

NOTES

INTRODUCTION: FROM SPORTS IN THE MIDDLE EAST TO MIDDLE EASTERN SPORTS

1. See for example Omer Aziz and Murtaza Hussain, 'Qatar's Showcase of Shame', *New York Times*, 6 January 2014, www.nytimes.com/2014/01/06/opinion/qatars-showcase-of-shame.html, last accessed 18 January 2019.

2. Di-Capua, Yoav, 'Sports, Society and Revolution: Egypt in the Early Nasserite Period', in *Rethinking Nasserism*, ed. Elie Podeh and Onn Winckler, Gainesville, FL: University Press of Florida, 2004; Walseth, Kristin and Kari Fasting, 'Islam's View on Physical Activity and Sport: Egyptian Women Interpreting Islam', *International Review for the Sociology of Sport* 38, 1 (2003), pp. 45–60; Jacob, Wilson, *Working Out Egypt: Masculinity and Subject Formation between Colonial Modernity and Nationalism, 1870–1940*, New York: New York University Press, 2005.

3. Stokes, Martin, '"Strong as a Turk": Power, Performance and Representation in Turkish Wrestling', in *Sport, Identity, and Ethnicity*, ed. Jeremy MacClancy, Oxford: Berg, 1996; Kari Fasting and Gertrud Pfister, *Opportunities and Barriers for Women in Sport: Turkey*, Women of Diversity Productions, 1999; Cünayd Okay, 'The introduction, early development and historiography of soccer in Turkey: 1890–1914', *Soccer and Society* 3, 3 (2002), pp. 1–10.

4. Chehabi, Houchang E., 'A Political History of Football in Iran', *Iranian Studies* 35, 4 (2002), pp. 371–402; Marcus Gerhardt, 'Sport and Civil Society in Iran', in *Twenty Years of Islamic Revolution: Political and Social Transition in Iran*, ed. E. Hooglund, Syracuse: Syracuse University Press, 2002; Cyrus Schayegh, 'Sport, Health, and the Iranian Middle Class in the 1920s and 1930s', *Iranian Studies* 35, 4 (2002), pp. 1–30; Babak Fozooni, 'Religion, Politics, and Class: Conflict and Contestation in the Development of Football in Iran', *Soccer and Society* 5, 3 (2004), pp. 356–70.

5. Stevenson, Thomas and Abdul-Karim Alaug, 'Football in Yemen: Rituals of

Resistance, Integration and Identity', *International Review for the Sociology of Sport* 32, 3 (1997), pp. 251–65.

6. Kaufman, Haim, 'The Zionist Sports Association: From National Sport to Political Sport', *Zmanim* 63, 1998, pp. 81–91; Ben Porat, Amir, 'The Commodification of Football in Israel', *International Review for the Sociology of Sport* 3, 33 (1998), pp. 269–76; '"Linesmen, Referees and Arbitrators": Politics, Modernization and Soccer in Palestine', in *Europe, Sport, World: Shaping Global Societies*, ed. J. A. Mangan, London and Portland, OR: Frank Cass, 2001; Sorek, Tamir, 'The Islamic Soccer League in Israel: Setting Moral Boundaries by Taming the Wild', *Identities: Global Studies in Culture and Power* 9, 4 (2002), pp. 445–70.

7. Tuastad, Dag, 'The Political Role of Football for Palestinians in Jordan', in *Entering the Field—New Perspectives on World Football*, ed. Gary Armstrong and Richard Giulianotti, Oxford, Berg, 1997.

8. Stanton, Andrea L., 'Syria and the Olympics: national identity on an international stage', *The International Journal of the History of Sport*, 31.3 (2014), pp. 290–305; Baun, Dylan, 'Lebanon's Youth Clubs and the 1936 Summer Olympics: Mobilizing Sports, Challenging Imperialism and Launching a National Project.' *The International Journal of the History of Sport* (2018), pp. 1–19.

9. Tinaz, Cem, Douglas Michele Turco, and Paul Salisbury, 'Sport policy in Turkey', *International Journal of Sport Policy and Politics* 6, 3 (2014), pp. 533–45; Danyel Reiche, 'Investing in sporting success as a domestic and foreign policy tool: the case of Qatar', *International Journal of Sport Policy and Politics* 7, 4 (2015), pp. 489–504. Nassif, Nadim and Mahfoud Amara, 'Sport, policy and politics in Lebanon', *International Journal of Sport Policy and Politics* 7, 3 (2015), pp. 443–55. David Hassan, 'Sport event management in the Gulf: a focus on strategy and promotion', in *Sport Management in the Middle East*, eds Mohammed Ben Sulayem, Sean O'Connor, David Hassan, Oxford: Routledge, 2013.

10. Hong, Fan, *Sport in the Middle East: Power, Politics, Ideology and Religion*, London and New York: Routledge, 2014; Ben-Sulayem, Mohammed, Sean O'Connor, and David Hassan, *Sport Management in the Middle East: A Case Study*, London and New York, Routledge, 2013; Amara, Mahfoud *Sport, Politics and Society in the Arab World*, London: Palgrave Macmillan, 2012; Dorsey, James M. *Shifting Sands: Essays On Sports And Politics In The Middle East And North Africa*, World Scientific Publishing Company, 2017; Nicholas Hopkins and Sandrin Gamblin, *Sports and Society in the Middle East*, Cairo Papers in Social Science, Cairo: American University in Cairo Press, 2016.

11. Raab, Alon and Issam Khalidi, *Soccer in the Middle East*, London and New York: Routledge, 2016; Dorsey James M. *The Turbulent World of Middle East Soccer*, London: Hurst, 2016.

12. Amanat, Abbas, 'Introduction: Is There a Middle East? Problematizing a Virtual Space.' In *Is There a Middle East? The Evolution of a Geopolitical Concept*, edited by Michael E. Bonine, Aabbas Amanat and Michael E. Gasper. 1–7. Stanford: Stanford University Press, 2012.

13. Reiche, Danyel, 'Investing in sporting success as a domestic and foreign policy tool: the case of Qatar', *International Journal of Sport Policy and Politics* 7, 4 (2015).
14. Pfister, Gertrud, 'Outsiders: Muslim Women and Olympic Games–barriers and Opportunities.' *The International Journal of the History of Sport* 27, 16–18 (2010), pp. 2925–2957.
15. See 2018 World Press Freedom Index at https://rsf.org/en/ranking?#; Freedom in the World 2018 index at https://freedomhouse.org/report/freedom-world/freedom-world-2018; Gender Inequality Index 2015 at http://hdr.undp.org/en/data, last accessed 22 January 2019.
16. See Al-Khuli, A., *Al-Riada wal-Hadara al-Islamiya*, Cairo: Dar al-Fikr al-'Arabi, 1995; 'Alawi, M. K., *Al-Riyada al-Badaniya 'Ind al-'Arab*, Cairo: Maktabat al-Nahda al-Misriya, 1947.

1. MAPPING THE 'SPORTS *NAHDA*': TOWARD A HISTORY OF SPORTS IN THE MODERN MIDDLE EAST

1. Author's Note: I wish to thank Arash Davari, Chris Silver, Suzi Mirgani, Tamir Sorek, Danyel Tobias Reiche, Samuel Dolbee, Juliette Rosenthal, Hadia Bakkar, Issam Nassar, Idan Barir, Mina Khalil, Ziad Abu-Rish, Tania El Khoury, Lara Ayad, Dylan Baun, Muhannad Salhi, Mikiya Koyagi, Hussein Omar, Shawki Ebeid El-Zatmah, and the peer reviewers. I would also like to thank the participants in the 'Sports, Society, and the State in the Middle East' working group at the Center for International and Regional Studies (CIRS), Georgetown University Qatar. This research was supported in part by the Maurice Amado research and travel grant (UCLA) and the American Research Institute in Turkey.
2. The official state visit reflects the close relationship that Egypt and Italy maintained during the 1930s. King Fuad spent a considerable amount of time in Italy during his youth. King Fuad's first official state trip was to Italy. See Starr, Deborah, *Remembering Cosmopolitan Egypt: Literature, Culture, and Empire*, London & New York, Routledge, 2009, p. 31; Borsoi, Marzia, 'Alexandria and Cairo: The "Balad" or "Terra Nostra" of the Italians in Egypt: 1860–1956', MA Thesis, University of North Carolina at Wilmington, 2010, p. 56.
3. 'Egyptians Welcome Italian Royal Party', *The New York Times* (21 February 1933), p. 22, www.nytimes.com/1933/02/21/archives/egyptians-welcome-italian-royal-party-great-political-importance-is.html; *The Illustrated London News* (11 March 1933), p. 348.
4. 'Al-hafla al-riyadiyya al-kubra li-wizara al-ma'arif bi munasiba tashrif hadrati sahibi al-jalala malik wa malika Italiya' [The Ministry of Education's large sports festivity on the occasion of honoring the presence of Italy's King and Queen], *al-Abtal* (4 March 1933), p. 4.
5. 'Al-hafla al-riyadiyya al-kubra li-wizara al-ma'arif', p. 4.
6. Ibid; This term, 'sports awakening' (*al-nahda al-riyadiyya*), was used in an article describing sports in Egypt during the 1930s.

7. See, for instance, Hourani, Albert Habib, *Arabic Thought in the Liberal Age, 1798–1939*, New York: Cambridge University Press, 1983; Wehr, Hans, and J. Milton Cowan, *Arabic–English Dictionary*, 3rd ed., Ithaca: Spoken Language Services, 1976, p. 1004.

8. In the past decade, historians of the Middle East have challenged the dominant narrative of the *nahda* as exclusively an Arabic literary renaissance. Notable contributions include the following: Khuri-Makdisi, Ilham, *The Eastern Mediterranean and the Making of Global Radicalism, 1860–1914*, Berkeley & Los Angeles: University of California Press, 2010; Elshakry, Marwa, *Reading Darwin in Arabic, 1860–1950*, Berkeley & Los Angeles: University of California Press, 2013; Seikaly, Sherene, *Men of Capital: Scarcity and Economy in Mandate Palestine*, Stanford: Stanford University Press, 2016; and Hanssen, Jens, and Max Weiss (eds.), *Arabic Thought Beyond the Liberal Age: Towards an Intellectual History of the Nahda*, Cambridge: Cambridge University Press, 2016.

9. Wilson Chacko Jacob's study of physical culture and masculinity focuses on the centrality of sports and corporeal reform to modern Egyptian subject formation. Jacob, Wilson Chacko, *Working Out Egypt: Effendi Masculinity and Colonial Modernity, 1870–1940*, Durham: Duke University Press, 2011.

10. For works on Egypt, Iran, Israel, Palestine, Turkey, and the Ottoman Empire, see Jacob, *Working Out Egypt*; Lopez, Shaun, 'Football as National Allegory: Al Ahram and the Olympics in 1920s Egypt', *History Compass* 7, 1 (2009), pp. 282–305; El-Zatmah, Shawki Ebeid, 'Aha Goal!: A Social and Cultural History of Football in Egypt', PhD diss., University of California, Los Angeles, 2014; Chehabi, Houchang, 'The Juggernaut of Globalization: Sport and Modernization in Iran', *The International Journal of the History of Sport* 19, 2–3 (2010), pp. 275–94; Fozooni, Babak, 'Religion, Politics and Class: Conflict, Contestation in the Development of Football in Iran', *Soccer and Society* 5, 3 (2004), pp. 356–70; Koyagi, Mikiya, 'Molding Future Soldiers and Mothers of the Iranian Nation: Gender and Physical Education under Reza Shah, 1921–41', *The International Journal of the History of Sport* 26, 11 (2009), pp. 1668–96; Schayegh, Cyrus, 'Sport, Health, and the Iranian Middle Class in the 1920s and the 1930s', *Iranian Studies* 35, 4 (2002), pp. 341–69; Sorek, Tamir, *Arab Soccer in a Jewish State: The Integrative Enclave*, Cambridge: Cambridge University Press, 2007; Spiegel, Nina S., *Embodying Hebrew Culture: Aesthetics, Athletics, and Dance in the Jewish Community of Mandate Palestine*, Detroit: Wayne State University Press, 2013; Khalidi, Issam, 'Body and Ideology: Early Athletics in Palestine (1900–1948)', *Jerusalem Quarterly* 27 (2006), pp. 44–58; Khalidi, Issam, 'Coverage of Sports News in 'Filistin', 1911–1948', *Jerusalem Quarterly* 44 (2010), pp. 45–69; Khalidi, Issam, 'Sports and Aspirations: Football in Palestine 1900–1948', *Jerusalem Quarterly* 58 (2014), pp. 74–89; Krawietz, Birgit, 'Sport and Nationalism in the Republic of Turkey', *The International Journal of the History of Sport* 31, 3 (2014), pp. 336–46; Akın, Yiğit, '*Gürbüz ve Yavuz Evlatlar:*' *Erken Cumhuriyet'te Beden*

Terbiyesi ve Spor, İstanbul: İletişim Yayınları, 2004; Cora, Yaşar Tolga, 'Constructing and Mobilizing the Nation through Sport: State, Physical Education, and Nationalism under the Young Turk Rule (1908–1918)', M.A. thesis, Central European University, 2007; and Yıldız, Murat C., 'Strengthening Male Bodies and Building Robust Communities: Physical Culture in the Late Ottoman Empire', PhD diss., University of California, Los Angeles, 2015.

11. For studies on the Arab world, see Amara, Mahfoud, *Sport, Politics and Society in the Arab World*, London: Palgrave Macmillan, 2012.

12. For studies of sports and football in the Middle East, respectively, see Raab, Alon K., 'Sport in the Middle East', in *The Oxford Handbook of Sports History*, eds. Robert Edelman and Wayne Wilson, Oxford University Press, 2017, pp. 287–300; Khalidi, Issam, and Alon K. Raab, *Soccer in the Middle East*, London and New York: Routledge, 2013; and Dorsey, James M., *The Turbulent World of Middle East Football*, London: C. Hurst & Co, 2016.

13. For a discussion about collective and individual reading practices, see Ayalon, Ami, *Reading Palestine: Printing and Literacy, 1900–1948*, Austin: University of Texas Press, 2004, pp. 79–131.

14. Goldstein, Laurence, *The Male Body: Features, Destinies, Exposures*, vol. 1, Ann Arbor: University of Michigan Press, 1994, p. 33.

15. For a discussion about the integration of the Middle East into the global world economy and nation-state system, see Gelvin, James L., *The Modern Middle East: A History*, 4th ed., Oxford: Oxford University Press, 2015.

16. See Yıldız, 'Strengthening Male Bodies and Building Robust Communities'.

17. See El-Zatmah, 'Aha Goal!'; Lopez, 'Football as National Allegory'; Raab, Alon K., 'Sport in the Middle East'.

18. See Chehabi, 'The Juggernaut of Globalization', 278; Fozooni, 'Religion, Politics and Class', pp. 356–70.

19. Russell, Mona, *Creating the New Egyptian Woman: Consumerism, Education, and National Identity, 1863–1922*, New York: Palgrave, 2004, p. 31.

20. Mak, Lanver, *The British in Egypt: Community, Crime, and Crisis, 1822–1922*, New York: I. B. Tauris. 2012, p. 94. Personal memoirs from the 1930s also reveal the importance of 'lawn tennis' for Britons in Egypt. Mabel Caillard writes, 'Everybody played [tennis]. Hostesses availed themselves a popular form of entertainment by holding their 'at homes' in the form of tennis days'. Mabel Caillard, *A Lifetime in Egypt, 1876–1835*, London: Grant Richards, 1935, p. 47. In addition to tennis, racing was very popular. Racing, according to William M. Welch, Jr., was 'the favorite spectator sport'. Welch, William M. Jr., *No Country For a Gentleman: British Rule in Egypt, 1883–1907*, New York: Greenwood Press, 1988, p. 33.

21. Ibid.

22. Khalidi, 'The Coverage of Sports News in "Filistin", 1911–1948', p. 46.

23. Ben Prestel, Joseph, *Emotional Cities: Debates on Urban Change in Berlin and Cairo, 1860–1910*, New York: Oxford University Press, 2017, p. 179; 'Nadi' [Club], *al-Hilal* (1 May 1904), p. 538.

24. Prestel, *Emotional Cities*, 179; 'Nadi,' *al-Hilal*, p. 538.

25. 'Umar discusses sports in his section 'need of the youth' (*haja al-shaban*) which was aimed at Egypt's middle stratum. 'Umar, Muhammad, *Hadir al-misriyyin aw sir ta'akhkhurihim* [The Present State of the Egyptians, or, the Cause of their Retrogression], Cairo: Matba'at al-Muqtataf, 1902, pp. 199–201. For a discussion about Muhammad Umar's book, see Lockman, Zachary, 'Imagining the Working Class: Culture, Nationalism, and Class Formation in Egypt, 1899–1914', *Poetics Today* 15, 2 (1994), pp. 157–190.

26. Musallam, Akram, ed., *Yawmiyyat Khalil al-Sakakini: yawmiyyat—rasa'il ve ta'ammulat. al-kitab al-awwal, New York, Sultana, Jerusalem, 1907–1912* [Diaries of Khalil al-Sakakini: Diaries, Letters, and Reflections. The First Book, New York, Sultana, Jerusalem, 1907–1912], Ramallah: Markaz Khalil al-Sakakini al-thaqafi, Mu'assasat al-dirasat al-qudsiyya, 2003, p. 340.

27. There were also important class distinctions across the region. For example, sociologist Tamir Sorek highlights the fact that many Arab sports clubs in Palestine attracted 'working-class individuals and petits bourgeois while the upper classes remained uninvolved'. Sorek, *Arab Soccer in a Jewish State*, p. 16.

28. For a discussion of Jewish sports clubs in urban centers of the Middle East, see Bashkin, Orit, *New Babylonians: A History of Jews in Modern Iraq*, Stanford: Stanford University Press, 2012, p. 61; Beinin, Joel, *The Dispersion of Egyptian Jewry: Culture, Politics, and the Formation of Modern Diaspora*, Los Angeles: University of California Press, 1998, p. 79, p. 120; Cabasso, Gilbert, *Juifs d'Egypte: Images et Textes*, Paris: Éditions du Scribe, 1984, p. 107, p. 171; Chehabi, Houchang E., 'Jews and Sport in Modern Iran', in *The History of Contemporary Iranian Jews*, eds. Homa Sarshar and Houman Sarshar, Beverly Hills: Center for Iranian Jewish Oral History, 2001, pp. 11–12; Krämer, Gudrun, *The Jews in Modern Egypt, 1914–1952*, New York: I.B. Tauris, 1989, p. 111, p. 180; Saposnik, Arieh Bruce, *Becoming Hebrew: The Creation of a Jewish National Culture in Ottoman Palestine*, New York: Oxford University Press, 2008, p. 116; Schulze, Kirsten E., *The Jews of Lebanon: Between Coexistence and Conflict*, Portland: Sussex Academic Press, 2001, pp. 48–53; and Yıldız, 'Strengthening Male Bodies and Building Robust Communities', chapter 2. Ofer Idel's dissertation at the Tel Aviv University, tentatively entitled, '*Atehlethim Ve-Halutzim: Aliyato Shel Ha-sport Ve-Hagof Ha-Tsyony Bpalestina, 1918–1939*' [Athletes and Pioneers: The Ascent of Modern Sport and the Zionist Body in Interwar Palestine], promises to offer insights into Jewish sports clubs in Mandate Palestine.

29. Many of the Maccabi clubs were Zionist. Nevertheless, it was only until the formation of the Maccabi World Union in the 1920s that institutional and ideolog-

ical connections were formally established. See Sorek, *Arab Soccer in a Jewish State*, pp. 16–17; Galily, Yair and Amir Ben-Porat, eds., *Sport, Politics and Society in the Land of Israel: Past and Present*, London and New York: Routledge, 2009; and Yıldız, Murat C., 'Discourses and Institutions of Sports in the Modern Middle East', in *Sports and Society in the Middle East*, eds. Hopkins, Nicholas S. and Sandrine Gamblin, Cairo Papers in Social Science 34, 2 (2016), pp. 12–47.

30. For example, see CZA A192/42 Letter from the Committee of Union Juive Sportive et Litteraire Macchabée to its members (15 November 1912).

31. *Al-Abtal* (11 March 1933), p. 22.

32. Toprak, Zafer, 'Istanbul'da Spor: Vay Em Si Ey (YMCA) Jimnastikhaneleri' [Sports in Istanbul: YMCA Gymnasiums], *Toplumsal Tarih* 2 (1994), pp. 8–12; Yıldız, 'Discourses and Institutions of Sports in the Modern Middle East'; and Sharkey, Heather J., *American Evangelicals in Egypt: Missionary Encounters in an Age of Empire*, Princeton: Princeton University Press, 2008.

33. Gershoni, Israel and James P. Jankowski, eds., *Redefining the Egyptian Nation, 1930–1945*, Cambridge: Cambridge University Press, 1995, p. 21; Baron, Beth, *The Orphan Scandal: Christian Missionaries and the Rise of the Muslim Brotherhood*, Stanford: Stanford University Press, 2014, p. 121.

34. Matthews, Weldon, *Confronting an Empire, Constructing a Nation: Arab Nationalists and Popular Politics in Mandate Palestine*, New York: I. B. Tauris, 2006, pp. 56–60.

35. For a discussion about sports in Ottoman and Egyptian government schools, see Yıldız, 'Discourses and Institutions of Sports in the Modern Middle East', pp. 12–47; Jacob, *Working Out Egypt*, p. 88.

36. See, for example, Prestel, *Emotional Cities*, 166–7;'Abd al-'Aziz Jawish, *Ghunyat al-mu'addibin fi al-turuq al-haditha lil-taribiyya wa-l-ta'lim* [Wealth of the educated in the current path for education], Cairo: Matba'at al-Hadiya, 1910.

37. Sadiq, Issa Khan, *Modern Persia and her Educational System*, PhD diss., Columbia University, 1931, pp. 79–80.

38. Ibid., p. 80.

39. Wasif Jawhariyyeh's memoirs refer to the school as the National Constitutional School (al-madrasa al-dusturiyya al-wataniyya). Wasif Jawhariyyeh, *Al-Quds al-'uthmaniyya fil-mudhakkirat al-Jawhariyyeh: Al-Kitab al-awwal min mudhakkirat al-musiqi Wasif Jawhariyyeh 1904–1917*, eds. Tamari, Salim and Issam Nassar [Ottoman Jerusalem in the memoirs of al-Jawhariyyeh: the First Book from the memoirs of the musician Wasif al-Jawhariyyeh, 1904–1917], Beirut: Mu'assasah al-dirasat al-Filastiniyya, 2005, p. 126.

40. Musallam, *Yawmiyyat Khalil al-Sakakini*, pp. 347–8.

41. Jawhariyyeh, *Al-Quds al-'uthmaniyya fil-mudhakkirat al-Jawhariyyeh*, p. 128.

42. Ibid., p. 127.

43. During the late nineteenth and early twentieth century, educators translated the

concept slightly differently. For example, al-Sakakini translates 'a sound mind [lives] in a sound body' as *al-'aql al-sahih fil-jism al-sahih*, whereas Jurj Atlas, a Syrian educator living in Brazil and writing in Arabic, renders the concept as *'al-'aql al-salim fil-jism al-salim'*. For Atlas' use of the mantra in Arabic, see Fahrenthold, Stacy, 'Sound Minds in Sound Bodies: Transnational Philanthropy and Patriotic Masculinity in al-Nadi al-Homsi and Syrian Brazil, 1920–1932', *International Journal of Middle East Studies* 46, 2 (2014), pp. 259–83. For the localization and spread of the maxim in Iran, see Schayegh, Cyrus, '"A Sound Mind lives in a Healthy Body": Texts and Contexts in the Iranian Modernists' Scientific Discourse of Health, 1910s–40s', *International Journal of Middle East Studies* 37 (2005), pp. 167–88.

44. There is a large literature on the AIU. See, for example, Laskier, Michael M., *The Alliance Israélite Universelle and the Jewish Communities of Morocco: 1862–1962*, Albany: State University of New York Press, 1983; Rodrigue, Aron, *French Jews, Turkish Jews: The Alliance Israélite Universelle and the Politics of Jewish Schooling in Turkey, 1860–1925*, Bloomington: Indiana University Press, 1990; Sciarcon, Jonathan, *Educational Oases in the Desert: The Alliance Israelite Universelle's Girls' Schools in Ottoman Iraq, 1895–1915*, Albany: State University of New York Press, 2017; and Cohen, Avraham, 'Iranian Jewry and the Educational Endeavors of the Alliance Israélite Universelle', *Jewish Social Studies* 48, 1 (1986), pp. 15–44.

45. *Instructions Générales pour les Professeurs*, Paris, 1903, p. 47.

46. Ibid.

47. 'Mr. V. Everit Macy Makes Gift to Build New Athletic Field', *The News Letter—Robert College, Constantinople Women's College, American University of Beirut*, March 1924.

48. Ibid.

49. Note, Howard Bliss is referring to soccer, not American football.

50. Bliss, Howard, 'Sunshine in Turkey', *National Geographic Magazine* (20 January 1909), p. 75.

51. Ibid. Bliss more than likely was not exaggerating when he wrote this.

52. Schayegh, 'Sport, Health, and the Iranian Middle Class in the 1920s and the 1930s', p. 22.

53. 'Basket Ball is A.U.C. Major Sport', *The A.U.C. Review* (1 November 1927), p. 4.

54. 'Basketball Schedule to December 31', *The A.U.C. Review* (13 December 1926), p. 4.

55. 'Football Coach is Encouraged, He Says—Prospects for Season are Fair, is Belief', *The A.U.C. Review* (29 November 1926), p. 3.

56. For a discussion about the emergence of basketball at the American University of Beirut, see McClenahan, William, 'Lebanese Sport from a Basketball Perspective', MA thesis, American University of Beirut, 2007.

57. Jacob, *Working Out Egypt*, p. 80; Al-doktor 'Abd al-Aziz 'Abd al-Mowjud, 'al-riyada al-badaniyya 'and al-masriyyin al-qudama' [Physical Exercise among the Ancient Egyptians], *al-Hilal* (1 April 1902), pp. 403–6.

58. The press in postwar Beirut and Damascus also featured magazines devoted to sports. See Elizabeth Thompson, *Colonial Citizens: Republican Rights, Paternal Privilege, and Gender in French Syria and Lebanon*, New York: Columbia University Press, 2000, p. 212.

59. For example, *Al-Musawar* (the illustrated), one of Egypt's leading illustrated weekly magazines, ran a sports edition, entitled '*al-musawar al-riyadi*' (sports illustrated), *Al-Musawar* (9 January 1931).

60. Jacob, Wilson C., 'Overcoming Simply Being: Straight Sex, Masculinity, and Physical Culture in Egypt', *Gender and History* 22, 3 (2010), pp. 1–19; Schayegh, 'Sport, Health, and the Iranian Middle Class in the 1920s and the 1930s'.

61. Ibid., 14. This process was inextricably connected to the merging of the sacred and the profane through the construction of the concept of physical culture as *al-riyada al-badaniyya*, in Arabic. See Jacob, *Working Out Egypt*, pp. 72–3.

62. Koyagi, 'Molding Future Soldiers and Mothers of the Iranian Nation'; Schayegh, 'Sport, Health, and the Iranian Middle Class in the 1920s and the 1930s'.

63. Asıf, Burhan, 'Nasıl Futbol Oynuyoruz?' [How Do We Play Football?], *Spor Alemi* (30 November 1920), pp. 8–9.

64. 'Tarbiyya al-badaniyya' [Physical Training], *Al-Abtal* (4 February 1933), p. 10.

65. 'Athar al-Riyada fil-Akhlaq' [Effects of Sports on Morality], *al-Abtal* (14 January 1933), p. 1.

66. Ibid.

67. Ibid.

68. See, for example, *Spor Alemi* (8 July 1925).

69. Frierson, Elizabeth B., *Unimagined Communities: State, Press, and Gender in the Hamidian Era*, PhD diss., Princeton University, 1996.

70. 'İstanbul Kız Lisesi'nde Spor' [Sports in Istanbul Girls' High School], *Spor Alemi* (3 March 1926), pp. 10–11.

71. 'Afdal anwa' al-riyada lil-nisa' [Best type of sports for women], *al-Muqtataf* (June 1920), p. 529.

72. Ibid.

73. Koyagi, 'Molding Future Soldiers and Mothers of the Iranian Nation', p. 1683.

74. Schayegh, 'Sport, Health, and the Iranian Middle Class in the 1920s and the 1930s', p. 13; Koyagi, 'Molding Future Soldiers and Mothers of the Iranian Nation', p. 1674.

75. For a discussion about the transnational spread of ideas, practices, and institutions in the *mahjar*, see Arsan, Andrew, John Karam, and Akram Khater, 'On Forgotten Shores: Migration in Middle East Studies and the Middle East in Migration Studies', *Mashriq&Mahjar* 1, 1 (2013), pp. 1–7; Arsan, Andrew, '"This Age is the

Age of Associations": Committees, Petitions, and the Roots of Interwar Middle Eastern Internationalism', *Journal of Global History* 7, 2 (2012), pp. 166–88; Bailony, Reem, 'Transnationalism and the Syrian Migrant Community: The Case of the 1925 Syrian Revolt', *Mashriq&Mahjar* 1, 1 (2013), pp. 8–29; Balloffet, Lily Pearl, 'From the Pampa to the Mashriq: Arab-Argentine Philanthropy Networks', *Mashriq&Mahjar* 4, 1 (2017), pp. 4–28; Fahrenthold, Stacy, 'Sound Minds in Sound Bodies: Transnational Philanthropy and Patriotic Masculinity in al-Nadi al-Homsi and Syrian Brazil, 1920–1932', *International Journal of Middle East Studies* 46, 2 (2014), pp. 259–83.

76. Fahrenthold, 'Sound Minds in Sound Bodies', p. 275.

77. For a more extensive treatment of *al-Abtal*, *al-Riyada al-Badaniyya*, and the presence semi-nude male bodies, see Jacob, *Working Out Egypt*, pp. 142–55.

78. *Al-Abtal* (28 January 1933), p. 20.

79. Ibid.

80. *Al-Abtal* created an entire section dedicated to sports in Iraq: 'al-Riyada fil-'Iraq' [Sports in Iraq], *Al-Abtal* (14 January 1933), p. 21.

81. For a discussion on the emergence, dissemination, and growing popularity of the sportsman genre of photography among Muslims, Christians, and Jews of late Ottoman Empire, see Yıldız, Murat C., '"What is a Beautiful Body?" Late Ottoman "Sportsman" Photographs and New Notions of Male Corporeal Beauty' in 'Critical Histories of Photography in the Middle East', Special Issue of the *Middle East Journal of Culture and Communication* 8, 2–3 (2015), pp. 192–214.

82. Baun, Dylan, 'Lebanon's Youth Clubs and the 1936 Summer Olympics: Mobilizing Sports, Challenging Imperialism and Launching a National Project', *The International Journal of the History of Sport* 34, 13 (2017), pp. 1347–65.

83. Lopez, *'Football as National Allegory'*.

84. Dolbee, Samuel, *'Mandatory Body Building, Nationalism, Masculinities, Class*, and *Physical Activity* in 1930s *Syria'*, M.A. Thesis, Georgetown University, 2009.

85. Yildiz, 'Discourses and Institutions of Sports in the Modern Middle East'.

86. Sorek, *Arab Soccer in a Jewish State*; Khalidi, 'Coverage of Sports News in Filistin, 1911–1948'.

87. Schayegh, 'Sport, Health, and the Iranian Middle Class in the 1920s and the 1930s'.

88. See Ayalon, *Reading Palestine*.

89. The February 1926 'Cairo Football Calendar', for example, consisted of games played in the Cairo Military Football League, the Command Cup, Sultan's Cup, YMCA, and other matches, *The Egyptian Gazette* (19 February 1926), p. 5.

90. For a discursive reading of Egypt's performance at the Olympics in 1924, see Lopez, 'Football as National Allegory'; Jacob, *Working Out Egypt*; and Baun, 'Lebanon's Youth Clubs and the 1936 Summer Olympics'.

91. For a discussion about department stores in Egypt, see Reynolds, Nancy Y., 'Entangled Communities: Interethnic Relationships among Urban Salesclerks and

Domestic Workers in Egypt, 1927–1961', *The European Review of History/Revue européenne d'histoire* 19, 1 (2012), pp. 113–39.

92. *Spor Alemi* (19 April 1922), p. 10.

93. For a discussion about the store, see Abdulhaq, Najat, *Jewish and Greek Communities in Egypt: Entrepreneurship and Business before Nasser*, New York: I.B. Tauris, 2016.

94. *Program Fifth Annual Sports Day of the College of Arts and Sciences of the American University at Cairo* (1925), advertisement section.

95. Ibid.

96. Khalidi, Walid, *Before their Diaspora: A Photographic History of the Palestinians, 1876–1948*, Washington, D.C.: Institute for Palestine Studies, 1991; Tamari, Salim, *The Great War and the Remaking of Palestine*, Berkeley & Los Angeles: the University of California Press, 2017, pp. 53–57.

97. The two most important were Union Club and Taksim Stadium. Union Club predates Taksim Stadium; however, Taksim Stadium became the more popular venue during the Allied occupation of the city from 1918 until 1923.

98. El-Zatmah, 'Aha Goal!'; Dolbee, 'Mandatory Body Building'.

99. El-Zatmah, 'Aha Goal!'

100. 'Football', *The Egyptian Gazette* (11 February 1918), p. 5.

101. Presented and annotated by Rifat N. Bali, *Sports and Physical Education in Turkey in the 1930s: a Report by Eugene M. Hinkle*, Istanbul: The Isis Press, 2009, p. 46.

102. Ibid., 47.

103. 'Egyptian Football: Prince Farouk's Cup Final', *The Egyptian Gazette* (28 March 1925), p. 5.

104. Ibid.

105. See, for example, Cromer, Lord, *Modern Egypt*, New York: The Macmillan Company, 1916. Cromer, who was the British agent and consul general of Egypt from 1883 to 1907, often refers to fundamental differences between Europeans and people of the East. For a discussion about the transitional state of Egypt, see Cromer's reference to Stephen Cave, a British official who had been sent to Cairo to write a report on the financial state of Egypt: 'Egypt may be said to be in a transitional state, and she suffers from the defects of the system out of which she is passing, as well as from those of the system into which she is attempting to enter. She suffers from the ignorance, dishonesty, waste, and extravagance of the East, such as have brought her suzerain to the verge of ruin, and at the same time from the vast expense caused by hasty and inconsiderate endeavors to adopt the civilisation of the West', *Modern Egypt*, p. 4.

106. 'Neutral Referees: Dissatisfaction in Cairo Match', *The Egyptian Gazette* (13 February 1924), p. 5.

107. Ibid.

108. Ibid.

109. 'Football in Cairo: E.S.R.I V. R.A.F. Eleven—Abandoned', *The Egyptian Gazette* (1 March 1924), p. 5.

110. Ibid.

111. See, for example, Faraj, Al-Sayid, *Kabtin Masr: Hussein Higazi* [Captain Egypt: Hussein Higazi], Cairo: al-Majlis al-A'la li-Ri'ayat al-Shabab, 1961.

112. This discussion about punctuality in sports can contribute to the literature on temporality in the Middle East. For example, see Barak, On, *On Time: Technology and Temporality in Modern Egypt*, Los Angeles: University of California Press, 2013; Wishnitzer, Avner, *Reading Clocks, Alla Turca: Time and Society in the Late Ottoman Empire*, Chicago: Chicago University Press, 2015; and Ogle, Vanessa, *The Global Transformation of Time 1870–1950*, Cambridge: Harvard University Press, 2015.

113. Ibid. 'Maalesh', according to many nineteenth- and twentieth-century descriptions of Egypt, meant 'it does not matter'. See, for example, Griffiths, Arthur, 'Egyptian Prisons', *The North American Review* 165, 490 (1897), p. 282; Madden, R. R., M. D., *Travels in Turkey, Egypt, Nubia and Palestine: In 1824, 1825, 1826, and 1827*, London: Whittaker Treacher, and Co., 1883, p. 319; and Cocteau, Jean, *Maalesh: A Theatrical Tour in the Middle-East*, P. Owen, 1956.

114. For a discussion about the discursive framing of Egypt's participation in the Olympics, see Lopez, Shaun, 'Football as National Allegory', pp. 282–305.

115. Ibid.

116. 'Avrupalılar Türkleri nasıl biliyorlar?' [How do Europeans know Turks], *Spor Alemi* (8 February 1922), p. 2.

117. 'Umar, *Hadir al-misriyyin aw sir ta'akhkhurihim*, p. 199.

118. Sorek, *Arab Soccer in a Jewish State*, p. 24.

1119. Khuri-Makdisi, *The Eastern Mediterranean and the Making of Global Radicalism*, pp. 26–27.

2. FOOTBALL'S ROLE IN HOW SOCIETIES REMEMBER: THE SYMBOLIC WARS OF JORDANIAN–PALESTINIAN FOOTBALL

1. Halbwachs, Maurice, *Collective Memory*, Chicago: Chicago University Press, 1992.

2. Ibid.

3. Olick, Jeffrey K., and Joyce Robbins, 'Social Memory Studies: From "Collective Memory" to the Historical Sociology of Mnemonic Practices', *Annual Review of Sociology* 24, (1998), p. 133.

4. Olick and Robbins, 'Social Memory Studies', p. 126.

5. Among the exceptions are: King, Anthony, 'Violent Pasts: Collective Memory and Football Hooliganism', *The Sociological Review* 49, 4 (2001), pp. 568–85; Robson, Garry, *No One Likes Us, We Don't Care: The Myth and Reality of Millwall Fandom*, Oxford: Berg, 2000.

6. Gilen, Signe, Are Hovenak, Rania Maktabi, Jon Pedersen, and Dag Tuastad, *Finding Ways: Palestinian Coping Strategies in Changing Environments*, Oslo: Fafo, 1994.

7. Tuastad, Dag, 'The Political Role of Football for Palestinians in Jordan', in *Entering the Field: New Perspectives on World Football*, ed. Gary Armstrong and Richard Giulianotti, Oxford: Berg Publishers, 1997, pp. 105–22.

8. Tuastad, Dag, 'From Football Riot to Revolution. The Political Role of Football in the Arab World', *Soccer and Society* 14, 2 (February 2013), pp. 1–13; Tuastad, Dag, '"A Threat to National Unity"—Football in Jordan: Ethnic Divisive or a Political Tool for the Regime?' *The International Journal of the History of Sport* 31, 14 (July 2014), pp. 1774–88; Tuastad, Dag, 'The Challenges of Managing Sport in a Divided Society', in *Managing Sport: Social and Cultural Perspectives*, ed. David Hassan and Jim Lusted, New York: Routledge, 2013, pp. 171–85.

9. *Mulukhiya* is a plant-based stew popular in the Middle East, North Africa, and Eastern Mediterranean.

10. Cleveland, William L., *A History of the Modern Middle East*, Oxford: Westview Press, 2000, pp. 347.

11. Rogan, Eugene, *The Arabs: A History*, New York: Basic Books, 2009, pp. 345.

12. Sayigh, Yezid, *Armed Struggle and the Search for State: The Palestinian National Movement, 1949–1993*, Oxford: Oxford University Press, 1997.

13. On the Palestinian quest for victory, see chapter 10 in Sorek, Tamir, *Palestinian Commemoration in Israel: Calendars, Monuments, and Martyrs*, Stanford: Stanford University Press, 2015, pp. 199–216.

14. Tuastad, 'The Political Role of Football,' 114.

15. Interview by author with Sobhi Ibrahim, Vice President of Wihdat, Amman, June 1997.

16. Brand, Laurie A., *Palestinians in the Arab World: Institution Building and the Search for State*, New York: Colorado University Press, 1988, p. 53.

17. Alon, Yoav, *The Making of Jordan*, London: I. B. Tauris, 2009.

18. Ibid., p. 157.

19. Ibid., p. 152.

20. Watson, Russel, 'A Lion in Winter', *Newsweek*, 7 February 1999, www.newsweek.com/lion-winter-169032; Wurmser, David, 'The Forces that Brought Crown Prince Hassan Down', *Behind the News in Israel*, 2 February 1999, http://israel-behindthenews.com/the-forces-the-brought-crown-prince-hassan-down/3126/.

21. Tell, Tariq, 'Early Spring in Jordan: The Revolt of the Military Veterans', *Carnegie Middle East Center*, 4 November 2015, http://carnegieendowment.org/files/ACMR_Tell_Jordan_Eng_final.pdf, last accessed 23 January 2019.

22. 'Jordanian Football Game Halted Amidst Anti-Regime Chants, Hooliganism Towards Palestinians', WikiLeaks Updates, 7 December 2010, http://wikileaks-supdates.blogspot.com/2010/12/jordanian-soccer-game-halted-amidst.html; last

accessed 23 January 2019; Jacobson, Philip 'Jordan Cracks Down amid Fears of Spreading Palestinian Unrest,' *The Telegraph*, 10 June 2001, www.telegraph.co.uk/news/worldnews/middleeast/jordan/1309922/Jordan-cracks-down-amid-fears-of-spreading-Palestinian-unrest.html, last accessed 23 January 2019.

23. Raed Omari, 'Probe Continues into Friday Football-related Violence', *Jordan Times*, 12 December 2010, www.jordantimes.com/?news=32549, last accessed 23 Jan, 2019.

24. Roey Simioni, 'Queen Rania is a Corrupt Thief,' *Ynet.news.com*, 14 February 2011, www.ynetnews.com/articles/0,7340,L-4028607,00.html.

25. Simioni, 'Queen Rania is a Corrupt Thief.'

26. Interview with author, Amman, March, 2011.

27. Although the Palestinians constitute a majority of the Jordanian population, only 25 percent of the parliament may be elected from the areas where Palestinians live. Within the ethnic homogenous Karak electoral district there are 50,000 inhabitants who elect six members to the parliament (only East Bankers). From the largely homogenous Palestinian electoral district of Zarqa, 500,000 Palestinians elect seven representatives. In other words, the vote of one East Banker equals ten Palestinian votes. See Adnan Abu-Odeh, *Jordanians, Palestinians, and the Hashemite Kingdom in the Middle East Peace Process* (Washington, DC: United States Institute of Peace Press, 1999), 250.

28. Daoud Kuttab, 'Jordan, Fatah's Achilles' Heel,' *Al Monitor*, 29 November 2016, www.al-monitor.com/pulse/en/originals/2016/11/palestine-fatah-seventh-congress-jordan-tension.html.

29. Interview with author, Amman, May 2014.

30. Lapidoth, Ruth, 'A Recent Agreement on the Holy Places in Jerusalem', *Israel Journal of Foreign Affairs* 7, 3 (2013), p. 65.

31. Groisman, Maayan, 'After Losing to a Palestinian-affiliated Team, Jordanian Soccer Fans Chant Pro-Israeli Slogans', *Jerusalem Post*, 2 May 2016, www.jpost.com/Middle-East/After-losing-to-a-Palestinian-affiliated-team-Jordanian-soccer-fans-chant-pro-Israel-slogans-452859, last accessed 23 January 2019.

32. Conversation with contributor to Wihdat's official magazine who also handed me a copy of the magazine with a picture showing the burning incident, Amman, May 2014.

33. Tuastad, 'A Threat to National Unity.'

34. McDonald, David A., 'Poetics and the Performance of Violence in Israel/Palestine', *Ethnomusicology* 53, 1 (2009), pp. 58–85.

35. McDonald, David A., *My Voice Is My Weapon: Music, Nationalism and the Poetics of Palestinian Resistance*, Durham, NC: Duke University Press, 2014), pp. 64–5.

36. Cleveland, *A History*, p. 347.

37. Barakat, Halim, *The Arab World: Society, Culture, and State*, Durham, NC: University of California Press, 1993, p. 55.

38. Swedenburg, Ted, 'The Palestinian Peasant as National Signifier', *Anthropological Quarterly* 63, 1 (1990), p. 22.

39. Abu-Odeh, *Jordanians, Palestinians*, p. 253.

40. Delgado, Fernando, 'Sport and Politics: Major League Soccer, Constitution, and (the) Latino Audience(s)', *Journal of Sport and Social Issues* 23, 1 (1999), p. 41; Stroeken, Koen, 'Why "the World" Loves Watching Football (and "the Americans" Don't),' *Anthropology Today* 18, 3 (2002), pp. 9–13.

41. Archetti, Eduardo and Romero, Amílcar G., 'Death and Violence in Argentinian Football', in *Football, Violence and Social Identity*, ed. Richard Guilianotti, London: Routledge, 1994, p. 39.

3. HAPOEL TEL AVIV AND ISRAELI LIBERAL SECULARISM

1. Smooha, Sammy, *Still Playing by the Rules: Index of Arab-Jewish Relations in Israel 2012*, Jerusalem: The Israel Democracy Institute and University of Haifa, 2013.

2. Elias, Norbert and Elias Dunning, *Quest for Excitement: Sport and Leisure in the Civilising Process*, Oxford: Blackwell, 1986.

3. Ben Porat, Amir, *Ho, eizo milhama me'aneget: ohadei kaduregel yisraelim* [*Oh, such a delighted war: Israelis football fans*], Haifa: Pardes, 2007, p. 24.

4. The survey was conducted by Avichai Shuv Ami from the College of Management at Tel Aviv.

5. Data courtesy of the Guttman Center for Public Opinion and Policy Research at the Israel Democracy Institute.

6. Shafir, Gershon, and Yoav Peled, *Being Israeli: The Dynamics of Multiple Citizenship*, Cambridge and New York: Cambridge University Press, 2002.

7. Sternhell, Zeev, *The Founding Myths of Israel: Nationalism, Socialism, and the Making of the Jewish State*, Princeton, NJ: Princeton University Press, 1998.

8. For some indications of the association between religiosity and an exclusionary vision of citizenship, see Hermann, Tamar, Chanan Cohen, Ella Heller, and Dana Bublil, *The Israeli Democracy Index 2015*, Jerusalem: The Guttman Center for Public Opinion and Policy Research, 2015, https://en.idi.org.il/media/3585/democracy_index_2015_eng.pdf, last accessed 23 January 2019.

9. De Picciotto, Motti, 'Ha-smalim ha-hadashim: seqer ha-ohadim ha-gadol shel ligat ha-'al', [The New Symbols: the Great Premier League Fan Survey], *Walla*, 2 April 2014, http://sports.walla.co.il/?w=/7/2734410, last accessed 23 January 2019.

10. 'Maccabi' is the singular form of the people known in English as Maccabees, warriors in ancient Judaea who overthrew Greek-Syrian rule around 165 BCE. The Hannukah holiday was born from this revolt.

11. Ben-Porat, Amir, 'The Commodification of Football in Israel', *International Review for the Sociology of Sport* 33, 3 (1998), pp. 269–76.

12. The Ultras phenomenon has different origins, mainly in Brazil and Italy. In Italy, they have existed since the 1950s and they gradually globalized since the 1980s.

13. Interview with the author, 21 January 2013.

14. See 'Antifa Football Teams', Facebook, www.facebook.com/AntifaFootballTeams. AFT, last accessed 23 January 2019.

15. Between 1995 and 2015, Hapoel Tel Aviv represented Israel sixteen times in various European competitions, and in the 2001–2002 season the team reached the UEFA Cup quarter-final.

16. The main motivation for this support was their objection to the mayor, Ron Huldai, because of his decision to destroy the historical auditorium of the basketball club. Anger at this move enabled Hanin to get support from larger circles of Hapoel fans, beyond the ideologically committed Ultras. Hanin got 34 percent of the votes and lost the elections. For more on the political activism of the Ultras, see Daniel Regev, '"meyatsgim et Hapoel ve-lo et yisrael"' [We represent Hapoel and not Israel] in *Kaduregel Shayakh La-Ohadim!* [Football belongs to the fans!], ed. Tamar Rapoport, Resling, 2016, pp. 149–178.

17. Shlomo Resnik, 'Agudat ha-sport beitar—sport u-politiqa be-hevra mefuleget' [The sport association Beitar: Sport and politics and a divided society], in *Tarbut ha-guf ve-hasport be-yisrael ba-meah ha-'esrim* [Body culture and sport in Israel in the twentieth century], eds. Haim Kaufman and Hagai Harif, Jerusalem: Yad Ben-Zvi 2002, pp. 159–183.

18. The data is based on an online survey conducted in September 2012 by Avichai Shuv Ami and Tamir Sorek. The sample included 500 respondents who constitute a representative sample of the adult Hebrew-speaking population in Israel.

19. See the documentary movie on Betar, *Forever Pure*, Yes Docu, Duckin' & Divin' Films, and Maya Films, directed by Maya Zinshtein, 2016.

20. Ben Porat, *Ho, eizo milhama me'aneget*, p. 191.

21. Betar and Kach share the same colors, black and yellow. It is likely that when Kach was founded in 1971 by the Jewish American Rabbi Meir Kahana his choice of color was not incidental.

22. Peled, Yoav, 'Labor Market Segmentation and Ethnic Conflict: The Social Basis of Right-wing Politics in Israel', in *The Elections in Israel 1988*, eds. Asher Arian and Michal Shamir, Boulder: Westview Press, 1990, pp. 93–113.

23. Shohat, Ella, 'Sephardim in Israel: Zionism from the Standpoint of Its Jewish Victims', *Social Text* 19–20 (1988), pp. 1–35.

24. Regev, 'meyatsgim et Hapoel ve-lo et yisrael,' p. 155

25. On the marginality of Arab citizens in Israeli basketball, see Tamir Sorek, 'Sport, Palestine, and Israel', in *A Companion to Sport*, eds. David L. Andrews and Ben Carrington, Oxford, UK: John Wiley & Sons, 2010, pp. 257–69.

26. See the project website, 'Homepage', Mifalot Education and Society Enterprises, http://mifalot.co.il, last accessed 23 January 2019.

27. Hermann, Cohen, Heller, and Bublil, *The Israeli Democracy Index 2015*.
28. About 8 percent of Israeli Jews defined themselves as Haredim, commonly translated as ultra-Orthodox. These people are strictly observant of Jewish religious law and highly segregated from the rest of society. The Haredi group arose in reaction to secular Enlightenment, its members sharply separating themselves from both non-Jews and relatively assimilated Jews.
29. Sometimes referred to as national-religious or Zionist-religious, Israeli Jews who view themselves as 'religious' constitute between 10 and 12 percent of the Jewish population. The origins of this group are found in those parts of the Jewish Orthodoxy reacting moderately to the Enlightenment and later adopting Zionism—aspects that distance them from the ultra-Orthodox.
30. The 'traditional' Jew is a relatively recent invention, a category aimed at covering the large 'grey' area between religious and non-religious. See Yaacov Yadgar and Charles Liebman, 'Me-'ever la-dikhotomya dati-hiloni: ha-masortiyim be-yisrael' [Beyond the religious-secular dichotomy: Masortim in Israel], in *Yisrael Ve-Hamoderniyut* [Israeli and modernity], eds. Uri Cohen, Eliezer Ben Rafael, Avi Bareli and Ephraim Ya'ar, Jerusalem: The Ben Gurion Research Institute for the Study of Israel and Zionism, 2006, pp. 337–366.
31. Ibid.
32. Ram, Uri, 'Jerusalem, Tel Aviv and the Bifurcation of Israel', *International Journal of Politics, Culture and Society* 19, 1/2 (2005), pp. 21–33.
33. Author's translation of 'simu et yerushalayim be-yarden', [Put Jerusalem in Jordan], YouTube, 2010, www.youtube.com/watch?v=Z7-keT45suI, last accessed 23 January 2019.
34. Sorek, Tamir, 'Between Football and Martyrdom: The Bi-focal Localism of an Arab-Palestinian Town in Israel', *British Journal of Sociology* 56, 4 (2005), pp. 635–61.
35. Regev, 'meyatsgim et Hapoel ve-lo et yisrael.'
36. Zertal, Idith, *Israel's Holocaust and the Politics of Nationhood*, Cambridge and New York: Cambridge University Press, 2005.
37. Liebman, Charles and Eliezer Don-Yehiye, *Civil Religion in Israel: Traditional Judaism and Political Culture in the Jewish State*, Berkeley and Los Angeles: University of California Press, 1983.
38. Zertal, *Israel's Holocaust*.
39. Swidler, Ann, 'Culture in Action: Symbols and Strategies', *American Sociological Review* 51, 2 (1986), pp. 273–86.
40. Eran, Shor, 'Utilizing Rights and Wrongs: Right-wing, the 'Right' Language, and Human Rights in the Gaza Disengagement', *Sociological Perspectives* 51, 4 (2008), pp. 803–26.
41. Rimon-Or, Anat, 'Mi-mot ha-'aravi ad 'mavet la-'aravim': ha-yehudi ha-moderni mul ha-'aravi ha-hai be-tokho' [From the death of the Arab to 'death for the Arabs':

221

The modern Jew and the Arab who lives inside him], *Teorya u-Viqoret* 20 [Theory and criticism 20] (2002), pp. 23–56.

42. 'Im yatsi'a shar shoah le-makabi zo lo 'avera,' [If the audience in the bleacher sings a holocaust song, it is not a crime], *Walla*, 9 November 2011, http://sports.walla.co.il/item/1875623, last accessed 23 January 2019.

43. Clip uploaded by Yahav Marom to YouTube, 1 May 2007, www.youtube.com/watch?v=ZPVa8pQW4F4, last accessed 23 January 2019.

44. A commonly parodied clip from the film *Downfall*, based on the scene where Hitler receives news of the advancing Red Army, in which subtitles from the original movie are replaced with different ones.

45. Author's translation of Salonim, Amit, 'Auschwitz Biblumfield: Eikh kavshu bituyey ha-sina et ha-yetsi'im', [Auschwitz in Bloomfield: How hate expressions conquered the bleachers], *Mako*, 11 April 2010, www.mako.co.il/Sports-football-il/premier-league/Article-4a3332d7ff4c021006.htm, last accessed 23 January 2019.

46. Sorek, Tamir and Alin M. Ceobanu, 'Religiosity, National Identity, and Legitimacy: Israel as an Extreme Case', *Sociology* 43, 3 (2009), pp. 477–96.

47. A survey conducted by Israel Democracy Institute's Guttman Center for Surveys in 2009, N=2803.

48. 'The Social Survey Table Generator of the Israeli Central Bureau of Statistics,' Central Bureau of Statistics, http://surveys.cbs.gov.il/Survey/surveyE.htm, last accessed 23 January 2019.

49. Ibid.

50. Claire Mitchell, 'The Religious Content of Ethnic Identities', *Sociology* 40, 6 (2006), pp. 1137.

51. Sorek and Ceobanu, 'Religiosity, National Identity, and Legitimacy.'

52. Liebman and Don-Yehiye, *Civil Religion in Israel*.

53. Kimmerling, Baruch, 'Religion, Nationalism and Democracy in Israel', *Constellations* 6, 3 (1999), pp. 339–63.

54. Kimmerling, 'Religion, Nationalism and Democracy in Israel', pp. 341.

55. Liebman and Don-Yehiye, *Civil Religion in Israel*, p. 129.

56. Ibid., p. 131.

4. QATARI FEMALE FOOTBALLERS: NEGOTIATING GENDERED EXPECTATIONS

1. Bayat, Asef, *Life as Politics: How Ordinary People Change the Middle East*, Amsterdam: Amsterdam University Press, 2013, pp. 116.

2. Whannel, Garry, *Culture, Politics and Sport: Blowing the Whistle, Revisited*, London: Routledge, 2008.

3. Jayne Caudwell, 'Gender, Feminism and Football Studies', *Soccer & Society* 12, 3 (2011), pp. 330–44.

4. For discussions on football and identity relating to the Middle East, see Tuastad, Dag, 'From Football Riot to Revolution: The Political Role of Football in the Arab World', *Soccer & Society* 15, 3 (2014), pp. 376–88; Stevenson, Thomas B., and Abdul Karim Alaug, 'Football in Newly United Yemen: Rituals of Equity, Identity, and State Formation', *Journal of Anthropological Research* 56, 4 (2000), pp. 453–75.

5. Web Desk, 'Seven Reasons Why World Cup 2022 in Qatar will be more Sand than Sail', *Tribune*, 2 March 2015, www.tribune.com.pk/story/846587/seven-reasons-why-world-cup-2022-in-qatar-will-be-more-sand-than-sail, last accessed 23 January 2019; Joe Hall, 'Qatar 2022 World Cup: The Six Biggest Problems with the Controversial Tournament', *CITYA.M.*, 25 February 2015, www.cityam.com/210256/qatar-2022-world-cup-eight-biggest-problems-controversial-tournament, last accessed 23 January 2019; John Duerden, 'Qatar's World Cup Résumé: Zero Games. 2022 Host' *The New York Times*, 1 April 2017, www.nytimes.com/2017/04/01/sports/soccer/qatar-world-cup-2022.html, last accessed 23 January 2019; Robert Booth, '"We will be Ready, Inshallah": Inside Qatar's $200bn World Cup', *The Guardian*, 14 November 2015, www.theguardian.com/football/2015/nov/14/qatar-world-cup-200-billion-dollar-gamble, last accessed 23 January 2019.

6. Ministry of Development Planning and Statistics, *Sports in Qatari Society: A Statistical Overview*, 2016, www.mdps.gov.qa/en/statistics/Statistical%20Releases/Social/Sport/2016/Sport_In_Qatar_2016_En.pdf, last accessed 23 January 2019.

7. For a discussion of Qatari sports investments and the FIFA 2022 World Cup, see Lysa, Charlotte, 'Gåten Qatar 2022', [The Qatar 2022 Enigma] *Babylon—Nordic Journal for Middle East Studies* 1 (2016) (in Norwegian); Brannagan, Paul Michael and Richard Giulianotti, 'Soft Power and Soft Disempowerment: Qatar, Global Sport and Football's 2022 World Cup Finals', *Leisure Studies* 34, 6 (2015), pp. 703–19; Reiche, Danyel, 'Investing in Sporting Success as a Domestic and Foreign Policy Tool: The Case of Qatar', *International Journal of Sport Policy and Politics* 7, 4 (2015), pp. 489–504; Dorsey, James M., 'The 2022 World Cup: A Potential Monkey Wrench for Change', *The International Journal of the History of Sport* 31, 14 (2014), pp. 1739–54; Scharfenort, Nadine, 'Urban Development and Social Change in Qatar: The Qatar National Vision 2030 and the 2022 FIFA World Cup', *Journal of Arabian Studies* 2, 2 (2012), pp. 209–30.

8. 'Women and Sport', Qatar Olympic Committee, www.olympic.qa/en/SportInQatar/Pages/WomenAndSport.aspx, last accessed 12 November 2016.

9. Kelly Knez, Tansin Benn, and Sara Alkhaldi, 'World Cup Football as a Catalyst for Change: Exploring the Lives of Women in Qatar's First National Football Team—a Case Study,' *The International Journal of the History of Sport* 31, no. 14 (2014): 1755–73.

10. 'Reem,' working with the national women's team, interview with the author, October 2016.

11. All names have been changed for the sake of anonymity. The majority of the interviews were carried out in public or semi-private places, and lasted around an hour.

12. Bernard, H. Russell, *Research Methods in Anthropology: Qualitative and Quantitative Approaches*, Lanham, MD: Rowman Altamira, 2011.

13. Education City is a campus in Doha, and the site for a number of foreign and local universities. It is an initiative of the nonprofit, government supported Qatar Foundation (QF), and includes Hamad bin Khalifa University (HBKU).

14. Asrar, Shakeeb, 'Education City Student Demographics 2014–15', *The Daily Q*, 31 January 2015, www.thedailyq.org/4436/features/education-city-student-demographics-2014–15/, last accessed 23 January 2019.

15. 'Amna', interview with the author, Doha, December 2016.

16. 'Haya', interview with the author, Doha, December 2016.

17. She later (by WhatsApp message to the author, December 2016) estimated that there were around 450 players and referees involved in the Education City female football teams, and between 300–400 spectators. This number seem too high. The numbers of players estimated in interviews by the captains of two teams was twenty-three and eighteen players respectively, and although these are teams from two of the smaller universities of Education City, they are also well organized, meaning the total number of players is more likely to be around 100. For the league, teams can sign up twelve players each although the teams have a larger number of players coming to practice.

18. See a discussion on this development in Sehlikoglu, Sertaç, 'Revisited: Muslim Women's Agency and Feminist Anthropology of the Middle East', *Contemporary Islam* 1, no. 20 (2017), pp. 73–92.

19. Abu-Lughod, Lila, 'The Romance of Resistance: Tracing Transformations of Power through Bedouin Women', *American Ethnologist* 17, 1 (1990), pp. 42.

20. Mahmood, Saba, *Politics of Piety: The Islamic Revival and the Feminist Subject* (Berkeley, CA: University of California Press, 2005).

21. Sehlikoglu, 'Revisited: Muslim Women's Agency.'

22. Bayat, *Life as Politics: How Ordinary People Change the Middle East*, p. 43.

23. Ibid., p. 17.

24. Ibid., p. 116.

25. Stewart, Kenda R., 'A Hobby or Hobbling? Playing Palestinian Women's Soccer in Israel', *Soccer & Society* 13, 5–6 (2012), pp. 739–763.

26. Altorki, Soraya, 'Some Considerations on the Family in the Arabian Peninsula in the Late Ottoman and Early Post-Ottoman Period', in *Gulf Women*, ed. Amira El-Azhary Sonbol, Syracuse, NY: Syracuse University Press, 2012.

27. Qatar General Secretariat for Development Planning, *Qatar National Development Strategy*, 2011–2016.

28. 'Maryam', interview with the author, Doha, November 2016.

29. An 'abaya' is a loose garment worn over clothes, covering the body from the neck to the ankles and wrists.
30. Ministry of Development Planning and Statistics, *Education Statistics Chapter IV*, 2016, www.mdps.gov.qa/en/statistics/Statistical%20Releases/Social/Education/2016/Education_Chapter_4_2016_AE.pdf, last accessed 23 January 2019.
31. Ministry of Development Planning and Statistics, *Labor Force Statistics*, 2016, www.mdps.gov.qa/en/statistics/Statistical%20Releases/Social/LaborForce/2016/Labour_force_2016_AE.pdf, last accessed 23 January 2019.
32. Maktabi, Rania, 'Female Citizenship and Family Law in Kuwait and Qatar: Globalization and Pressures for Reform in Two Rentier States', *Nidaba* 1, 1 (2016), pp. 20–34.
33. Ulrichsen, Kristian, *Qatar and the Arab Spring*, Oxford: Oxford University Press, 2014.
34. AFP, 'Qatar appoints women to Shura council for the first time', *The Peninsula Qatar*, 9 November 2017, www.thepeninsulaqatar.com/article/09/11/2017/Qatar-appoints-women-to-Shura-Council-for-first-time, last accessed 23 January 2019.
35. *Majālis*, plural of *majlis*, literally 'a place to sit', in Gulf culture refers to a place where people gather, often at someone's home.
36. Jocelyn Sage Mitchell et al., 'In Majaalis Al-Hareem: The Complex Professional and Personal Choices of Qatari Women', *DIFI Family Research and Proceedings* 4 (2015), pp. 1–12.
37. Qatar National Vision 2030.
38. Qatar Olympic Committee, 'Sports Sector Strategy 2011—2016' (2011), p. 197.
39. Susan Dun, 'Role Models in the Media and Women's Sport Participation in Qatar', *Nidaba* 1, 1 (2016), pp. 48–58.
40. Dun, 'Role Models in the Media and Women's Sport Participation in Qatar.'
41. None of the women actually qualified for the Olympics, and were thus given this status by the IOC in order for Qatar to be able to have female representatives at all.
42. Dun, 'Role Models in the Media and Women's Sport Participation in Qatar.'
43. 'Football History,' The Supreme Committee for Delivery and Legacy, www.sc.qa/en/qatar/football-history, last accessed 23 January 2019.
44. 'About Qatar Stars League,' Qatar Football Association, 2018, www.qfa.qa, last accessed 23 January 2019.
45. Ibid.
46. 'Haya,' interview with the author, November 2016.
47. 'Aljohara,' interview with the author, November 2016.
48. 'Maryam,' interview with the author, November 2016.
49. 'Mohammed,' interview with the author, November 2016.

50. 'Reem,' working with the national women's team, interview with the author, October 2016.

51. According to Doha News, citing the QWSC, the first women futsal tournament took place in 2009 'despite cultural resistance', and the Qatar Women's Football League, consisting of 7 teams, were set up in 2012. Doha News Team, 'Women's Football in Qatar Making Strides, but more Young Talent Needed', *Doha News*, 25 February 2014, https://dohanews.co/womens-football-in-qatar-making-strides-but-more-young-talent-needed, last accessed 23 January 2019.

52. 'Reem', working with the national women's team, interview with the author, October 2016.

53. According to the Ministry of Planning and Statistics, the average monthly income of a Qatari household is QR 72,715 compared to an average of QR 24,415 for a non-Qatari household. In addition, Qatari nationals have free water and electricity. See Ministry of Planning and Statistics, 'Final Results of Household Expenditure and Income Survey (HEIS)' (2013), www.mdps.gov.qa/en/statistics/Statistical%20Releases/Social/HouseholdIncomeAndExpenditure/2013/Household_Expenditure_2012_2013_Eng.pdf, last accessed 23 January 2019.

54. 'Roberto', sports official, interview with the author, November 2016.

55. The women playing for the national team are given provisional passports, called a 'mission passport', one that is temporary and taken away after their careers finish. Besides being counted as Qatari in any football-related situation, the passports have limited benefits.

56. Geoff Harkness, 'Out of Bounds: Cultural Barriers to Female Sports Participation in Qatar', *The International Journal of the History of Sport* 29, 15 (2012), pp. 2162–2183.

57. This difference was pointed out in a number of interviews with different actors carried out in Doha in the fall of 2016.

58. 'Haya', interview with the author, November 2016.

59. 'Hessa', interview with the author, Doha, November 2016.

60. Knez et al., 'World Cup Football as a Catalyst for Change.'

61. Harkness, 'Out of Bounds: Cultural Barriers to Female Sports Participation in Qatar.'

62. 'Aljohara', interview with the author, November 2016.

63. Ibid.

64. This statement was repeated in all of my interviews with young Qataris.

65. 'Aljohara', interview with the author, November 2016.

66. Mahmood, *Politics of Piety: The Islamic Revival and the Feminist Subject*, pp. 155–161.

67. 'Sheikha', interview with the author, 2016.

68. 'Asian Games: Qatar Women's Team Pull out over Hijab Ban', *BBC Sport*, 26 September 2014, www.bbc.com/sport/basketball/29342986, last accessed 23 January 2019.

NOTES pp. [84–90]

69. 'Maryam,' interview with the author, November 2016.
70. 'Noura,' interview with the author, October 2016.
71. This was pointed out in several interviews with young women, Doha, October–December 2016.
72. 'Aljohara', interview with the author, November 2016.
73. *Būyāt*, plural of *būya*. This word is used in the Gulf countries to describe women who dress or act in a masculine way. It comes from the English 'boy' with the Arabic suffix–a (tā' marbūṭa), which is used to make a word feminine. Even though the word could be translated as 'tomboy', it is often used interchangeably with 'lesbian'.
74. 'Alanood', interview with the author, December 2016.
75. 'Aljohara,' interview with the author, November 2016.
76. Amélie Le Renard, *A Society of Young Women: Opportunities of Place, Power, and Reform in Saudi Arabia* (Stanford: Stanford University Press, 2014), 155.
77. Le Renard, *A Society of Young Women: Opportunities of Place, Power, and Reform in Saudi Arabia*, 155.
78. See for example Caudwell, Jayne, 'Women's Football in the United Kingdom: Theorizing Gender and Unpacking the Butch Lesbian Image' *Journal of Sport and Social Issues* 23, 4 (1999), pp. 390–402. Caudwell found that heterosexual women playing football are sometimes labeled butch or lesbian, which the women in question experience as problematic.
79. Stated by several sources, including players, and officials of the universities and the Supreme Committee.
80. 'Alanood', interview with the author, December 2016.
81. 'Haya', interview with the author, November 2016.
82. 'Hessa', interview with the author, November 2016.
83. 'Amna', interview with the author, November 2016.
84. 'Alanood', interview with the author, December 2016.
85. Stewart, 'A Hobby or Hobbling? Playing Palestinian Women's Soccer in Israel.'
86. 'Alanood', interview with the author, December 2016.
87. 'Hessa', interview with the author, November 2016.
88. Sobh, Rana and Russell Belk, 'Domains of Privacy and Hospitality in Arab Gulf Homes,' *Journal of Islamic Marketing* 2, 2 (2011), pp. 125–137.
89. Sobh and Belk, 'Domains of Privacy and Hospitality in Arab Gulf Homes,' p. 126.
90. Mitchell et al., 'In Majaalis Al-Hareem: The Complex Professional and Personal Choices of Qatari Women.'
91. Bayat, *Life as Politics*, pp. 116.
92. Lila Abu-Lughod, 'The Romance of Resistance: Tracing Transformations of Power through Bedouin Women.'
93. Bayat, *Life as Politics*, p. 97.
94. 'Haya', interview with the author, November 2016.

227

95. Saba Mahmood, 'Feminist Theory, Embodiment, and the Docile Agent: Some Reflections on the Egyptian Islamic Revival', *Cultural Anthropology* 16, 2 (2001), pp. 202–236.
96. 'Mozah', interview with the author, November 2016.

5. SPORTSWOMEN'S USE OF SOCIAL MEDIA IN THE MIDDLE EAST AND NORTH AFRICA (MENA)

1. Deborah Lupton, *Digital Sociology*, (New York, NY: Routledge, 2015), pp. 1–20.
2. Anna Piela, 'How do Muslim Women who wear the Niqab Interact with Others Online? A Case Study of a Profile on a Photo-Sharing Website', *New Media & Society* 19, no. 1 (2017), pp. 67–80; Jan H. Kietzmann, Kristopher Hermkens, Ian P. McCarthy, Bruno S. Silvestre, 'Social Media? Get Serious! Understanding the Functional Building Blocks of Social Media', *Business Horizons* 54, no. 3 (2011), pp. 241–251; Lupton, *Digital Sociology*.
3. Eickelman, Dale F. and Jon W. Anderson, *New Media in the Muslim World: The Emerging Public Sphere*, Bloomington: Indiana University Press, 2003, pp. 45–61.
4. Vieweg, Sarah and Adam Hodges, 'Surveillance & Modesty on Social Media: How Qataris Navigate Modernity and Maintain Tradition', (*Proceedings of the 19th ACM Conference on Computer-Supported Cooperative Work & Social Computing*, ACM, San Francisco, CA: ACM, USA, 27 February–2 March 2016.
5. Eickelman and Anderson, *New Media*; Brown, Sophia, 'Blogging the Resistance: Testimony and Solidarity in Egyptian Women's Blogs', *Contention: The Multidisciplinary Journal of Social Protest* 2, 1 (2014), pp. 41–55; Nouraie-Simone, Fereshteh, 'Wings of Freedom: Iranian Women, Identity, and Cyberspace', in *On Shifting ground: Muslim Women in the Global Era*, ed. Fereshteh Nouraie-Simone, New York, NY: Feminist Press, 2014, pp. 61–79.
6. Piela, 'Photo-sharing Website New Media'; Vieweg and Hodges, 'Surveillance & Modesty.'
7. Nouraie-Simone, 'Wings of Freedom'; Peila, 'Photo-sharing website New Media.'
8. Stuart Hall, 'Introduction: Who Needs 'Identity'?' in *Questions of Cultural Identity*, ed. Stuart Hall and Paul du Gay, London: SAGE Publication, 1996, pp. 1–17.
9. Hall, 'Introduction,' p. 4.
10. Ibid.
11. Ahmed, Sara, *Strange Encounters: Embodied Others in Post-Coloniality*, London: Routledge, 2000; Kassam, Shelina 'Marketing an Imagined Muslim Woman: Muslim Girl Magazine and the Politics of Race, Gender and Representation,' *Social Identities* 17, 4 (2011), pp. 543–64.
12. Geurin-Eagleman, Andrea N. and Lauren M. Burch, 'Communicating via Photographs: A Gendered Analysis of Olympic Athletes' Visual Self-presentation on Instagram', *Sport Management Review* 19, 2 (2016), pp. 133–45; Toffoletti, Kim and Holly Thorpe, 'Female Athletes' Self-representation on Social Media:

A Feminist Analysis of Neoliberal Marketing Strategies in 'Economies of Visibility', *Feminism and Psychology* 28, 1 (2018), pp. 11–31; Chawansky, Megan 'Be Who You are and be Proud: Brittney Griner, Intersectional Invisibility and Digital Possibilities for Lesbian Sporting Celebrity', *Leisure Studies* 35, 6 (2016), pp. 771–82.

13. Murthy, Dhiraj 'Emergent Digital Ethnographic Methods for Social Research', in *Handbook of Emergent Technologies in Social Research*, ed. Sharlene Nagy Hesse-Biber, New York: Oxford University Press, 2011, pp. 158–79.

14. Interviews lasted from one to three hours, with most conducted via digital platforms like Skype, Zoom, and Google Hangouts. Interviews were conducted from New Zealand, where I am based.

15. Denzin, Norman K. 'Cybertalk and the Method of Instances', in *Doing Internet Research: Critical Issues and Methods for Examining the Net*, ed. Steve G. Jones, Thousand Oaks, CA: SAGE Publications, 1999, pp. 107–26.

16. Markham, Annette N. 'Fieldwork in Social Media', *Qualitative Communication Research* 2, 4 (2013) pp. 434–46; Wittkower, Dyan Eric, 'Lurkers, Creepers, and Virtuous Interactivity: From Property Rights to Consent and Care as a Conceptual Basis for Privacy Concerns and Information Ethics', *First Monday* 21, 10 (2016), online only.

17. Ellison, Nicole B. and Danah M. Boyd, 'Sociality through Social Network Sites', in *The Oxford Handbook of Internet Studies*, ed. William H. Dutton, Oxford: Oxford University Press, 2013, pp. 158–80.

18. Ellison and Boyd, 'Sociality through Social Network Sites.'

19. Radcliffe, Damian 'Social Media in the Middle East: The Story of 2016', December 2016, https://damianradcliffe.files.wordpress.com/2016/12/social-media-in-the-middle-east-the-story-of-2016-final.pdf, last accessed 21 January 2019.

20. Lupton, *Digital Sociology*.

21. 'Arab Youth Media Initiative Launched', Ministry of Cabinet Affairs and the Future, 1 March 2017, www.mocaf.gov.ae/en/media/news/arab-youth-media-initiative-launched, last accessed 21 January 2016.

22. Howard, Philip N., Aiden Duffy, Deen Freelon, Muzammil M. Hussain, Will Mari, and Marwa Maziad. 'Opening Closed Regimes: What Was the Role of Social Media during the Arab Spring?' *Project on Information Technology & Political Islam* (PITPI), Working Paper, (2011).

23. Brown, 'Blogs Contention;' Nouraie-Simone, 'Wings of Freedom'; Mohamed Zayani and Suzi Mirgani, eds. *Bullets and Bulletins: Media and Politics in the Wake of the Arab Uprisings*. Oxford University Press/Hurst, 2016.

24. Hilleary, Cecily 'Tunisian Blogger Undeterred by Censorship', *VOA*, 4 January 2011, www.voanews.com/content/tunisian-blogger-undeterred-by-censorship-112948869/157156.html, last accessed 21 January 2019.

25. Brown, 'Blogs Contention.'

26. Nouraie-Simone, 'Wings of Freedom.'

27. Ibid.

28. Brown, 'Blogging the Resistance'.

29. Prodanovic, Branka and Susie Khamis, 'Representing the Veil in Contemporary Australian Media', in *The Routledge International Handbook to Veils and Veiling*, ed. Anna-Mari Almila and David Inglish, Oxford: Routledge, 2017, pp. 125–35.

30. Heinecken, Dawn '"So Tight in the Thighs, So Loose in the Waist": Embodying the Female Athlete Online', *Feminist Media Studies* 15, 6 (2015), pp. 1035–52; Geurin-Eagleman and Burch, 'Self-presentation on Instagram'; Clavio, Glen 'Emerging Social Media and Applications in Sport', in *Routledge Handbook of Sport Communication*, ed. Paul M. Pedersen, New York, NY: Routledge, 2013, pp. 259–69; Thorpe, Holly 'Action Sports, Social Media, and New Technologies Towards a Research Agenda', *Communication & Sport* 5, 5 (2016), pp. 554–578; Sanderson, Jimmy, 'Facebook, Twitter, and Sports Fans: Identity Protection and Social Network Sites in US Sports', in *Digital Media Sport: Technology, Power, and Identity in the Network Society*, ed. Brett Hutchins and David Rowe, New York, NY: Routledge, 2013, pp. 124–38; Sanderson, Jimmy 'What do we do with Twitter?' *Communication & Sport* 2, 2 (2014), pp. 127–31; Olive, Rebecca 'Reframing Surfing: Physical Culture in Online Spaces', *Media International Australia* 155, 1 (2015), pp. 99–107; Toffoletti and Thorpe, 'Economics of Visibility'.

31. Filo, Kevin, Daniel Lock, and Adam Karg, 'Sport and Social Media Research: A Review', *Sport Management Review* 18, 2 (2015), pp. 166–81; Ballouli, Khalil, and Michael Hutchinson, 'Digital-Branding and Social-Media Strategies for Professional Athletes, Sports Teams, and Leagues: An Interview with Digital Royalty's Amy Martin', *International Journal of Sport Communication* 3, 4 (2010), pp. 395–401; Chawansky, 'Sporting Celebrity'; Antunovic, Dunja and Marie Hardin, 'Activism in Women's Sports Blogs: Fandom and Feminist Potential', *International Journal of Sport Communication* 5, 3 (2012), pp. 305–22; Geurin-Eagleman and Burch, 'Self-Presentation on Instagram'; Weathers, Melina et al., 'The Tweet Life of Erin and Kirk: A Gendered Analysis of Professional Sports Broadcasters' Self-presentation on Twitter', *Journal of Sports Media* 9, 2 (2014), pp: 1–24; Toffoletti and Thorpe, 'Economics of Visibility'.

32. Kietzmann et al., 'Social Media'.

33. Gilchrist, Paul and Belinda Wheaton, 'New Media Technologies in Lifestyle Sport', in *Digital Media Sport: Technology, Power and Culture in the Network Society*, ed. Brett Hutchins and David Rowe, New York, NY: Routledge, 2013, pp. 169–85.

34. Antunovic and Hardin, 'Feminist Potential'; Sanderson, Jimmy, and Kelly Gramlich, '"You Go Girl!"': Twitter and Conversations about Sport Culture and Gender', *Sociology of Sport Journal* 33, 2 (2016), pp. 113–23; M. LaVoi, Nicole and Austin S. Calhoun, 'Digital Media and Women's Sport: An Old View on "New" Media?' in *Handbook of Sport and New Media*, ed. Andrew C. Billings and Marie Hardin, New York, NY: Routledge, 2014, pp. 320–30; Sanderson, 'Facebook, Twitter, and Sports Fans'; Sanderson, 'What do we do with Twitter?'

35. Piela, Anna, 'Challenging Stereotypes: Muslim Women's Photographic Self-representations on the Internet', *Online-Heidelberg Journal of Religions on the Internet* 4, 1 (2010), pp. 87–110; Gilchrist and Wheaton, 'New Media', 169–85; Bonilla, Yarimar, and Jonathan Rosa, '#Ferguson: Digital Protest, Hashtag Ethnography, and the Racial Politics of Social Media in the United States', *American Ethnologist* 42, 1 (2015), pp. 4–17.

36. Brown, 'Blogs Contention;' Nouraie-Simone, 'Wings of Freedom.'

37. Bonilla and Rosa, '#Ferguson;' Gilchrist and Wheaton, 'New Media;' Piela, 'Challenging Stereotypes.'

38. Messner, Michael A., Margaret Carlisle Duncan, and Cheryl Cooky, 'Silence, Sports Bras, and Wrestling Porn: Women in Televised Sports News and Highlights Shows', *Journal of Sport and Social Issues* 27, 1 (2003), pp. 38–51.

39. Dumont, 'Rock Climbing', p. 2.

40. Interview was conducted online via Zoom on 29 March 2017, and it was conducted in English.

41. Hashtags (#) aid in organizing events, controlling communication through the use of a specific word along with the (#) symbol. This helps to amplify a cause and reach large audiences: Nathan Gilkerson and Kati Tusinski, 'Social Media, Hashtag Hijacking, and the Evolution of an Activist Group Strategy', in *Social Media and Crisis Communication*, ed. Lucinda L. Austin, New York: Taylor & Francis, 2017, pp. 141–54.

42. An individual who is able to create compelling content through social media, allowing audience members or fans to respond, engage or get information.

43. Arai, Akiko, Yong Jae Ko, and Stephen Ross, 'Branding Athletes: Exploration and Conceptualization of Athlete Brand Image', *Sport Management Review* 17, 2 (2014), pp. 97–106; Dumont, Guillaume 'The Beautiful and the Damned: The Work of New Media Production in Professional Rock Climbing', *Journal of Sport and Social Issues* 41, 2 (2017), pp. 99–117; Hambrick, Marion E. and Sun J. Kang, 'Pin it: Exploring how Professional Sports Organizations Use Pinterest as a Communications and Relationship-Marketing Tool', *Communication & Sport* 3, 4 (2015), pp. 434–57.

44. Arai, Jae Ko, Stephen Ross, 'Branding Athletes.'

45. Instagram, 'Instagram Statistics', 2017, www.instagram.com/press, last accessed 21 Jan 2019.

46. Eagleman, Andrea N. 'Acceptance, Motivations, and Usage of Social Media as a Marketing Communications Tool amongst Employees of Sport National Governing Bodies', *Sport Management Review* 16, 4 (2013), pp. 488–97.

47. Interview conducted online via Zoom on 30 April 2017, in English.

48. Action sports refers to surfing, skateboarding, snowboarding, BMX-riding, climbing, and mountain biking; Thorpe, 'Action Sports', p. 559.

49. This quote was edited for clarity.

50. Coche, Roxane, 'How Golfers and Tennis Players Frame Themselves: A Content

Analysis of Twitter Profile Pictures', *Journal of Sports Media* 9, 1 (2014), pp. 95–121; Toffoletti and Thorpe, 'Economics of Visibility'.

51. Gill, Rosalind 'Postfeminist Media Culture: Elements of a Sensibility', *European Journal of Cultural Studies* 10, 2 (2007), pp. 147–166.

52. Banet-Weiser, Sarah '"Confidence you can Carry!": Girls in Crisis and the Market for Girls' Empowerment Organizations', *Continuum* 29, 2 (2015), pp. 182–93.

53. Sanderson, Jimmy, 'The Blog is Serving its Purpose: Self-Presentation Strategies on 38pitches.com', *Journal of Computer-Mediated Communication* 13, 4 (2008), pp. 912–36; Lebel, Katie and Karen Danylchuk, 'How Tweet it is: A Gendered Analysis of Professional Tennis Players' Self-presentation on Twitter', *International Journal of Sport Communication* 5, 4 (2012), pp. 461–80.

54. Hambrick and Kang, 'Pin it.'

55. Rose, Jessica, et al., 'Face it: The Impact of Gender on Social Media Images', *Communication Quarterly* 60, 5 (2012), pp. 588–607.

56. Toffoletti and Thorpe, 'Economics of Visibility'.

57. Sanderson, 'The Blog is Serving its Purpose'.

58. Farooq Samie, Sumaya and Sertaç Sehlikoglu, 'Strange, Incompetent and Out-Of-Place: Media, Muslim Sportswomen and London 2012', *Feminist Media Studies* 15, 3 (2015), pp. 363–81; Benn, Tansin, Gertrud Pfister, and Haifaa Jawad, *Muslim Women and Sport*, New York: Routledge, 2010; Benn, Tansin and Symeon Dagkas, 'The Olympic Movement and Islamic Culture: Conflict or Compromise for Muslim Women?' *International Journal of Sport Policy and Politics* 5, 2 (2013), pp. 281–94.

59. Trolan, Eoin J. 'The Impact of the Media on Gender Inequality within Sport', *Procedia-Social and Behavioral Sciences* 91 (2013), pp. 215–27.

60. LaVoi and Calhoun, 'Digital Media and Women's Sport'; Sanderson and Gramlich, 'You Go Girl!'; Sanderson, 'Facebook, Twitter, and Sports Fans'; Sanderson, 'What do we do with Twitter?'

61. Hambrick and Kang, 'Pin it'.

62. Sanderson, 'The Blog is Serving its Purpose'.

63. 'Saudi Woman who Climbed Everest tells Countrywomen: Challenge Yourselves', *The Raw Story*, 27 May 2013, www.rawstory.com/rs/2013/05/27/saudi-woman-who-climbed-everest-tells-countrywomen-challenge-yourselves/, last accessed 21 Jan 2019.

64. Toffoletti and Thorpe, 'Economics of Visibility.'

65. Benn and Dagkas, 'The Olympic Movement and Islamic Culture'; Samie and Sehlikoglu, 'Strange, Incompetent and Out-Of-Place.'

6. THE WORLD CUP AND FREEDOM OF EXPRESSION IN QATAR

1. The Gulf Cooperation Council states are Qatar, Bahrain, Kuwait, Oman, Saudi Arabia and the United Arab Emirates. The GCC was founded in 1981.

2. See Reiche, Danyel, 'Investing in Sporting Success as a Domestic and Foreign Policy Tool: The Case of Qatar', *International Journal of Sport Policy and Politics* 7, 4 (2015), pp. 489–504; and Mahfoud Amara, 'The Pillars of Qatar's International Sport Strategy', *E-International Relations*, 29 November 2013, www.e-ir.info/2013/11/29/the-pillars-of-qatars-international-sport-strategy/, last accessed 23 January 2019.

3. See Liam Morgan, 'Qatar to Host almost 90 Major Sporting Events this Year, Olympic Committee Reveals', *Inside the Games*, 20 April 2015, www.insidethegames.biz/articles/1026862/qatar-to-host-89-major-sporting-events-this-year-qoc-reveals, last accessed 23 January 2019.

4. 'Qatar Accused of Blocking Doha News Website', *BBC News*, 1 December 2016, www.bbc.com/news/world-middle-east-38169032, last accessed 23 January 2019. Shortly after the 2017 blockade began, VoiP services (Skype, WhatsApp, etc.) in Qatar were also interrupted.

5. For context, the media in all the countries of the Arab peninsula rate as unfree on all three of the major international media freedom indices (explained in more detail later in the paper). Importantly, the indices have reported steady declines in media freedom everywhere in the world for more than a decade now, including in the United States and Western Europe. Qatar's decline was due in part to its blocking of the *Doha News*, an online news site without the required publication license.

6. 'Recommendations of the International Conference, "Freedom of Expression, Facing up to the Threat,"' 24–25 July 2017, Doha, Qatar, www.fnsi.it/upload/9b/9bf31c 7ff062936a96d3c8bd1f8f2ff3/06f90f53aa785615e1729b2dea077256.pdf, last accessed 23 January 2019.

7. The Foreign Minister, Sheikh Mohammed bin Abdulrahman Al Thani, spoke at Chatham House on the blockade in July 2017; 'The Crisis in the Gulf: Qatar Responds', Chatham House, 5 July 2017, www.youtube.com/watch?v=8ksR1 C8B2HA, last accessed 23 January 2019.

8. 'Qatar's Emir Stands Defiant in Face of Blockade', *CBS News*, 29 October 2017, www.cbsnews.com/news/qatars-emir-stands-defiant-in-face-of-blockade/, last accessed 23 January 2019.

9. There is a long history of researchers attempting to measure press freedom using quantifiable measures, and today there are at least three internationally known indices that rate and compare national media systems and, explicitly or implicitly, their degree of freedom. The oldest is the annual 'Survey of Press Freedom' done by the British NGO Freedom House, which includes rankings for almost all of the world's countries; the second is a 'Media Sustainability Index' (MSI) created jointly by the US Agency for International Development (USAID) and the International Research Exchange Board (IREX) in 2000; and a third, more recent entry to the field, is the 'Press Freedom Index' from the French NGO Reporters sans Frontières (RSF). Each has over time developed substantial resources and sophisticated measures, but each also relies on values that are, if not subjective, at least not universal even in established democracies.

10. On the topic of media freedom measures, see generally Price, Monroe, Susan Abbott and Libby Morgan, eds., *Measures of Press Freedom and Media Contributions to Development: Evaluating the Evaluators*, New York: Peter Lang, 2011; and LaMay, Craig, *Exporting Press Freedom: Economic Dilemmas in Media Assistance*, New Brunswick, NJ: Transaction, 2007.

11. Few sources in Qatar, when talking about sensitive issues, are willing to be identified or quoted. Another sourcing problem to note is that the news reports cited in this paper are primarily from Western news organizations, not Qatari ones, because Qatari newspapers do not make archives available online except as individual copies in PDF format that are searchable only within each issue. While Qatari newspapers sometimes do carry critical stories about the country, they are usually from Western news sources.

12. Brannagan, Paul and Richard Giulianotti, 'Soft Power and Soft Disempowerment: Qatar, Global Sport and Football's 2022 World Cup Finals,' *Leisure Studies* 34, 6 (2014), pp. 707.

13. The term 'mega-event' has several similar definitions in economics literature, but a widely accepted one comes from Maurice Roche, who describes them as 'large-scale cultural events which have dramatic character, mass popular appeal and international significance.' The two key characteristics of the modern mega-events are that they leave a 'legacy' for the host city, region or country where they occur; and that they receive global media coverage. See Roche, Maurice, *Mega-events and Modernity*, London: Routledge, 2000; and Roberts, Kenneth, *The Leisure Industries*, London: Palgrave, 2004. On Qatar and the legacies of its sports tourism strategy, see Grichting, Anna, 'Scales of Flows: Qatar and the Urban Legacies of Mega Events', *International Journal of Architecture and Urban Planning* 7, 2 (July 2013), pp. 173–91.

14. Nye, Joseph, 'Soft Power and American Foreign Policy', *Political Science Quarterly* 119, 2 (2004), pp. 256.

15. See Amara, Mahfoud, '2006 Qatar Asian Games: A "Modernization" Project from Above?' *Sport in Society* 8, 3 (2005), pp. 493–514.

16. According to FIFA, 3.2 billion people watched some part of the 2014 World Cup in Brazil, and almost a billion watched some part of the final. See FIFA's '2014 FIFA World Cup Brazil: Television Audience Report', Fédération Internationale de Football Association (FIFA), https://resources.fifa.com/mm/document/affederation/tv/02/74/55/57/2014fwcbraziltvaudiencereport(draft5)(issue-date14.12.15)_neutral.pdf, last accessed 23 January 2019.

17. Brannagan and Giulianotti, 'Soft power and Soft Disempowerment,' p. 707.

18. Higham, James, 'Commentary-Sport as an Avenue of Tourism Development: An Approach to Qatar and Abu Dhabi', *African Journal of Business Management* 5 (2011), p. 84.

19. As part of Qatar's sports strategy, it has made major investments in European sports

facilities and football clubs; hosted dozens of international sporting events and sport conferences; and bid to become a significant voice in international sport governance.

20. Scott, Matt, 'Millions Paid in Bribes for Qatar's 2022 World Cup, Report Claims', *The Guardian*, 10 May 2011, www.theguardian.com/football/2011/may/10/millions-bribes-qatar-2022-world-cup-claims, last accessed 23 January 2019.

21. Sam Borden, 'FIFA Confirms Winter World Cup for 2022', *New York Times*, 19 March 2015, www.nytimes.com/2015/03/20/sports/soccer/fifa-confirms-winter-world-cup-for-2022.html, last accessed 23 January 2019; Jacob Murtagh, 'What Will Qatar Winter World Cup Mean for the Premier League, Transfer Window and Players?' *Mirror*, 25 September 2015, www.mirror.co.uk/sport/football/news/what-qatar-winter-world-cup-6514982, last accessed 23 January 2019.

22. 'Court hears how Senior FIFA Exec took Bribes to back Qatar's World Cup Bid', *Sport Business*, 15 November 2017, www.sportbusiness.com/sport-news/court-hears-how-senior-fifa-exec-took-bribes-back-qatar%E2%80%99s-world-cup-bid?0=ip_login_no_cache%3Ddf847e41037bc13c856e6bcfc72e115a, last accessed 23 January 2019.

23. Rivenburgh, Nancy K., 'The Olympic Games, Media and the Challenges of Global Image Making', paper presentation, Centre d'Estudis Olimpics, International Chair in Olympism, Barcelona, Spain, 2004, http://ceo.uab.cat/download/rivenburgh_eng.pdf, last accessed 23 January 2019.

24. See Kuper, Simon, 'Soccer's Culture of Corruption', *New York Review of Books*, 28 September 2017, www.nybooks.com/articles/2017/09/28/soccers-culture-of-corruption/, last accessed 23 January 2019.

25. See Garcia, Michael J., *Report on the Inquiry into the 2018/2022 World Cup Bidding Process*, Fédération Internationale de Football Association (FIFA), 2014, http://resources.fifa.com/mm/document/affederation/footballgovernance/02/89/87/97/aus_bel-ned_eng_esp-por_jpn_kor_qat_report_neutral.pdf, last accessed 23 January 2019. The 'Garcia Report' by American federal judge Michael Garcia, is the FIFA examination of its own bidding process, only portions of which were released before 2017, when the full report was leaked to the German newspaper *Bild*.

26. 'US Jury Convicts Two FIFA Soccer Bosses in Corruption Trial', *Deutsche Welle.com*, 23 December 2017, www.dw.com/en/us-jury-convicts-two-fifa-soccer-bosses-in-corruption-trial/a-41913989, last accessed 23 January 2019.

27. Ruggie, John J., '*For the Game. For the World: FIFA & Human Rights*', April 2016, www.sportandhumanrights.org/wordpress/wp-content/uploads/2015/07/Ruggie_human-rights_FIFA_report_April_2016.pdf, last accessed 23 January 2019.

28. Dorsey, James M., 'Qatar's World Cup Sparks Battle for Legal, Social and Political Reform,' in *The Turbulent World of Middle East Soccer*, 25 January 2017, http://

mideastsoccer.blogspot.com/2017/01/qatars-world-cup-sparks-battle-for.html, last accessed 23 January 2019.

29. Lobel, Mark, 'Arrested for Reporting on Qatar's World Cup Labourers', *BBC News*, 18 May 2015, www.bbc.com/news/world-middle-east-32775563, last accessed 23 January 2019; 'Qatar Detains International Journalists for the Second Time this Year', Committee to Protect Journalists, 18 May 2015, https://cpj.org/2015/05/qatar-detains-international-journalists-for-the-se.php, last accessed 23 January 2019.

30. Allison, Lincoln and Alan Tomlinson, *Understanding International Sport Organizations: Principles, Power and Possibilities*, London: Routledge, 2017, p. xii.

31. Cottrell, M. Patrick and Travis Nelson, 'Not Just the Games? Power, Protest and Politics at the Olympics', *European Journal of International Relations* 17, 4 (2011), pp. 729–53.

32. Corrarino, Megan, '"Law Exclusion Zones": Mega-events as Sites of Procedural and Substantive Human Rights Violations', *Yale Human Rights & Development Law Journal* 17 (2014), pp. 180–204.

33. 'Olympic Charter', International Olympic Committee, September 2015, https://stillmed.olympic.org/Documents/olympic_charter_en.pdf, last accessed 23 January 2019.

34. Owen Gibson, 'Olympic Anti-discrimination Clause Introduced after Sochi Gay Rights Row,' *The Guardian*, 25 September 2014, www.theguardian.com/sport/2014/sep/25/olympic-anti-discrimination-clause-sochi-gay-rights-row, last accessed 29 January 2019.

35. 'IOC and UN Secretariat Agree Historic Deal to Work Together to Use Sport to Build a Better World,' Olympic.org, 28 April 2014, at www.olympic.org/news/ioc-and-un-secretariat-agree-historic-deal/230542, last accessed 23 January 2019.

36. Historically, sporting mega-events have featured several moments that have cemented their link to human rights promotion: Jesse Owen's victories in 1936 at the summer Olympic Games in Berlin; the medal-stand salute and protests of Americans John Carlos and Tommy Smith, and Australian Peter Norman, at the 1968 Mexico City games; the promotion of Aboriginal rights by Australian Cathy Freeman at the 2000 Sydney Olympics; and, most recently, the participation of women athletes from Saudi Arabia, Qatar and Brunei at the 2012 London Olympics.

37. Article 4, FIFA Statutes, April 2016 edition, http://resources.fifa.com/mm/document/affederation/generic/02/78/29/07/fifastatutsweben_neutral.pdf, last accessed 23 January 2019.

38. 'Our Strategy,' Fédération Internationale de Football Association, 2018, www.fifa.com/about-fifa/who-we-are/explore-fifa.html, last accessed 29 January 2019.

39. Paul Doyle, 'How football can help bring new hope to a neglected region of Uganda', *The Guardian*, 30 April 2019, www.theguardian.com/katine/2009/may/01/football.

40. Ruggie, *For the Game*. Ruggie's recommendations for, among other things, a permanent human rights advisory board within FIFA to meet twice a year and to monitor bids and contracts, were adapted later the same year in a new FIFA mission document, '*FIFA 2.0: The Vision for the Future*', 13 October 2016, http://resources.fifa.com/mm/document/affederation/generic/02/84/35/01/FIFA_2.0_Vision_LOW_neu.17102016_Neutral.pdf, last accessed 23 January 2019. The advisory board met for the first time in March 2017. The Ruggie Report also raised human rights concerns about Russia, host of the 2018 World Cup, and Papua New Guinea, host of the 2016 Under-20 Women's World Cup. Ruggie's report came a year after another internal investigation into FIFA ethics violations in the 2018 and 2022 bidding processes by Michael Garcia, a former U.S. Attorney. The FIFA Ethics Committee refused to release the full report, leading Garcia to resign his position in protest. While the Garcia report contained no new revelations, it is not correct to say, as some sources do, that Qatar was 'cleared' of allegations of bribery in relation to its World Cup bid.

41. Perlman, Matthew, 'FIFA Report Offers Ways Group Can Protect Human Rights', *Law360*, 14 April 2016, www.law360.com/articles/784594/fifa-report-offers-ways-group-can-protect-human-rights, last accessed 23 January 2019.

42. An 'illiberal' country, to borrow from journalist Fareed Zakaria, is one that routinely fails to hold free and fair elections; that lacks rule of law; that represses political opposition; and that fails to protect basic liberties of speech, press, assembly, religion and property. Obviously, the extent to which any country is illiberal is a matter of degree depending on how one scores these measures. See Fareed Zakaria, 'The Rise of Illiberal Democracy', *Foreign Affairs* 76, 6 (1997), pp. 22–43.

43. See Kilgore, Adam, 'Want to Host the Olympics? Most Western Cities Would Rather Not', *Washington Post*, 29 July 2015, www.washingtonpost.com/sports/olympics/for-citizens-in-many-locales-hosting-games-no-longer-has-same-ring-to-it/2015/07/29/10ac4c12–355a-11e5–94ce-834ad8f5c50e_story.html?utm_term=.6d6bd96b77ee, last accessed 23 January 2019; Abend, Lisa, 'Why Nobody Wants to Host the 2022 Winter Olympics', *Time*, 3 October 2014, http://time.com/3462070/olympics-winter-2022/, last accessed 23 January 2019; and Morgan, Liam, 'Budapest Withdrawal Deals Blow to IOC and Casts Further Doubt over Agenda 2020', *Inside the Games*, 25 February 2017, www.insidethegames.biz/articles/1047470/liam-morgan-budpest-withdrawal-deals-blow-to-ioc-and-casts-further-doubt-over-agenda-2020, last accessed 23 January 2019.

44. Worden, Minky, 'Human Rights and the 2022 Olympics', *New York Times*, 18 January 2015, www.nytimes.com/2015/01/19/opinion/human-rights-and-the-2022-olympics.html, last accessed 23 January 2019.

45. See Zimbalist, Andrew, *Circus Maximus: The Economic Gamble Behind Hosting the Olympics and the World Cup*, Washington, DC: Brookings Institution Press, 2016; Mehrotra, Anita, 'To Host or Not to Host?' A Comparison Study on the

Long-run Impact of the Olympic Games', *Michigan Journal of Business* 5, 2 (2012), pp. 62–92.

46. See for example Nauright, John, 'Selling Nations to the World through Sports: Mega-events and Nation Branding as Global Diplomacy', *Public Diplomacy Magazine*, Winter 2013, http://publicdiplomacymagazine.com/wp-content/uploads/2013/02/Selling-nationS-to-the-World-through-SportS-Mega-eventS-and-nation-Branding-aS-gloBal-diploMacy.pdf, last accessed 23 January 2019.

47. See, for example, 'Games That Must Stop: Major International Sporting Events Must not Become the Preserve of Autocrats', *The Economist*, 26 February 2015, www.economist.com/news/leaders/21645194-major-international-sporting-events-must-not-become-preserve-autocrats-games-must; Suzanne Nossel, 'Faster, Higher, More Oppressive: International Mega-sporting Events like the Olympics Have Become the Playthings of Authoritarian Regimes', *Foreign Policy*, 19 May 2015, http://foreignpolicy.com/2015/05/19/faster-higher-more-oppressive-olympics-world-cup-russia-qatar/; Jonathan Grix, 'Sport, Politics and the Olympics', *Political Studies Review* 11, no. 1 (January 2013): 15–25; and Alexander Lord, 'A Game Changer; Mega-sporting Events, Illiberal Regimes, and Political Liberalization' (master's thesis, City University of New York, 2014), academicworks.cuny.edu/cc_etds_theses/304.

48. Consider that the IOC had 207 member countries, FIFA has 210, and the United Nations 193 in February 2018. Excluding the IOC and FIFA, a conservative number of ISNGOs in the world is about 213—because no sport is a sport without an international governing body—most of which are under the aegis of the IOC. A complete list of summer and winter sport federations is at www.olympic.org/ioc-governance-international-sports-federations, last accessed 23 January 2019. Through its relationships with the World Anti-Doping Association (WADA) and the Court of Arbitration for Sport (CAS), the IOC essentially claims authority over *all* sport, everywhere.

49. See Allison and Tomlinson, *Understanding International Sport Organizations*, 2017.

50. 'Soccer: Less Democracy Makes for an Easier World Cup—Valcke', *Reuters*, 24 April 2013, www.reuters.com/article/us-soccer-fifa-idUSBRE93N18F201 30424; see also 'Too Much Democracy—FIFA's Valcke', *BBC Sport*, 24 April 2013, www.bbc.com/sport/football/22288688.

51. Neither the IOC nor FIFA—nor indeed any international sports governing body—maintains any US-based operations, in order to avoid US law. FIFA's criminal problems in the US arose as a result of a single person in the FIFA chain who failed to report taxable income.

52. Zaggar, Zachary, 'Panama Papers Breathe New Life into FIFA Corruption Scandal', *Law360*, 7 April 2016, www.law360.com/articles/781948/panama-papers-breathe-new-life-into-fifa-corruption-scandal, last accessed 23 January 2019.

53. Jefferson Lenskyj, Helen, 'The Olympic Industry and Civil Liberties: The Threat to Free Speech and Freedom of Assembly', in *Sport, Civil Liberties and Human Rights*, eds., David Giulianotti and David McArdle, New York: Routledge, 2006, pp. 78–92. See also Marthoz, Jean-Paul, 'Mega-Events, Mega Media Restrictions', speech at Play the Game, Aarhus, 30 October 2013, www.playthegame.org/fileadmin/image/PtG2013/Presentations/30_October_Wednesday/Jean-Paul_Marthoz_30_okt.pdf, last accessed 23 January 2019.

54. The IOC, for example, launched a streaming channel in 2014, and in 2017 launched a broadcast channel in partnership with NBCUniversal. In the United States, Europe, East Asia and Australia, virtually all major sports leagues now have both streaming and broadcast channels.

55. Digital media have also changed the job of sports reporters. They are now less in the business of breaking stories and more in the business of verifying and contextualizing stories generated by non-journalists—fans and athletes. Journalists also use social media—Twitter primarily—to break news, promote their own work, and connect to audiences. But the live audience can also break news, and the trend of social media conversation can quickly and dramatically change the mainstream media narrative around any sporting event.

56. IOC Article 48, bylaw 3: 93, https://stillmed.olympic.org/Documents/olympic_charter_en.pdf, last accessed 23 January 2019.

57. IOC Article 50, bylaw 2: 94.

58. Claire Stocks, 'Beijing Olympics pose internet challenges', *BBC Sport*, 3 April 2008, www.bbc.co.uk/blogs/sporteditors/2008/04/why_the_beijing_olympics_chall.html.

59. 'Accredited persons' in the IOC guidelines include 'all athletes, coaches, officials, personnel of the National Olympic Committees and of International Federations and members of accredited media.' The IOC has no guidelines for non-accredited media, which instead get accreditation from the host city or country.

60. According to the guidelines, 'Only the persons who are accredited as media may act as journalists, reporters or in any other media capacity while they are at the Games.' *IOC Social and Digital Media Guidelines for Persons Accredited to the Games of the XXXI Olympiad Rio 2016*, International Olympic Committee, October 2015, https://stillmed.olympic.org/media/Document%20Library/OlympicOrg/Documents/Games-Rio-2016-Olympic-Games/Social-Media-Blogging-Internet-Guidelines-and-News-Access-Rules/IOC-Social-and-Digital-Media-Guidelines-Rio-2016.pdf, last accessed 23 January 2019.

61. See Rowe, David, 'Sport, Sochi and the Rising Challenge of the Activist Athlete', *The Conversation*, 5 February 2014, http://theconversation.com/sport-sochi-and-the-rising-challenge-of-the-activist-athlete-22491, last accessed 23 January 2019.

62. See, for example, Chadwick, Simon, 'Euro 2016 Sponsors Being Ambushed on Social Media by 'Unofficial' Brands,' *The Conversation*, 1 July 2016, http://the-

conversation.com/euro-2016-sponsors-being-ambushed-on-social-media-by-unof-ficial-brands-61880, last accessed 23 January 2019; and Pathak, Shareen, 'Activist Athletes Pose an "Unprecedented" Threat to Sponsor Brands', *Digiday*, 13 February 2017, https://digiday.com/marketing/activist-athletes-pose-unprecedented-threat-sponsor-brands/, last accessed 23 January 2019.

63. In 2009, a dispute arose in Australia over the rights to cricket video that entangled the Australian Cricket Council, several news organizations, mobile and internet companies, and fans. The controversy became the focus of a national election and resulted in a formal government inquiry that ended with the investigating parlia-mentary committee recommending the parties sue one another.

64. John Ruggie, quoted in Pearlman, Matthew, 'FIFA Report Offers Ways Group Can Protect Human Rights', *Law360*, 14 April 2016, www.law360.com/arti-cles/784594/fifa-report-offers-ways-group-can-protect-human-rights, last accessed 23 January 2019.

65. See Reiche, 'Investing in Sporting Success as a Domestic and Foreign Policy Tool: The Case of Qatar.'

66. There are exceptions to this openness. The Qatar Radio and Television Corporation and customs officials censor both domestic and foreign print and broadcast media for religious, political and sexual content. Online content is reviewed and blocked in the same way by the country's sole internet service provider, state-owned Qtel. See *Media Use in the Middle East 2016: A Six-Nation Survey*, Northwestern University in Qatar, Doha: 2016, www.qatar.northwestern.edu/docs/publica-tions/research-media-use/2016-middle-east-media-use-report.pdf, last accessed 23 January 2019.

67. 'Homepage,' Josoor Institute, www.josoorinstitute.qa, last accessed 23 January 2019.

68. Constitution of Qatar 2004, Article 47, http://portal.www.gov.qa/wps/portal/!ut/p/a0/04_Sj9CPykssy0xPLMnMz0vMAfGjzOIt_S2cDS0sDNwtQg KcDTyNfAOcLD3cDdw9zfULsh0VAQl92_s!/, last accessed 23 January 2019.

69. 'World Press Freedom Index, Qatar, 2017', Qatar, Reporters San Frontières, https://rsf.org/en/qatar, last accessed 23 January 2019; see also 'Freedom of the Press 2016, Qatar', Freedom House, https://freedomhouse.org/report/freedom-press/2016/qatar, last accessed 23 January 2019.

70. 'Freedom of the Press 2011 Qatar', Freedom House, https://freedomhouse.org/sites/default/files/FOTP%202011%20Final%20Full%20Report.pdf, pp. 249.

71. Lambert, Jennifer, 'Qatari Law Will Test Media Freedom', Carnegie Endowment for International Peace, 1 December 2010, http://carnegieendowment.org/sada/42049, last accessed 23 January 2019.

72. Duffy, Matt, *Media Laws and Regulations of the GCC Countries: Summary, Analysis and Recommendations*, Doha Centre for Media Freedom, 2013, www.dc4mf.org/wp-content/uploads/2013/04/gcc_media_law_en_0.pdf, last accessed 23 January 2019.

73. *Law No. 8 of the Year 1979 on Prints and Publications*, Articles 2 and 5, www. dc4mf.org/wp-content/uploads/2013/04/press_law_qatar.pdf, last accessed 23 January 2019.

74. Ibid., Article 9.

75. Ibid., Articles 10, 11, and 12. Though the law refers to the Ministry of Information as the licensing authority, former Emir Sheikh Hamad bin Khalifa Al Thani abolished that ministry when he came to power in 1995. The Ministry of Culture, Arts and Heritage is now responsible for the enforcement of the press law. See David Salt and Emma Higham, "Qatar's 'Press Law'" *Qatar Juris Updates* 11, 6 (2013), www.inhousecommunity.com/wp-content/uploads/2016/07/v11i6_Qatar_JURIS_UPDATES.pdf, last accessed 23 January 2019.

76. *Law No. 8 of the Year 1979*, Articles 17, 24, and 25.

77. Lambert, 'Qatar Law Will Test Media Freedom;' Duffy, *Media Laws and Regulations of the GCC Countries*.

78. *Law No. 11 of 2004, Penal Code*, http://portal.www.gov.qa/wps/wcm/connect/8abaea8046be1deaae97ef70b3652ad8/Penal+Code.pdf?MOD=AJPERES&useDefaultText=0&useDefaultDesc=0, last accessed 23 January 2019.

79. 'Qatar: Revise Draft Media Law to Allow Criticism of Rulers,' Human Rights Watch, 30 October 2013, www.hrw.org/news/2012/10/30/qatar-revise-draft-media-law-allow-criticism-rulers; Duffy, *Media Laws and Regulations of the GCC Countries*.

80. Law No. 11 of 2004, *Penal Code*, http://portal.www.gov.qa/wps/wcm/connect/8abaea8046be1deaae97ef70b3652ad8/Penal+Code.pdf?MOD=AJPERES&useDefaultText=0&useDefaultDesc=0.

81. Law No. 14 of 2014, *Cybercrime Prevention Law*, http://chato.cl/blog/files/QatarCybercrimeLaw_unofficial_translation.pdf.

82. Non-Western countries come in for particularly intense scrutiny by Western media. See John Hargreaves, 'Olympism and Nationalism: Some Preliminary Considerations,' *International Review for the Sociology of Sport* 27, no. 2 (1992): 119–35.

83. An obvious question is why sports journalism is not more rigorous. The reasons are many, and beyond the scope of this paper, but the short answer is that sports journalism has never been rigorous. Sports divisions in most media companies continue to be regarded as the 'toy department,' not a place where serious reporters ply their trade. Most of the major international sports stories of the last decade—match-fixing in tennis and football, money-laundering in football, the risks of concussive injury, doping in cycling, athletics and in other sports, corruption and self-dealing in ISNGOs, the sexual abuse of child athletes—were not developed by sports reporters but reporters working other news beats. There are some superb sports media (such as Play the Game, Edge of Sports, Transparency in Sport, Around the Rings, Inside the Games, 3Wire Sports, Engaging Sports, the Allrounder, The Turbulent World of Middle East Soccer, VICE Sports, the New

York Times), but most mainstream sports reporters continue to be dependent for their livelihoods on the sports teams, leagues and competitions they cover. This is all the more so where accreditation to cover an event or an organization comes with exclusive access to sport venues.

84. The PRC refused to participate in the Olympics for almost four decades in a battle over whether the IOC would recognize it or Taiwan as the 'real' China.

85. There is a history of illiberal host countries attempting to control or suppress press coverage before and during a sport mega-event. In the run-up to the 1978 World Cup, for example, the military government in Argentina cracked down on domestic journalists, issuing guidelines that detailed subjects forbidden in news coverage or commentary. Between 1976 and 1978, seventy-two journalists disappeared or were jailed, and about 400 went into exile. Several European human rights groups protested Argentina's games, as did some football associations and players. The Argentine government had attempted to mollify international criticism by inviting Amnesty International to visit the country in 1976, but the organization's subsequent report documented the regime's ongoing human rights violations. See Smith, Bill L., 'The Argentinian Junta and the Press in the Run-up to the 1978 World Cup', *Soccer and Society* 3, 1 (2002), pp. 69.

86. In 2006, China issued regulations giving foreign journalists more freedom to report in the country in the run-up to and during the games, but only for a year. More generally, see Rowe, David, 'The Bid, the Lead-up, the Event and the Legacy: Global Cultural Politics and Hosting the Olympics', *British Journal of Sociology* 63, 2 (June 2012), pp. 285–305.

87. Batty, David, 'Media Face Web Censorship at Beijing Olympics', *The Guardian*, 30 July 2008, www.theguardian.com/world/2008/jul/30/china.olympic-games2008, last accessed 23 January 2019.

88. Jacobs, Andrew, 'China to Limit Web Access during Olympic Games', *New York Times*, 31 July 2008, www.nytimes.com/2008/07/31/sports/olympics/31china.html, last accessed 23 January 2019.

89. Batty, 'Media Face Web Censorship at Beijing Olympics.'

90. Worden, Minky, 'No medals for the IOC', *New York Times*, 15 August 2008, www.nytimes.com/2008/08/15/opinion/15iht-edworden.1.15328869.html.

91. In response to these episodes, and to criticism of human rights abuses in Brazil in advance of the 2016 games, the IOC, in cooperation with the US-based Committee to Protect Journalists, launched a confidential, registration-based 'press freedom reporting tool' for the 2016 Rio Games with which journalists could report any instances of official interference with their ability to report and publish. If the IOC thought the complaints legitimate it would 'follow-up with the relevant stakeholders.' See the 'Media Complaints Reporting Tool', Olympic.org, https://secure.registration.olympic.org/en/media-complaint/, last accessed 23 January 2019.

92. Shahine, Alaa, 'Game-Changing Qatar Law to Grant Expats Permanent Residency', *Bloomberg*, 2 August 2017, www.bloomberg.com/news/articles/2017–08–02/ qatar-passes-landmark-law-to-grant-permanent-residency-to-expats, last accessed 23 January 2019.

93. Adly, Ayman, 'End-of-service Benefits for Domestic Hands', *Gulf Times*, 23 August 2017; and Aljundi, Hisham, 'Domestic Helps Entitled to End-of-Service Gratuity', *Qatar Tribune*, 23 August 2017, www.gulf-times.com/story/561223/End-of-service-benefits-for-domestic-hands, last accessed 23 January 2019.

94. See Kamrava, Mehran, 'Royal Factionalism and Political Liberalization in Qatar' *Middle East Journal*, Summer 2009. DOI: 10.3751/63.3.13.

95. See Dennis, Everette, et al., *Media Use in the Middle East, 2016*, Northwestern University in Qatar, Doha: 2016, pp. 20–22, www.qatar.northwestern.edu/docs/ publications/research-media-use/2016-middle-east-media-use-report.pdf, last accessed 23 January 2019.

96. 'Is it Time for Northwestern to Quit Qatar?' *The Daily Northwestern*, 10 June 2017, https://dailynorthwestern.com/2017/06/10/opinion/letter-to-the-editor-is-it-time-for-northwestern-to-quit-qatar/, last accessed 23 January 2019.

7. TURKISH SPORTS: LOST IN POLITICS?

1. Smith, Andy, and Daniel Bloyce, *Sport Policy and Development: An Introduction*, London: Routledge, 2010.

2. King, Neil, *Sport Policy and Governance: Local Perspectives*, Oxford: Elsevier, 2009.

3. Kissoudi, Penelope, 'Sport, Politics and International Relations in the Twentieth Century', *International Journal of the History of Sport* 25, 13 (2008), pp. 1689–706.

4. Hoye, Russell, et al., *Sport Management: Principles and Applications*, 4th ed., Oxford: Elsevier, 2015.

5. Green, Mick, 'Olympic Glory or Grassroots Development? Sport Policy Priorities in Australia, Canada and the United Kingdom, 1960–2006', *International Journal of the History of Sport* 24, 7 (2007), pp. 921–53.

6. Reiche, Danyel, 'Investing in Sporting Success as a Domestic and Foreign Policy Tool: The Case of Qatar', *International Journal of Sport Policy and Politics* 7, 4 (2015), pp. 490.

7. Leftwich, Adrian, *What is Politics? The Activity and its Study*, Oxford: Blackwell, 1984.

8. Aykin, Alparslan Gazi, and Fatma Pervin Bilir, 'Hükümet Programları ve Spor Politikaları' [Government Programs and Sport Policies], *Ç.Ü. Journal of Social Sciences Institute* 22, 2 (2013), pp. 239–54. All Turkish quotes in this chapter were translated from Turkish to English by the author.

9. Akça, Yaşar, and Gökhan Özer, 'Sports Policy of Turkey in Development Plans', *International Journal of Science Culture and Sport* 4, 2 (2016), pp. 177–86.

10. Devlet Planlama Teşkilatı [State Planning Organization], Kalkınma Planı İkinci Beş Yıl [Second Five-Year Development Plan], Ankara: State Planning Organization Publications, 1968.

11. Devlet Planlama Teşkilatı [State Planning Organization], Kalkınma Planı Üçüncü Beş Yıl [Third Five-Year Development Plan], Ankara: State Planning Organization Publications, 1972.

12. Devlet Planlama Teşkilatı [State Planning Organization], Kalkınma Planı Dördüncü Beş Yıl [Fourth Five-Year Development Plan], Ankara: State Planning Organization Publications, 1978.

13. Fişek, Kurthan, *Dünyada ve Türkiye'de Spor Yönetimi* [Sport Management in Turkey and in the World], Ankara: Ankara University Press, 1981; Original quote is in Turkish. All Turkish quotes in this chapter were translated from Turkish to English by the author.

14. Okumus, Fevzi, 'Impact of an Economic Crisis: Evidence from Turkey', *Annals of Tourism Research* 32, 4 (2005), pp. 942–961.

15. Çolakoğlu, Tekin, and Erturan, Esra, 'Spor Federasyonlarının Özerkleşmeleri ve Hukuksal Boyutunda Spor Hukuku Gereksinimleri', [Autonomy of sport federations and sport law requirements in forensic dimensions], *Electronic Journal of Social Sciences* 8, 27 (2009), pp. 323–35.

16. Tinaz, Cem, Douglas Michele Turco, and Paul Salisbury, 'Sport Policy in Turkey', *International Journal of Sport Policy and Politics* 6, 3 (2014), pp. 533–545.

17. Law no. 5105, Law for the Amendment of the Law on the Organization and Duties of the General Directorate of Youth and Sports (2004).

18. Erturan, Esra, and Faik İmamoğlu, 'Özerkleşen Spor Federasyonlarının İdari ve Mali Açıdan Değerlendirilmesi' [Administrative and Financial Evaluation of Autonomous Sports Federations], paper presented at the 9th International Sport Sciences Congress, Muğla, Turkey, 20–22 October 2006.

19. Author's interview with former Sports Minister Mehmet Ali Şahin, 10 July 2012, Ankara.

20. Law no. 7258, Regulation of Betting and Lottery Games in Soccer and Other Sports, 2007.

21. Aksar, Tuğrul, 'Iddaanin futbola katkisi', [The contribution of Iddaa to Football], *Futbol Ekonomi*, 2009, www.futbolekonomi.com/index.php?option=com_cont ent&view=article&id=575:ddaann-futbola-katks&catid=35:tugrulaksar&Ite mid=57, last accessed 23 January 2019.

22. Author's interview with former Sports Minister Faruk Nafiz Özak, 12 July 2012, Ankara.

23. Law no. 6222, Law for the Prevention of Violence and Match-fixing in Sports, 2011.

24. Üstünel, Rüstem, and Zafer Alkurt, 'Futbolda şiddet ve düzensizliğin önlenmesi için 6222 sayılı yasanın getirdiği yeni bir uygulama: Elektronik Bilet ve Yaşanan

Sorunlar' [A New Application by Law No. 6222 for Prevention of Football Violence and Disorder: Electronic Ticket and Problems Experienced], *Science Journal of Turkish Military Academy* 25, 2 (2015), pp. 141–75.

25. Üstünel and Alkurt, 'Elektronik Bilet ve Yaşanan Sorunlar,' p. 148.

26. Breuer, Christoph, Remco Hoekman, Siegfried Nagel, and Harold Van Der Werff, eds. *Sport Clubs in Europe a Cross-national Comparative Perspective*, Cham: Springer, 2015.

27. Author's interview with former Sports Minister Mehmet Ali Şahin, 10 July 2012, Ankara.

28. Law no. 5253, Law of Associations, 2004.

29. Ministry of Youth and Sport, Ulusal Gençlik ve Spor Politikası Belgesi [National youth and sport policy paper], Ankara, 2013, www.gsb.gov.tr/public/edit/files/Mevzuat/ulusal_genclik_ve_spor_politikasi.pdf, 7–21, last accessed 23 January 2019.

30. Regulations on Rewarding of Success in Youth and Sports Service and Activities (2000).

31. Ministry of Youth and Sports, *Ödül Yönetmeliği Değişiyor* [Regulation on awards is changing], 2013, http://gsb.gov.tr/HaberDetaylari/3/1982/odul-yonetmeligi-degisiyor.aspx, last accessed 23 January 2019.

32. Phone interview with athlete manager Önder Özbilen, 6 March 2018.

33. General Directorate of Sport, *Stratejik Plan 2015–2019* [Strategic plan for 2015–2019], 2015. https://sgm.gsb.gov.tr/Public/Edit/images/SGM/StratejiB%C3%BCt%C3%A7e/SGM_Stratejik%20Plan%20_%202015–2019_(04,01).pdf, last accessed 23 January 2019.

34. Author's interview with former Sports Minister Faruk Nafiz Özak, 12 July 2012, Ankara.

35. Author's interview with the president of the Turkish National Olympic Committee, Uğur Erdener, 3 July 2017, Ankara.

36. Author's interview with the president of the Turkish National Olympic Committee, Uğur Erdener, 3 July 2017.

37. 'Türkiye Olimpiyatlarda Ne Yaptı' [What Turkey did at the Olympic Games], Al Jazeera Türk, 22 August 2016, www.aljazeera.com.tr/haber/turkiye-olimpiyat-larda-ne-yapti, last accessed 23 January 2016.

38. Hacer Akyüz (President of the Orienteering Federation), Gülkız Tülay (President of the Chess Federation), Özlem Akdurak (President of the Sailing Federation).

39. Başbakanlık İletişim Merkezi (Bimer) [Presidential Communication Centre], communication with the organization via e-mail, 11 December 2017.

40. Author's interview with the Secretary General of the Turkish Tennis Federation, Serhat Altınel, 2 February 2018, Istanbul.

41. 'Yaklaşık 3 milyon Suriye'li kayıt altında' [Nearly 3 million Syrians are registered], *Haberturk.com.tr*, 15 March 2017, www.haberturk.com/gundem/haber/1427703-yaklasik-3-milyon-suriyeli-kayit-altinda, last accessed 23 January 2019.

42. Zengin, Eyüp and Cemal Öztaş, 'Yerel Yönetimler ve Spor' [Local municipalities and sport], *Sosyal Siyaset Konferansları Dergisi* 55 (2010), pp. 49–78.

43. Law no. 5393, Belediyeler Kanunu [The Law of Municipalities], 2005.

44. Author's interview with Yalçın Aksoy, liaison for Istanbul's 2000, 2004, 2008 and 2012 Olympic Bids, 23 June 2017, Istanbul.

45. Whitson, David, and John Horne, 'Underestimated Costs and Overestimated Benefits? Comparing the Outcomes of Sports Mega-Events in Canada and Japan', in *Sports Mega-Events: Social Scientific Analyses of a Global Phenomenon*, ed. John Horne and Wolfram Manzenreiter, Oxford: Blackwell, 2006, pp. 73–89; Waitt, Gordon, 'The Olympic Spirit and Civic Boosterism: The Sydney 2000 Olympics', *Tourism Geographies* 3, 3 (2001), pp. 249–78; Essex, Stephen, and Brian Chalkley, 'Mega-Sporting Events in Urban and Regional Policy: A History of the Winter Olympics', *Planning Perspectives* 19, 2 (2006), pp. 201–32.

46. Author's interview with the Secretary General of the Turkish Olympic Committee Neşe Gündoğan, 2 June 2017, Istanbul; author's interview with the CEO of Istanbul's 2020 Olympic Bid Ali Kiremitçioğlu, 2 May 2017.

47. Houlihan, Barrie, 'Public Sector Sport Policy', *International Review for the Sociology of Sport* 40, 2 (2005), pp. 165–85.

48. Latouche, Daniel, 'Montreal 1976', in *Olympic Cities: City Agendas, Planning, and the World's Games, 1896–2012*, eds. J. Gold and M. Gold, London: Routledge, 2007; Searle, Glen, 'Uncertain Legacy: Sydney's Olympic Stadiums', *European Planning Studies* 10, 7 (2002), pp. 845–60.

49. Zimbalist, Andrew, *Circus Maximus: The Economic Gamble Behind Hosting the Olympics and the World Cup*, Washington: The Brookings Institution, 2015.

50. See for example, Andranovich, Greg, Matthew Burbank, and Charles Heying, 'Olympic Cities: Lessons Learned from Mega-Event Politics', *Journal of Urban Affairs* 23, 2 (2001), pp. 113–31; and Fourie, Johan, and Karly Spronk, 'South African Mega-Sport Events and Their Impact on Tourism', *Journal of Sport and Tourism* 16, 1 (2011), pp. 75–97.

51. Türkiye İstatistik Kurumu (TUIK), İstatistiklerle Gençlik,2017 [Turkish Statistical Institution, Youth in Statistics, 2017], Ankara, 2018.

52. Author's interview with former Sports Minister Faruk Nafiz Özak 12 July 2012, Ankara.

53. General Directorate of Sports Statistics, 2016, http://sgm.gsb.gov.tr/Sayfalar/175/105/Istatistikler, last accessed 23 January 2019.

54. Author's interview with the Sports Director of the Turkish Basketball Federation, İbrahim Erkan, 10 January 2018, Istanbul.

55. Author's interview with the Secretary General of the Turkish Tennis Federation Serhat Altınel, 2 February 2018, Istanbul.

56. Gedikoglu, Tokay, 'Avrupa Birliği Sürecinde Türk Eğitim Sistemi: Sorunlar ve Çözüm Önerileri' [Turkish Education System through the European Union

Process: Problems and Possible Solutions], *Mersin University Journal of the Faculty of Education* 1, 1 (2005), pp. 66–80.

57. Interview with former Sport Minister Faruk Nafiz Özak, personal communication with author, 12 July 2012, Ankara.

58. David Kirk and Trish Gorely, 'Challenging Thinking About the Relationship Between School Physical Education and Sport Performance,' *European Physical Education Review* 6 (2000): 119–34.

59. Author's interview with the president of the Turkish National Olympic Committee, Uğur Erdener, 3 July 2017, Ankara.

60. Author's interview with former Sports Minister Murat Başesgioğlu, 11 July 2012, Ankara; author's interview with former Sports Minister Mehmet Ali Şahin, 10 July 2012, Ankara.

61. 'Türkiye'nin Stadyum Yatırımlarında Son Durum,' [Latest stand of Turkey's stadium investments] 2016, www.ajanshaber.com/turkiyenin-dev-stadyum-yatirim-larinda-son-durum-haberi/338938, last accessed 23 January 2019.

62. Masterman, Guy, *Strategic Sports Event Management: An International Approach*, Oxford: Elsevier Butterworth-Heinemann, 2004, p. 78

63. Masterman, *Strategic Sports Event Management*.

8. DEVELOPING A NATIONAL ELITE SPORT POLICY IN AN ARAB COUNTRY

1. Beck, Peter, 'War Minus the Shooting: George Orwell on International Sport and the Olympics,' *Sport in History* 33, 1 (2013), pp. 72–94.

2. Colomb, Pierre, 'Sport et Etat,' (Sport and State), *Pouvoirs* 61 (1992), p. 41.

3. Nassif, Nadim, 'Elite Sport Ranking of the 'International Society of Sports Sciences in the Arab World': An Accurate Evaluation of all Nations' Performances International Sports Competitions,' *Athens Journal of Sport* 4, 1 (2017), p. 54.

4. Novikov, A.D. and A.M. Maximenko, 'The Influence of Selected Socio-economic Factors on the Level of Sports Achievements in the Various Countries (Using as an Example the 18th Olympic Games in Tokyo),' *International Review for the Sociology of Sport* 7, 1 (1972), p. 27.

5. Reiche, Danyel, 'Why Developing Countries are just Spectators in the "Gold War": The Case of Lebanon in the Olympic Games,' *Third World Quarterly* 38, 4 (2016), p. 996.

6. Reiche, Danyel, *Success and Failure of Countries at the Olympic Games*, London and New York: Routledge, 2017, pp. 3–4.

7. Ramadan, Mazen, Head of the 2016 Lebanese Olympic delegation, in discussion with the author, May 2016.

8. Ibid.

9. 'Estonia,' National Olympic Committees, www.olympic.org/Estonia, last accessed 23 January 2019.

10. 'Georgia', National Olympic Committees, www.olympic.org/georgia, last accessed 23 January 2019.

11. 'Jamaica', National Olympic Committees, www.olympic.org/jamaica, last accessed 23 January 2019.

12. Nassif, 'Elite Sport Ranking.'

13. Green, Mick, 'Changing Policy Priorities for Sport in England: The Emergence of Elite Sport Development as a Key Policy Concern', *Leisure Studies* 23, 4 (2004), pp. 365–85; Grix, Jonathan and Franklin Carmichael, 'Why do Governments Invest in Elite Sport? A Polemic', *International Journal of Sport Policy and Politics* 4, 1 (2012), pp. 73–90.

14. Novikov and Maximenko, 'The Influence of Selected Socio-economic Factors on the Level of Sports Achievements', pp. 27–44; Kiviaho, Pekka, and Pekka Mäkelä, 'Olympic Success: A Sum of Non-material and Material Factors', *International Review for the Sociology of Sport* 13, 2 (1978), p. 5.

15. Houlihan, Barrie, and Jinming Zheng, 'Small States: Sport and Politics at the Margin', *International Journal of Sport Policy and Politics* 7, 3 (2014), pp. 329–44; Bernard, Andrew B. and Meghan R. Busse, 'Who Wins the Olympic Games: Economic Resources and Medal Totals', *Review of Economics and Statistics* 86, 1 (2004, pp. 413–17; Andreff, Wladimir, 'Economic Development as Major Determinant of Olympic Medal Wins: Predicting Performances of Russian and Chinese Teams at Sochi Games', *International Journal of Economic Policy in Emerging Economies* 6, 4 (2013), pp. 314–40.

16. De Bosscher, Veerle, Simon Shibli, Hans Westerbeek, and Maarten van Bottenburg, eds., *Successful Elite Sport Policies*, Oxford: Meyer & Meyer Sport, 2015.

17. Reiche, Danyel, *Success and Failure of Countries at the Olympic Games*, London and New York: Routledge, 2017.

18. Grix and Carmichael, 'Why do Governments Invest in Elite Sport?', p. 73.

19. Riordan, Jim, 'Rewriting Soviet Sports History', *Journal of Sports History* 20, 3 (1993), p. 251.

20. Henry, Ian P., Mahfoud Amara, and Mansour Al-Tauqui, 'Sport, Arab Nationalism and the Pan-Arab Games', *International Review for the Sociology of Sport* 38, 3 (2003), p. 301.

21. Chehabi, Houchang E., 'Sport and Politics in Iran: The Legend of Gholamreza Takhti', *The International Journal of the History of Sport* 12, 3 (1995), pp. 52–8.

22. Chappell, Robert, 'Sport in Namibia: Conflicts, Negotiations and Struggles since Independence', *International Review for the Sociology of Sport* 40, 2 (2004), p. 241.

23. Bouchet, P. and M. Kaach, 'Existe-t-il un 'Modèle Sportif' dans les Pays Africains Francophones?' Does a 'sport model' exist in French-speaking African countries?, *Revue STAPS*, 65 (2005), pp. 7–8.

24. Callede, Jean-Paul, 'Les Politiques du Sport en France' (Sport policies in France), *L'Année sociologique* 52, 2 (2002), p. 447.

25. Callede, 'Les Politiques du Sport en France', 447.
26. Novikov and Maximenko, 'The Influence of Selected Socio-economic Factors', p. 27
27. Kiviaho and Mäkelä, 'Olympic Success', p. 5.
28. Rathke, Alexander, and Ulrich Woitek, 'Economics and the Summer Olympics: An Efficiency Analysis', *Journal of Sports Economics* 9, 5 (2008), p. 521.
29. Butter, Den and Casper M. van der Tak, 'Olympic Medals as an Indicator of Social Welfare', *Social Indicators Research* 35, 1 (1995), pp. 27–8.
30. Johnson, Daniel K. N., and Ayfer Ali, 'Coming to Play or Coming to Win', Working Paper, Wellesley College Department of Economics, 2000, p. 8.
31. Lui, Hon-Kwong and Wing Suen, 'Men, Money and Medals: An Econometric Analysis of the Olympic Games', *Pacific Economic Review* 13, 1 (2008), p. 1.
32. Van Tuyckom, Charlotte and Karl G. Jöreskog, 'Going for Gold! Welfare Characteristics and Olympic Success', *The Park Place Economist* 13 (2012), p. 67.
33. Andreff 'Economic Development as Major Determinant of Olympic Medal Wins', p. 314.
34. Kuper, Gerard, and Elmer Sterken, 'Olympic Participation and Performance since 1896', Working Paper, University of Groningen, Research Institute Systems, Organizations and Management, 2003.
35. Moosa, Imad. A. and Lee Smith, 'Economic Development Indicators as Determinants of Medal Winning at the Sydney Olympics: An Extreme Bounds Analysis', *Australian Economic Papers* 43, 3 (2004), p. 300.
36. Tcha, Moonjoong and Vitaly Pershin, 'Reconsidering Performance at the Summer Olympics and Revealed Comparative Advantage', *Journal of Sports Economics* 4, 3 (2003), p. 231.
37. Bernard, Andrew B. and Meghan R. Busse, 'Who Wins the Olympic Games: Economic Resources and Medal Totals', *Review of Economics and Statistics* 86, 1 (2004), p. 413.
38. Butter and van der Tak, 'Olympic Medals as an Indicator of Social Welfare', p. 31.
39. Houlihan and Zheng, 'Small States: Sport and Politics at the Margin', p. 330.
40. Nadim Nassif, *Sport Policy in Lebanon, 1975 to 2004: Lebanese Geopolitical Background, Lebanese Sport Characteristics and Difficulties Plan for Development* (Saarbrucken, Germany: Lambert Academic Publishing GMBH & Co.KG, 2010), p. 75.
41. 'United States of America', National Olympic Committees, www.olympic.org/united-states-of-america.
42. Steven J. Overman, *The Protestant Ethic and the Spirit of Sport: How Calvinism and Capitalism Shaped America's Games* (Mercer University Press, 2011), viii–viii.
43. Mick Green, 'Changing Policy Priorities for Sport in England: The Emergence of Elite Sport Development as a Key Policy Concern', *Leisure Studies* 23, no. 4 (2004): p. 365.

44. Houlihan, Barrie, 'Public Sector Sport Policy: Developing a Framework for Analysis', *International Review for the Sociology of Sport* 40, 2 (2005), p. 163.

45. De Bosscher, et al., eds., *Successful Elite Sport Policies*, p. 24.

46. Ibid., p. 42.

47. Ibid., p. 47.

48. Reiche, *Success and Failure of Countries at the Olympic Games*, pp. 3–4.

49. Ibid.

50. Ibid., p. 90.

51. Ibid., p. 97.

52. Ibid., p. 108.

53. Ibid., p. 126.

54. Nassif, 'Elite Sport Ranking.'

55. De Bosscher, Verlee, et al., *The Global Sporting Arms Race: An International Comparative Study on Sports Policy Factors Leading to International Sporting Success*, Oxford, UK: Meyer & Meyer Sport, 2008.

56. 'USA, Russia and Germany Ranked Top Three Countries in Elite Sport Ranking', *Association Internationale de la Presse Sportive*, 21 July 2015, www.aipsmedia.com/index.php?page=news&cod=17052, last accessed 23 January 2019; 'International Society of Sport Sciences in the Arab World Releases Elite Sport List', *Association Internationale de la Presse Sportive*, 14 April 2016, www.aipsmedia.com/index.php?page=news&cod=18503, last accessed 23 January 2019; 'USA and France Top I3SAW Ranking of Countries in Elite Sport', *Association Internationale de la Presse Sportive*, 18 January 2017, www.aipsmedia.com/2017/01/18/20160/best-of-2016-world-sport-i3saw-rankings-usa-France, last accessed 23 January 2019.

57. Novikov and Maximenko, 'Socio-economic Factors Influence on Sports Achievements in Countries', p. 27; Kiviaho and Mäkelä, 'Olympic Success: A Sum of Non-material and Material Factors'; Rathke and Woitek, 'Economics and the Summer Olympics', p. 521; Den Butter and van der Tak, 'Olympic Medals as an Indicator of Social Welfare', p. 27–8; Johnson and Ali, 'Coming to Play or Coming to Win', p. 8; Hon-Kwong and Suen, 'Men, Money and Medals', p. 1; Tuyckom and Joreskog, 'Going for Gold! Welfare Characteristics and Olympic Success', p. 67; Andreff, 'Economic Development as Major Determinant of Olympic Medal Wins', p. 314; Kuper and Sterken, 'Olympic Participation and Performance Since 1896'; Moosa and Smith, 'Economic Development Indicators as Determinants of Medal Winning at the Sydney Olympics', p. 300; Tcha and Pershin, 'Reconsidering Performance at the Summer Olympics', p. 232.

58. 'The World Factbook', Central Intelligence Agency, www.cia.gov/library/publications/the-world-factbook, last accessed 23 January 2019.

59. De Bosscher et al., *Successful Elite Sport Policies*, p. 24.

60. Reiche, *Success and Failure of Countries at the Olympic Games*, pp. 3–4.

61. 'Homepage', Scimago Journal & Country Rank, www.scimagojr.com, last accessed 23 January 2019.

62. 'CINC', The Index of National Power, www.nationalpower.info/cinc, last accessed 23 January 2019.

63. Angang, Hu, and Men Honghua, 'The Rising of Modern China: Comprehensive National Power and Grand Strategy', *Strategy and Management* 3, 2 (2002).

64. Houlihan and Zheng, *Small States: Sport and Politics at the Margin*, p. 330.

65. Andrew and Busse, 'Who Wins the Olympic Games', p. 413.

66. Den Butter and van der Tak, 'Olympic Medals as an Indicator of Social Welfare', pp. 31–2.

67. De Bosscher et al., *Successful Elite Sport Policies*, p. 24; Reiche, *Success and Failure of Countries at the Olympic Games*, pp. 3–4.

68. Sacre, Joseph, *Le Sport au Liban* (Sport in Lebanon), Beirut: Joseph Reayde Edition, 1980, pp. 79–90.

69. Nassif, *Sport Policy in Lebanon*, p. 52.

70. Ibid., p. 53.

71. Stanton, Andrea L., '"Pioneer of Olympism in the Middle East": Gabriel Gemayel and Lebanese Sport', *The International Journal of the History of Sport* 29, 15 (2012), p. 2119.

72. Stanton, 'Pioneer of Olympism in the Middle East', p. 2119.

73. Ibid., p. 2120.

74. Mazen Ramadan, Head of the 2016 Lebanese Olympic Delegation, in discussion with the author, May 2016.

75. Sanjay Myers, 'Government Serious about Sport, Says PM', *Jamaica Observer*, 30 January 2016, www.jamaicaobserver.com/sport/Government-serious-about-sport—says-PM, last accessed 23 January 2019.

76. European Programme of National Cultural Policy Reviews, Cultural Policy in Estonia, Council for Cultural Co-operation Strasbourg, 1996, p. 245

77. 'The primary project of the 2015 budget', [in Georgian], Civil Georgia, www.civil.ge/geo/article.php?id=28719, last accessed 23 January 2019.

78. De Bosscher et al., *Successful Elite Sport Policies*, p. 24.

79. Henry, Balford, 'Government Turns to Sport, Entertainment, Culture for Economic Growth', *Jamaica Observer*, 28 August 2016, www.jamaicaobserver.com/business/Government-turns-to-sport—entertainment—culture-for-economic-growth_72148, last accessed 23 January 2019.

80. Ibid.

81. De Bosscher, Verlee, Popi Sotiriadou, and Maarten van Bottenburg, 'Scrutinizing the Sport Pyramid Metaphor: An Examination of the Relationship between Elite Success and Mass Participation in Flanders', *International Journal of Sport Policy and Politics* 5, 3 (2013), p. 320.

82. Colomb, 'Sport et Etat', p. 41; Calmat, Alain, 'Sport et Nationalisme' (Sport and Nationalism), *Pouvoirs* 61 (1992), p. 51; Merkel, Udo, 'The Politics of Sport Diplomacy and Reunification in Divided Korea: One Nation, Two Countries and

Three Flags', *International Review for the Sociology of Sport* 43, 3 (2008), p. 289; Henry, Amara, and Al-Tauqui, 'Sport, Arab Nationalism and the Pan-Arab Games', 301; Adami, Sylvain, 'Les Jeux Méditerranéens: Un Reflet de la Situation Géopolitique de l'Espace Méditerranéen' (The Mediterranean Games: A reflection of the geopolitical situation in the Mediterranean space), *Les Cahiers de Confluence*, 50 (2004), p. 71; Chifflet, Pierre and S. Gouda, 'Sport et Politique Nationale au Bénin de 1975 à 1990' (Sport and National Policy in Benin from 1975 to 1990), *Revue STAPS* 13, 28 (1992), p. 71; Chifflet, Pierre and Souaïbou Gouda, 'Olympisme et Identité Nationale en Afrique Noire Francophone' (Olympism and national identity in Francophone Black Africa), *Revue STAPS* 17, 41 (1996), p. 93; Djirmey, Aboubacar et al., 'Lutte et Identité Culturelle au Niger' Wrestling and cultural identity in Niger, *Politique Africaine* 45 (1992), p. 142; Bergsgard, Nils Asle and Hilmar Rommetvedt, 'Sport and Politics: The Case of Norway,' *International Review for the Sociology of Sport* 41, 1 (2006), p. 7.

83. Salibi, Kamal, *A House of Many Mansions. The History of Lebanon Reconsidered*, London: I.B. Tauris, 2009, p. 35.

84. Nassif, Nadim, and Mahfoud Amara, 'Sport Policy and Politics in Lebanon,' *International Journal of Sport Policy and Politics* 7, 2 (2015), p. 1.

85. Ibid.

86. Ibid, p. 6.

87. Nassif, Nadim, ed. 'The Olympic Movement and the Arab World—History, Culture and Geopolitics, Factors Behind Lebanon's Difficulties to Achieve Success in the Olympics', *The International Journal of the History of Sport Journal* (forthcoming).

88. Reiche, Danyel, 'Why Developing Countries are just Spectators in the "Gold War": The Case of Lebanon in the Olympic Games,' *Third World Quarterly* 38, 4 (2017), pp. 1003–4.

89. Reiche, 'Why Developing Countries are just Spectators in the 'Gold War', p. 1002.

90. Reiche, *Success and Failure of Countries at the Olympic Games*, p. 97.

91. Ibid., p. 108.

92. Reiche, 'Why Developing Countries are just Spectators in the "Gold War"', p. 1002.

93. Nassif, Nadim, *Sport Policy in Lebanon*, p. 75.

94. Ibid., p. 76.

95. Ibid., p. 66.

96. Overman, *The Protestant Ethic and the Spirit of Sport*.

97. Decree 247 of the Ministry of Youth and Sports.

98. Nadim Nassif, 'Corruption in Sport: The Case of Lebanon,' *Middle East Law and Governance Journal* 6, no. 2 (2014): 139.

99. Raymond Touma, Financing Director of the Lebanese Ministry of Youth and Sports, in discussion with the author, March 2011.

100. Deputy Simon Abi Ramia, Head of the Lebanese Youth and Sports Parliamentary Committee, in discussion with the author, February 2010.

101. Antoine Chartier, Former President of the Lebanese Olympic Committee, in discussion with the author, March 2011.

102. Deputy Simon Abi Ramia, Head of the Lebanese Youth and Sports Parliamentary Committee, in discussion with the author, February 2010; Antoine Chartier, Former President of the Lebanese Olympic Committee, in discussion with the author, March 2011.

103. Callede, Jean-Paul, 'Les Politiques du Sport en France', p. 447.

104. Nassif, 'Corruption in Sport: The Case of Lebanon,' p. 133.

105. De Bosscher, et al., *Successful Elite Sport Policies*, p. 24; Reiche, *Success and Failure of Countries at the Olympic Games*, pp. 3–4.

106. De Bosscher, ed., Veerle, 'SPLISS Conference on Elite Sport Success: Society Boost or Not?' 13–14 November 2013, Antwerp, Conference Proceedings, Vrije Universiteit Brussel, Belgium, www.vub.ac.be/SBMA/sites/default/files/Conference%20Proceedings%20SPLISS.pdf, last accessed 23 January 2019.

9. LEGACIES OF MEGA-SPORTING EVENTS IN DEVELOPING COUNTRIES: A CASE STUDY OF LEBANON

1. Matheson, Victor A. and Robert A. Baade, 'Mega-sporting Events in Developing Nations: Playing the Way to Prosperity?' *South African Journal of Economics* 72, 5 (2004), pp. 1085–1096.

2. Cornelissen, Scarlett, 'The Geopolitics of Global Aspiration: Sport Mega-events and Emerging Powers', *The International Journal of the History of Sport* 27, 16–18 (2010), pp. 3008–3025.

3. Zimbalist, Andrew, *Circus Maximus: The Economic Gamble Behind Hosting the Olympics and the World Cup*, Washington, DC: The Brookings Institution, 2015.

4. Reiche, Danyel 'Investing in Sporting Success as a Domestic and Foreign Policy Tool: The Case of Qatar', *International Journal of Sport Policy and Politics* 7, 4 (2015), pp. 489–504.

5. 'National Olympic Committees', Olympic.org, 2018, www.olympic.org/national-olympic-committees, last accessed 23 January 2019.

6. Pettigrew, Stephen and Danyel Reiche, 'Hosting the Olympic Games: An Overstated Advantage in Sports History', *The International Journal of the History of Sport* 33, 6–7 (2016), p. 644.

7. 'FIFA Associations', Fédération Internationale de Football Association (FIFA), www.fifa.com/associations/index.html, last accessed 23 January 2019.

8. Horne, John, 'Sports Mega-events–three sites of Contemporary Political Contestation', *Sport in Society* 20, 3 (2017), p. 329.

9. Ibid., p. 331.

10. Cornelissen, 'Geopolitics of Global Aspiration,' p. 3008.
11. Nye, Joseph S., *Soft Power: The Means to Success in World Politics*, New York: Public Affairs, 2004, p. x.
12. Ibid., p. 89.
13. Horne, 'Sports Mega-events,' p. 332.
14. Harris, John, Fiona Skillen, and Matthew L. McDowell, 'Introduction: The Contested Terrain of Major Sporting Events', *Sport in Society* 20, 3 (2017), p. 325.
15. Horne, 'Sports Mega-events', p. 332.
16. Reiche, 'The Case of Qatar', p. 489–504.
17. Horne, 'Sports Mega-events', p. 334.
18. Henry, Ian P., Mahfoud Amara, and Mansour Al-Tauqi, 'Sport, Arab Nationalism and the Pan-Arab Games', *International Review for the Sociology of Sport* 38, 3 (2003), pp. 295–310; Luis Henrique Rolim Silva and Hans-Dieter Gerber, 'Our Games! The Pan-Arab Games (1953–1965)', *The International Journal of the History of Sport* 29, 15 (2012), pp. 2099–114.
19. Rowe, David, 'The AFC Asian Cup', in *Sport, Media and Mega-Events*, eds. Wenner, Lawrence A. and Andrew C. Billings, Abingdon, Oxon: Taylor & Francis, 2017, p. 185.
20. Khashan, Hilal, *Inside the Lebanese Confessional Mind*, Lanham, MD: University Press of America, 1992, p. xiii.
21. Personal communication with the author, 2014, Cambridge, Massachusetts.
22. Bryman, Alan, *Social Research Methods*. New York: Oxford University Press, 2012, p. 470.
23. 'Aoun: FIBA Asia Cup Proves International Trust in Lebanon', *National News Agency*, 27 July 2017, http://nna-leb.gov.lb/en/show-news/81796/Aoun-FIBA-Asia-Cup-proves-international-trust-in-Lebanon, last accessed 23 January 2019.
24. Henry, Amara, and Al-Tauqi, 'The Pan-Arab Games', p. 295.
25. Silva and Gerber, 'The Pan-Arab Games (1953–1965)', p. 2100.
26. Henry, Amara, and Al-Tauqi, 'The Pan-Arab Games', p. 295.
27. Robert Fisk, 'Saddam's Athletes Tripped up at Visa Hurdle', *The Independent*, 12 July 1997, p. 14. www.independent.co.uk/news/world/kuwait-up-in-arms-as-iraq-joins-arab-games-1249879.html, last accessed 23 January 2019.
28. Arnold Kemp, 'Iraq v Kazakhstan: What Happened Next?' *The Observer*, 20 July 1997, p. 1.
29. 'Syrian Soccer Fans Riot After Loss to Jordan in Arab Games Final', *The Jerusalem Post*, 29 July 1997, p. 13.
30. Silva and Gerber, 'The Pan-Arab Games (1953–1965)' p. 2108.
31. Amichai Alperovich, 'Israel in der Olympischen Bewegung' [Israel in the Olympic Movement] (PhD dissertation, Deutsche Sporthochschule, 2008), p. 254.
32. Reiche, Danyel, 'Not Allowed to Win: Lebanon's Sporting Boycott of Israel', *The Middle East Journal* 72, 1 (2018), p. 39.

33. Rowe, 'The AFC Asian Cup' p. 190.

34. Ibid., p. 194–195.

35. Megheirkouni, Majd, 'Arab Sport between Islamic Fundamentalism and Arab Spring', *Sport in Society* 20, 11 (2017), p. 1494.

36. Beard, 'Lebanon's Asian Odyssey: Battered Beirut has been Rejuvenated by Football', *The Observer*, 15 October 2000, p. 6, www.theguardian.com/football/2000/oct/15/newsstory.sport12, last accessed 23 January 2019.

37. 'Lebanon is not Ready to Host the Asian Cup', *Middle East News Online*, 9 August 2000.

38. 'The Asia Cup: Ultimatum to Lebanon', *Middle East News Online*, 15 August 2000.

39. Ghazi, Ayman, 'Sports in Lebanon, 8th Pan Arab Games: The Opening Ceremony', 4 August 1997, www.ghazi.de/panopen.html, last accessed 23 January 2019.

40. 'Aoun: FIBA Asia Cup Proves International Trust in Lebanon.'

41. 'Spectacular Ceremony Kicks off Francophone Games in Lebanon', *The Daily Star*, 28 September 2009, www.dailystar.com.lb/News/Lebanon-News/2009/Sep-28/55614-spectacular-ceremony-kicks-off-francophone-games-in-lebanon.ashx, last accessed 23 January 2019.

42. Zaatari, Mohammed, 'Bahia Hariri Expresses Pride during Francophone Games', *The Daily Star*, 29 September 2009, www.dailystar.com.lb//News/Lebanon-News/2009/Sep-30/55637-bahia-hariri-expresses-pride-during-francophone-games.ashx, last accessed 23 January 2019.

43. Beard, 'Lebanon's Asian Odyssey', p. 6.

44. Nassif, Nadim, *Sport Policy in Lebanon, 1975 to 2004: Lebanese Geopolitical Background, Lebanese Sport Characteristics and Difficulties, Plan for Development*, Saarbrucken: Lambert Academic Publishing, 2009, p. 58.

45. Ibid.

46. Patrick Galey, 'Why People Only Chose to see the Worst in the Francophone Games.' *The Daily Star*, 9 October 2009, www.dailystar.com.lb/News/Lebanon-News/2009/Oct-09/55073-why-people-only-chose-to-see-the-worst-in-the-francophone-games.ashx, last accessed 31 January 2019.

47. 'Poor Media Coverage Blamed for Francophone Flop', *The Daily Star*, 5 November 2009, www.dailystar.com.lb/News/Lebanon-News/2009/Nov-05/56107-poor-media-coverage-blamed-for-francophone-flop.ashx, last accessed 23 January 2019.

48. Silva and Gerber, 'The Pan-Arab Games (1953–1965)', p. 2108.

49. The following cultural events are part of the Francophone Games: singing, story-telling, traditional dance, poetry, painting, photography, and sculpture. For more information see www.jeux.francophonie.org, last accessed 23 January 2019.

50. Henry, Amara, and Al-Tauqi, 'The Pan-Arab Games', p. 306.

51. Ibid.

52. 'With 50 days to #FIBAAsiaCup2017, Meet the Participating Teams', Fédération Internationale de Basketball (FIBA), 15 August 2017, www.fiba.com/asia-

cup/2017/news/fiba-asia-cup-2017-countdown-meet-the-16-teams, last accessed 23 January 2019.

53. Catacutan, Dodo, 'Andray Blatche unlikely to join Gilas in FIBA Asia Cup owing to Lebanon Security Concerns', *Sports Interactive Network Philippines*, 24 July 2017, www.spin.ph/basketball/fiba/news/andray-blatche-unlikely-to-join-gilas-in-fiba-asia-cup-owing-to-lebanon-security-concerns, last accessed 23 January 2019.

54. Ghazi, Ayman, 'Sports in Lebanon.'

55. 'War or Peace, Asia 2000 will Stay', *Middle East News Online*, 9 October 2000.

56. 'War or Peace, Asia 2000 will Stay.'

57. Personal communication with the author, 2017, Beirut.

58. Ibid.

59. Ibid.

60. Henry, Amara and Al-Tauqi, 'The Pan-Arab Games' p. 304.

61. Ghazi, Ayman, 'Sports in Lebanon: Sports City', 4 August 1997, www.ghazi.de/pancity.html, last accessed 23 January 2019.

62. 'Canada to Contribute $1 Million to Francophone Games', *The Daily Star*, 25 September 2009, www.dailystar.com.lb/News/Lebanon-News/2009/Sep-25/55575-canada-to-contribute-1-million-to-francophone-games.ashx, last accessed 23 January 2019; Galey, 'Why People Only Chose to See the Worst in the Francophone Games.'

63. Personal communication with author, 2017, Beirut.

64. Ibid.

65. Personal communication with author, 2017, Beirut.

66. 'Tripoli Stadium still an Asian Cup Problem,' *Middle East News Online*, 21 September 2000.

67. Personal communication with author, 2017, Beirut.

68. Rowe, 'The AFC Asian Cup,' 194.

69. James Young, 'South Africa, Brazil World Cup Stadia largely remain National Burdens,' *Sports Illustrated*, 2 February 2015, www.si.com/planet-futbol/2015/02/02/world-cup-stadiums-brazil-south-africa-fifa-white-elephants, last accessed 23 January 2019.

70. Personal communication with author, 2017, Beirut.

71. Ibid.

72. Ibid.

73. Ibid.

74. Ibid.

75. 'Corruption Perceptions Index 2016', Transparency International, 14 August 2017, www.transparency.org/news/feature/corruption_perceptions_index_2016, last accessed 23 January 2019.

76. Personal communication with author, 2017, Beirut.

77. Ibid.
78. Ibid.
79. Ibid.
80. Ibid.
81. Horne, 'Sports Mega-Events', p. 335.
82. 'Lebanon Expresses Willingness to Host any International Tournament', *Xinhuanet*, 19 August 2017, www.xinhuanet.com/english/2017–08/19/c_136538345.htm, last accessed 23 January 2019.

10. THE BUSINESS OF SPORTS IN THE GULF COOPERATION COUNCIL MEMBER STATES

1. Reardon, Jonathan, 'Developments in Saudi Sports Following Saudi Vision 2030', *Al Tamimi and Company*, 7 January 2017, www.tamimi.com/en/magazine/law-update/section-14/dec-jan-2017/developments-in-saudi-sports-following-saudi-vision-2030.html, last accessed 23 January 2019.
2. Qatar Olympic Committee, 'Qatar Sports Strategy 2011–2016', July 2011, www.aspire.qa/Document/Sports_sector_strategy_final-English.pdf, last accessed 23 January 2019.
3. 'The Economic Impact of the Premier League', Ernst and Young, 18 November 2015, www.ey.com/Publication/vwLUAssets/EY_-_The_economic_impact_of_the_Premier_League/$FILE/EY-The-economic-impact-of-the-Premier-League.pdf, last accessed 23 January 2019.
4. 'Qatar Spending $500m a Week on World Cup Infrastructure Projects', *BBC News*, 8 February 2017, www.bbc.co.uk/news/world-middle-east-38905510, last accessed 23 January 2019.
5. Beblawi, Hazem and Giacomo Luciani, ed. *The Rentier State*, London: Routledge, 1990.
6. Reiche, Danyel, 'Investing in Sporting Success as a Domestic and Foreign Policy Tool: The Case of Qatar', *International Journal of Sport Policy and Politics* 7, 4 (2015), pp. 489–504.
7. Grix, Jonathan, and Donna Lee, 'Soft Power, Sports Mega-events and Emerging States: The Lure of the Politics of Attraction', *Global Society* 27, 4 (2013), pp. 521–36; Håvard Mokleiv Nygård and Scott Gates, 'Soft Power at Home and Abroad: Sport Diplomacy, Politics and Peace-Building', *International Area Studies Review* 16, 3 (2013), pp. 235–43.
8. Brannagan, Paul, and Richard Giulianotti, 'Soft Power and Soft Disempowerment: Qatar, Global Sport and Football's 2022 World Cup Finals', *Leisure Studies* 34, 6 (2015), pp. 703–19; Reiche, 'Investing in Sporting', pp. 489–504.
9. Nye, Joseph S., *Soft Power: The Means to Success in World Politics*, New York: Public Affairs, 2004.

10. Chadwick, Simon, 'China and Qatar's Stadium Diplomacy: An East-West One-two for Oil and Power', *Policy Forum*, 19 December 2016, www.policyforum.net/china-qatars-stadium-diplomacy/, last accessed 23 January 2019.

11. Van Ham, Peter, 'Place Branding: The State of the Art', *The Annals of the American Academy of Political and Social Science* 16, 1 (2008), pp. 126–49; Fan, Ying, 'Branding the Nation: Toward a Better Understanding', *Place Branding and Public Diplomacy* 6, 2 (2010), pp. 97–103; Anholt, Simon, 'Why Brand? Some Practical Considerations for Nation Branding', *Place Branding and Public Diplomacy* 2, 2 (2010), p. 97.

12. Dinnie, Keith, *Nation Branding: Concepts, Issues, Practice*, Oxford: Routledge, 2015.

13. Govers, Robert, 'Brand Dubai and its Competitors in the Middle East: An Image and Reputation Analysis', *Place Branding and Public Diplomacy* 8, 1 (2012), pp. 48–57; Peterson, John E., 'Qatar and the World: Branding for a Micro-State', *The Middle East Journal* 60, 4 (2006), pp. 732–48; King, John Mark, 'Nation Branding: Coverage and Perceptions of Qatar in Major World Newspapers', *Business Research Yearbook* 15, 3 (2008), pp. 27–32.

14. 'Emerging Giants: Defining the Trend: How Increasing Investment from Asia and the Middle East is Turning Them into Sport's Emerging Giants', Nielsen Sports, December 2015, http://nielsensports.com/wp-content/uploads/Repucom-Emerging-Markets.pdf, last accessed 23 January 2019.

15. 'Qatar Tourism Authority Strategy', Qatar Tourism Authority, 23 February 2014, www.visitqatar.qa/corporate/planning/strategy-2030, last accessed 23 January 2019.

16. Warburton, Darren E.R., Crystal Whitney Nicol, and Shannon S. D. Bredin, 'Health Benefits of Physical Activity: The Evidence', *Canadian Medical Association Journal* 174, 6 (2006), pp. 801–09.

17. Alhyas, Layla, Ailsa McKay, Anjali Balasanthiran, and Azeem Majeed, 'Prevalence of Overweight, Obesity, Hyperglycaemia, Hypertension and Dyslipidaemia in the Gulf: Systematic Review', *JRSM Short Reports* 2, 7 (2011), pp. 1–16.

18. Colditz, Graham A., 'Economic Costs of Obesity and Inactivity', *Medicine and Science in Sports and Exercise* 31, 11 (1999), pp. S663–7.

19. Nicholl, Jon P., Patricia Coleman, and John E. Brazier, 'Health and Health Care Costs and Benefits of Exercise', *Pharmacoeconomics* 5, 2 (1994), pp. 109–22.

20. Penedo, Frank J, and Jason R. Dahn, 'Exercise and Well-being: A Review of Mental and Physical Health Benefits Associated with Physical Activity', *Current Opinion in Psychiatry* 18, 2 (2005), pp. 189–93.

21. Osman, Ossama T. and Mohammed Afifi, 'Troubled Minds in the Gulf: Mental Health Research in the United Arab Emirates (1989–2008)', *Asia Pacific Journal of Public Health* 22, 3 (2010), pp. 48S–53S.

22. Hallmann, Kirstin, Christoph Breuer, and Benedikt Kühnreich, 'Happiness, Pride

and Elite Sporting Success: What Population Segments Gain Most from National Athletic Achievements?', *Sport Management Review* 16, 2 (2013), pp. 226–35.

23. Kavetsos, Georgios and Stefan Szymanski, 'National Well-being and International Sports Events', *Journal of Economic Psychology* 31, 2 (2010), pp. 158–71.

24. 'Qatar National Sports Day Round-up 2017', *BQ Magazine*, 15 February 2017, http://www.bq-magazine.com/qatar-national-sports-day-roundup-2017, last accessed 23 January 2019.

25. Monetary values are in US dollars unless indicated otherwise; 'Sports and Recreation Business Statistics Analysis, Business and Industry Statistics', Plunkett Research Ltd., 19 October 2017, www.plunkettresearch.com/statistics/sports-industry, last accessed 23 January 2019.

26. 'Sports Industry Growing Faster than GDP', A.T. Kearney, 4 November 2014, www.middle-east.atkearney.com/communications-media-technology/winning-in-the-business-of-sports/news-release/-/asset_publisher/IozB7i6P4wkW/content/a-t-kearney-study-sports-industry-growing-faster-than-gdp/10192?_101_INSTANCE_IozB7i6P4wkW_redirect=%2Fcommunications-media-technology%2Fwinning-in-the-business-of-sports, last accessed 23 January 2019.

27. 'Changing the Game: Outlook for the Global Sports Market to 2015', PWC, December 2011, www.pwc.com/gx/en/hospitality-leisure/pdf/changing-the-game-outlook-for-the-global-sports-market-to-2015.pdf, last accessed 23 January 2019.

28. Ibid.

29. 'Sports Industry Growing Faster than GDP', A.T. Kearney.

30. 'Research of Sports and Events Industries', Josoor Institute, April 2017, www.josoorinstitute.qa/content/research-sports-and-events-industries, last accessed 23 January 2019.

31. 'Middle East Football Fan Engagement', Josoor Institute, April 2017, www.josoorinstitute.qa/content/middle-east-football-fan-engagement, last accessed 23 January 2019.

32. Sofotasiou, Polytimi, Benjamin Richard Hughes, and John Kaiser Calautit, 'Qatar 2022: Facing the FIFA World Cup Climatic and Legacy Challenges', *Sustainable Cities and Society* 14 (2015), pp. 16–30.

33. Binshtok, Noam, 'ISIS to FIFA: Cancel the World Cup or We'll Bomb It', *Vocativ*, 8 July 2014, www.vocativ.com/culture/religion/isis-tells-fifa-cancel-qatari-world-cup-face-scuds/, last accessed 23 January 2019.

34. '7 Important Shipping Routes Vulnerable to Maritime Piracy', *Maritime Insight*, 21 July 2016, www.marineinsight.com/marine-piracy-marine/7-important-shipping-routes-vulnerable-to-maritime-piracy/, last accessed 23 January 2019.

35. Khouri, Jean, 'Sustainable Development and Management of Water Resources in the Arab Region', *Developments in Water Science* 50 (2003), pp. 199–220.

36. Walker, Lesley, 'Formula One Chief Cools Qatar's Hopes of Hosting Grand Prix Races', *Doha News*, 21 April 2015, https://dohanews.co/formula-one-chief-cools-qatars-hopes-of-hosting-grand-prix-races/, last accessed 23 January 2019.

37. Chadwick, Simon, 'How a US-Qatar Takeover Will Take Formula 1 Up a Gear', *The Conversation*, 24 June 2015, https://theconversation.com/how-a-us-qatar-takeover-will-take-formula-1-up-a-gear-43790, last accessed 23 January 2019.

38. 'Banning All Things Qatar: UAE Censors FC Barcelona Sponsor Logo', *Al Araby*, 8 June 2017, www.alaraby.co.uk/english/blog/2017/6/8/banning-all-things-qatar-uae-censors-barcelona-shirt, last accessed 23 January 2019.

39. Hanif, Nadeem, 'BeIN Sports Blocked in the UAE as Diplomatic Row with Qatar Deepens', *The National*, 6 June 2017, www.thenational.ae/uae/bein-sports-blocked-in-the-uae-as-diplomatic-row-with-qatar-deepens-1.84232, last accessed 23 January 2019.

40. Holyman, Ian, 'PSG Mull Action over Controversial Bastia Banner Aimed at Club's Qatari Owners', *ESPN*, 12 January 2015, www.espn.co.uk/football/paris-saint-germain/story/2239890/psg-anger-at-controversial-bastia-banner-aimed-at-clubs-qatari-owners, last accessed 23 January 2019.

41. 'Europe's Pro Leagues: Rescheduling 2022 World Cup would be "Damaging"', *Sports Illustrated*, 24 October 2014, www.si.com/planet-futbol/2014/10/24/association-european-professional-football-leagues-2022-world-cup, last accessed 23 January 2019.

42. Khan, Azfar and Hélène Harroff-Tavel, 'Reforming the Kafala: Challenges and Opportunities in Moving Forward', *Asian and Pacific Migration Journal* 20, 3–4 (2011), pp. 293–313.

43. 'Qatar: Abuse of Migrant Workers Remains Widespread as World Cup Stadium Hosts First Match', *Amnesty International*, 18 May 2017, www.amnesty.org/en/latest/news/2017/05/qatar-world-cup-stadium-first-match, last accessed 23 January 2019.

44. Kamrava, Mehran, and Zahra Babar, eds., *Migrant Labor in the Persian Gulf*, London: Hurst, 2012.

45. 'Challenge 22', Supreme Committee for Delivery and Legacy, www.sc.qa/en/opportunities/challenge-22, last accessed 23 January 2019.

46. 'Qatar Handball Team Coach Faces Questions over Foreign Players', *BBC News*, 29 January 2015, www.bbc.co.uk/news/world-middle-east-31031852, last accessed 23 January 2019.

47. 'Fifa to Review Rules over Player Nationality', *BBC News*, 5 May 2011, http://news.bbc.co.uk/sport1/hi/football/africa/9475788.stm, last accessed 23 January 2019.

48. Alkhalisi, Zahraa, 'Qatar Slashes Budget for 2022 World Cup By at Least 40%', *CNN Money*, 5 April 2017, http://money.cnn.com/2017/04/05/news/economy/qatar-2022-budget-soccer/index.html, last accessed 23 January 2019.

49. Nicholson, Paul, 'China Wins the World Cup of Acquisitions with €2.1bn Buying Spree', *Inside World Football*, 12 June 2017, www.insideworldfootball.com/2017/06/12/china-wins-world-cup-acquisitions-e2–1bn-buying-spree/, last accessed 23 January 2019.

50. Chadwick, Simon, 'Privatisation of Saudi State Assets Set to Fuel Sports Boom', *Economic Journal Insight*, 31 October 2017, www.ejinsight.com/20171031-privatisation-of-saudi-state-assets-set-to-fuel-sports-boom/, last accessed 23 January 2019.

51. Jabir, Wael, 'Asia's Next Super Club? Lekhwiya and El Jaish Merge into Al Duhail SC', *Ahdaaf*, 10 April 2017, https://ahdaaf.me/2017/04/10/asias-next-super-club-lekhwiya-el-jaish-merge-into-al-duhail-sc/, last accessed 23 January 2019.

52. 'Sharjah Ruler orders the Merger of Two Sports Clubs', *Sharjah 24*, 16 May 2017 www.sharjah24.ae/en/sharjah/221991-sharjah-ruler-orders-the-merger-of-two-sports-clubs, last accessed 23 January 2019.

53. Dokoupil, Martin, 'In UAE, Horses are Big Business as Well as Passion', *Reuters*, 9 May 2012, www.reuters.com/article/us-emirates-horseracing-idUSBRE8480SC20120509, last accessed 23 January 2019.

54. 'Economic Impact of Sport in Dubai', Deloitte, 2015, www2.deloitte.com/content/dam/Deloitte/uk/Documents/sports-business-group/deloitte-uk-sbg-dubai-falcon-report.pdf, last accessed 23 January 2019.

55. 'GCC Nations Eye Greater Share of $600 bn Global Sports Tourism Industry', *Qatar Tribune*, 31 January 2017, www.qatar-tribune.com/news-details/id/46513, last accessed 23 January 2019.

INDEX